LEAVING CERTIF

LESS STRESS MORE SUCCESS

Home Economics
Revision

Mary Anne Halton

Gill & Macmillan

Gill & Macmillan

Hume Avenue

Park West

Dublin 12

with associated companies throughout the world

www.gillmacmillan.ie

978 07171 4684 0

Design by Liz White Designs
Artwork and print origination by MPS Limited, a Macmillan Company

The paper used in this book is made from the wood pulp of managed forests.
For every tree felled, at least one tree is planted, thereby renewing natural resources.

For permission to reproduce photographs, the author and publisher gratefully acknowledge the following:

© Alamy: 138; Courtesy of Batchelors: 137T; Courtesy of Bord Bia: 72, 119; Courtesy of Bord Iascaigh Mhara: 120T; Courtesy of BSI: 222C, 222CB; Courtesy of Clonarn Clover and Persona Design: 83; Courtesy of Enterprise Ireland: 120B; Courtesy of Flahavan's: 137BL; Courtesy of FSA: 120CB; Courtesy of Glanbia: 136; Courtesy of Guaranteed Irish: 222TC; Courtesy of IOFGA: 96BL; Courtesy of National Standards Authority of Ireland: 222T, 222B, 223B; Courtesy of Old McDonnell's Farm: 90; Courtesy of Teagasc: 120CT; Courtesy of the Brady Family & Rudd's: 137BR; Courtesy of the EU: 224BL; Courtesy of The Organic Trust: 96BR; Courtesy of The Soil Association: 96BC; Courtesy of the Tipperary Co-Op Creamery Ltd: 93.

The authors and publisher have made every effort to trace all copyright holders, but if any has been inadvertently overlooked we would be pleased to make the necessary arrangement at the first opportunity.

CONTENTS

✓ done
Revise
know

Electives

- Revise your chosen elective on **www.moresuccess.ie**:
  - **Elective 1:** Home Design and Management
  - **Elective 2:** Textiles, Fashion and Design
  - **Elective 3:** Social Studies
- **Chapter 3:** Extra revision on **Food Studies** builds your confidence in this extensive topic

Just search for Home Economics Leaving Cert and look under 'Additional Resources'.

Introduction and Exam Guidelines

This book covers the **key topics** of the **compulsory Core** area for your Leaving Certificate Home Economics: Scientific and Social examination. Extra material is provided online at **www.moresuccess.ie**:

- **Chapter 3:** Food Studies
  - Extension 1: Methods of Cooking
  - Extension 2: Soups, Sauces and Pastry
- **Elective 1:** Home Design and Management
- **Elective 2:** Textiles, Fashion and Design
- **Elective 3:** Social Studies

How to use this book

Each chapter/section includes:

- Aims
- Topics
- **Higher level** material identified **HL**
- **Links** between topics **LINKS**
- **Exam focus** with hints for the exam
- **Key points** with information to note
- Tables integrating the topics
- **Sample answers** to exam questions with summaries of key points.

The syllabus and the exam

Structure of the syllabus

The exam is offered at two levels, **Higher** and **Ordinary**. The syllabus is divided into a **core** section and a choice of three **electives**.

Syllabus	What is in this section?
Mandatory core topics – study *all* the core topics (80%)	1. Food Studies (45%) 2. Resource Management and Consumer Studies (25%) 3. Social Studies (10%)
Electives – choose *one* of the three topics (20%)	Elective 1: Home Design and Management OR Elective 2: Textiles, Fashion and Design OR Elective 3: Social Studies

How home economics is examined

If you choose **Elective 1: Home Design and Management** *or* **Elective 3: Social Studies,** the exam consists of:

- a written exam (80%)
- Food Studies coursework with a journal (20%)

If you choose **Elective 2: Textiles, Fashion and Design,** the exam consists of:

- a written exam (70%)
- Food Studies coursework with a journal (20%)
- Textiles, Fashion and Design Elective coursework (10%)

How the exam is marked

Marks are allocated to each component as follows.

- Candidates choosing **Home Design and Management** *or* **Social Studies Elective**:

Component of exam	Marks	Percentage
Written paper	320	80
Food Studies coursework	80	20
Total	400	100

- Candidates choosing **Textiles, Fashion and Design Elective**:

Component of exam	Marks	Percentage
Written paper	280	70
Food Studies coursework	80	20
Textiles, Fashion and Design coursework	40	10
Total	400	100

Structure, marking and timing of the exam paper

There are **three** sections in the exam paper: Section A, Section B and Section C (the elective). You have two hours and 30 minutes to do the exam paper.

The sections are structured and marked for Higher Level *and* Ordinary Level papers as follows:

Section	Requirements	Marks	Total marks	Time allocated
Section A (short questions)	Answer **10** out of 12 questions	6 marks per question	60 marks	25–30 minutes
Section B (long questions): Question 1	Question 1 is **compulsory**	80 marks	80 marks	30–35 minutes
Section B: Questions 2, 3, 4, 5	Answer any **two** questions from 2, 3, 4 and 5	50 marks *each*	100 marks	20 minutes × 2 = 40 minutes
Section C Electives 1 and 3	Answer a *and* b **or** c	80 marks	80 marks	30–35 minutes
Section C Elective 2 (Textiles)	Answer a *and* b **or** c	40 marks	40 marks	30–35 minutes

Do not forget to allow time for:

1. Reading through the paper before you start. Take ten minutes to read the questions and decide which questions you will answer. Underline *key words and phrases*.

2. Reading through your work at the end. Take 5–10 minutes to read over your work and make additions or adjustments.

The above timings are only a guideline. Practise answering questions within the times suggested in the table.

Budget your time carefully!

Make sure you complete **all** parts of the written exam.

Guidelines for each section

- **Section A**
  - Short, concise answers.
  - Answer the questions in the spaces provided in the exam booklet.
  - Hand the booklet to the superintendent.

- **Section B**
  - Question 1 is *compulsory*.
  - All questions in this section begin with a statement.
  - You will be asked to read and analyse tables, charts and pie diagrams in the questions and draw conclusions where appropriate.

- **Section C – The Electives**
  - Candidates *must answer* (a) *and either* (b) *or* (c).
  - Part (a) is compulsory.

Key words

Look out for these key words in questions. Make sure you understand what they mean.

Characteristics: Qualities.

Compare: Show the similarities or differences between two items; you could use a table to illustrate your answer.

> *Remember:* Home Economics involves **integration of topics** within questions. Sections B and C demonstrate this key principle. Learn all **linked material** when revising topics.

Define: Give the exact meaning of a word or phrase. Use examples if necessary to make your definitions clear.

Describe: Give the description in bullet/point form. Use a clearly labelled diagram to illustrate answers.

Discuss: Give a detailed description. Use a series of points.

Enumerate: List key points with a short explanation of each.

Evaluate: Refer to the positive and negative points.

Explain: Give a detailed account, with examples, and a diagram if appropriate.

Illustrate: Use a diagram to explain a point.

List: List the key points – a detailed explanation is not needed.

Name: One or two words; no details are necessary.

Outline: Give one or two sentences on each point.

Principle: Describe how something works or the reason for something.

Properties: The characteristics of something, e.g. a nutrient.

Suggest: State your answer in a few words.

Other key words and phrases:

- identify
- indicate
- give an account
- write

- summarise
- factors
- sources
- uses

Effective revision – setting smart goals

The best way to approach sections/topics is to:

- Make a revision time plan.
- Read the material carefully.
- Make notes as you revise (make these *visual*: do not simply copy notes from your class work/textbooks).
- Make tables of key information.

- Draw spider/web diagrams or mind maps for *each* topic.
- Revise linked material in each topic.
- Attempt past exam questions on each topic.

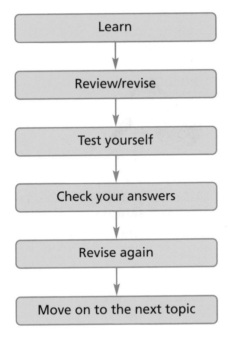

Tick (✓) each topic when you have read, learned and tested yourself.

Essential skills:
1. Recognising **key words** in questions.
2. **Analysing** case studies, charts and tables of information, labels and symbols, and drawing conclusions.
3. **Sketching** and **labelling** diagrams to illustrate an answer.
4. **Checking** and *knowing* the latest legislation/updates.

Final preparation for the written exam

1. Revise the complete course.
2. Note what to learn for Higher and Ordinary levels.
3. Be familiar with the layout of the exam paper.
4. Know how many questions you have to answer and how much time is needed to answer them.
5. Know which are the compulsory questions.
6. Know how the questions are marked.
7. Practise answering questions from past papers.

Guidelines on the day

1. Stay calm.
2. **Listen** to instructions given by superintendent.
3. Write your **exam number** in the box on the paper.
4. **Read** all questions and **highlight**/underline *key words*.

5. Mark the *compulsory* questions and choose which other questions you will answer.

6. Keep rigidly to your *time plan*.

7. Attempt *all* questions in Section A.

8. In Sections B and C, write neat *headings*, answer in *point form* and *elaborate* as appropriate.

9. *Attempt all parts*/sub-sections of a question. *Never* leave a section of a question unanswered: you could lose valuable marks.

10. *Label* all diagrams/sketches fully and clearly.

11. *Answer each new question on a new page.* Leave space at the end of each question in case you want to add more information when you read through your answers at the end of the exam.

12. Write *menus* in a box and use the correct *format*.

13. *Do not leave until the exam is finished.* Use all the time available to answer questions fully and to read over the questions and answers before the end.

exam focus

● **Use relevant** terminology/vocabulary.

● **Do not waffle** or write essay-style answers.

● **Do not repeat** information.

Study/revision plan

Overview of school year:

- Term 1 (September to December)
- Term 2a (December to mock exams)
- Term 2b (mock exams to Easter)
- Term 3 (Easter to Leaving Certificate exams)

Deadlines

Write down the dates/times for each of these:

- Submit Food Journal   _____
- Mid-term exam   _____
- Christmas exam   _____
- Mock exam   _____
- Easter exam   _____
- Leaving Certificate exam   _____

Your teacher will give you deadlines for homework (written and learning), classwork and revision. *Listen and take all the advice given*.

Check which topics have been covered

Make a list of topics. Tick each topic when you have learned it, practised exam questions and revised it.

For example:

Topic	Covered in class	Exam questions	Revised at home
Food choices			
Protein			
Carbohydrates			
Lipids			
Vitamins			
Minerals			
Water			
Energy			
Nutritional guidelines			
Dietary and food requirements			
Special diets			

Study plan

This is an example of an 11-week study plan. Modify the outline plan below to suit you and your ability to revise topics in a realistic time. Add in more linked topics. Make it an eight-week or nine-week study plan, whichever suits you best.

Week	Topics	Linked topics
1	Food choices, protein, dietary guidelines	Meat, poultry, eggs, menu management and planning
2	Lipids, fats/oils, dietary and food requirements, diet-related health problems	Energy, milk, cheese, dairy products, the Irish diet
3	Carbohydrates, cooking methods, resource management (finance, textiles)	Cereals, fruit, vegetables, nuts, legumes
4	Minerals, vitamins, household technology	Consumer studies
5	Fish, food profiles, alternative protein foods	

6	Microbiology, food spoilage and preservation	Food safety and hygiene, HACCP, food legislation and food agencies
7	Food additives	Sensory analysis
8	The Irish food industry, food legislation	Food processing, packaging and labelling, the Irish diet
9	Consumer studies	***
10	Social studies	***
11	Elective	***

*** List the topics you will be covering in this column.

Revise exam questions alongside topics. **Practise** past exam papers with each topic.

And finally: good luck!

Core Topics

1 Food Science and Nutrition

aims To learn and revise:
- Food choices
- Nutrients
- Water.

Food choices

Factors affecting food choices:

1. Specific countries, cultural beliefs and traditions.
2. Availability, convenience and access to food.
3. Nutritional awareness and health status.
4. Sensory aspects and food presentation.
5. Financial resources.
6. Eating patterns and lifestyle.
7. Personal preferences.
8. Advertising and marketing.

LINKS
- Individual dietary requirements (pp. 47–52)
- The Irish diet (p. 64)
- Meal management and planning (p. 106)

Nutrients

Macronutrients	Micronutrients
<ul><li>Protein</li><li>Lipids (fat)</li><li>Carbohydrates</li></ul>	<ul><li>Vitamins<ul><li>– fat-soluble</li><li>– water-soluble</li></ul></li><li>Minerals</li></ul>

exam focus

You must *understand* and *be able to explain* what is meant by these **nutritional terms**:

- Macronutrients
- Micronutrients
- Elemental composition
- Chemical formula or equation
- Classification
- Sources
- Properties

- Functions
- Biological value
- Energy value
- Digestion
- Absorption and utilisation of digested nutrients
- Enzymes

Protein

Elemental composition

- Carbon (C), hydrogen (H), oxygen (O) and nitrogen (N).
- Some contain sulphur (S), iron (Fe) and phosphorus (P).

Chemical structure

- Proteins are made up of amino acids.
- Amino acids contain carbon, hydrogen, a variable (R), an amino group (NH_2) and a carboxyl group (COOH).

H (hydrogen)

(variable) R—C—COOH (Acidic carboxyl group)

NH_2 (amino group)

Basic amino acid

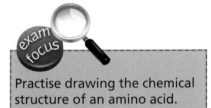

exam focus

Practise drawing the chemical structure of an amino acid.

H

$HSCH_2$—C—COOH (carboxyl group)

NH_2
(amino group)

Cysteine showing the R (variable) group

Essential and non-essential amino acids

HL

- There are 20 common amino acids.
- Eight are essential for adults.
- Children need these eight plus two more.

Essential amino acids	Non-essential amino acids
Cannot be made by the body	Can be made by the body
Must be supplied by food	
Examples: isoleucine, leucine, lycine, methionine, phenylanine, threonine, tryptophan, valine	*Examples:* alanine, aspargine, aspartic acid, cysteine, glutamic acid, glutamine, glycine, proline, serine, tyrosine
For children: histidine, arginine	

Peptides and peptide bonds

Amino acids are linked by a peptide bond. A carboxyl group (COOH) of one amino acid combines with an amino group (NH_2) of the next amino acid. A molecule of water (H_2O) is released (condensation) during this process.

H   O

NH_2—C—C   H—N—C—COOH

OH   H   R

R

| Removal H_2O → Condensation | Addition H_2O → Hydrolysis |

Hydrolysis

During digestion the reverse of the condensation process happens. Peptide bonds are broken by the addition of water, producing single amino acids. This is called hydrolysis.

exam focus

Practise drawing a peptide bond/link showing condensation and hydrolysis.

key point

- Two amino acids linked by peptide bond = **dipeptide**.
- Three amino acids linked = **tripeptide**.
- Ten or more amino acids linked = **polypeptide chain**.

LINKS

- Digestion of protein (p. 9)
- Absorption of amino acids/proteins (p. 10)

exam Q

Exam question and sample answer

HL

Higher Level 2006, Section B, Q1 (b), (c), (d)

Meat and Protein

(b) Name **two** proteins present in meat   (2 × 3 marks = 6 marks)

- *Actin is found in meat fibre.*   (3 marks)
- *Collagen is found in connective tissue.*   (3 marks)

(c) Explain:

   (i) High biological value protein   (2 points × 3 marks each = 6 marks)

- *HBV proteins contain all the essential amino acids.*
- *Generally from animal sources.*

   (ii) Essential amino acids   (2 points × 3 marks each = 6 marks)

- *Cannot be made by the body, e.g. lysine.*
- *Must be obtained from the foods that we eat.*

(d) Describe (i) the **primary** structure and (ii) the **secondary** structure of protein.

   (i) *Primary structure*   (3 points × 4 marks each = 12 marks)

- *Is the sequence of amino acids in a polypeptide chain.*
- *The chain is formed by peptide links.*
- *The OH from the carboxyl group of one amino acid joins with the H of an amino group of another amino acid, and water (H_2O) is released (condensation reaction).*

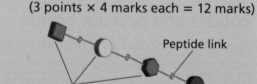

Peptide link

Different amino acids

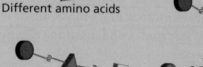

-Ala-Ser-Val-Tyr-Gly-Val-Ser-Cys-Ile-Ala-Val-Ser-

(ii) *Secondary structure*　　　　(3 points × 4 marks each = 12 marks)

- *Occurs when amino acids in the polypeptide chain are folded and cross-linked to create definite shapes and structures.*
- *Disulphide links occur when two sulphur molecules are linked together, e.g. cysteine.*
- *Hydrogen bonds occur when hydrogen (H) from an amino group and oxygen (O) in a carboxyl group join together, e.g. collagen. This can occur in the same chain or between neighbouring polypeptide chains.*

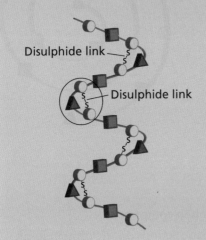

Disulphide link

Disulphide link

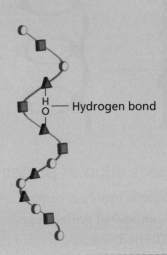

Hydrogen bond

Practise drawing and labelling all diagrams.

Tertiary structure

- Pattern of folding polypeptide chains into three-dimensional shapes.
- Shapes are held in place by cross-links and may be fibrous (straight, coiled or zigzag) or globular (ball-shaped).

Fibrous shapes	Globular shapes
Insoluble in water	Soluble in water
Examples: gluten (wheat), elastin (meat)	*Examples:* myoglobin (meat), haemoglobin (blood)

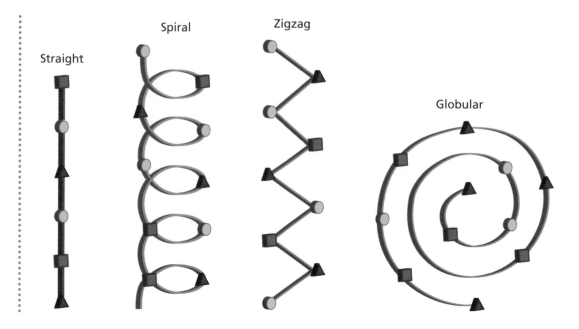

Classification of proteins

1. **Simple proteins:** contain amino acids.
2. **Conjugated proteins:** amino acids and a non-protein component.
3. **Derived proteins:** formed from chemical/enzymatic actions on the protein itself, e.g. rennin acts on caseinogen.

Simple proteins

Types	Examples	Sources
Animal		
Classified according to shape	HL (a) Fibrous	Collagen Elastin – connective tissue
	(b) Globular	Albumin – egg white
Plant		
Classified according to solubility	HL (a) Glutelins: ● insoluble in water ● soluble in acids and alkalis	Glutenin – wheat Oryzenin – rice
	(b) Prolamines: ● insoluble in water ● soluble in alcohol	Gliadin – wheat Zein – maize/corn

Conjugated proteins (protein + non-protein)

Types	Examples	Source
Lipoprotein	Lecithin	Eggs
Phosphoproteins	Casein	Milk
Glycoproteins	Ovomucin	Egg white
Chromoproteins	Haemoglobin Myoglobin	Blood Meat
Nucleoproteins	Chromosomes	DNA (Deoxyribonucleic Acid)

Sources of protein

Animal proteins	Plant proteins
Meat, fish, poultry, eggs, milk, cheese	Soya beans, whole cereals, nuts, pulses

Biological value (BV)

- Measures the quality of a protein as a percentage.
- Is determined by how many essential amino acids are in food.

LINK
- Food commodities (pp. 70–106)

High biological value (HBV) proteins or complete proteins:
- contain all the essential amino acids
- come mainly from animal sources (*exception*: soya beans – source of HBV protein).

Low biological value (LBV) proteins or incomplete proteins:
- lack one or more essential amino acids
- come mainly from plant sources (*exception*: gelatine – source of LBV protein).

Biological value of foods and distribution of proteins

Distribution of myosin, actin and collagen.

Foods	Biological value	Distribution of proteins
Eggs	100%	Ovalbumin, vitelin, livetin
Milk	95%	Casein, lacto albumin, lacto globulin
Meat	80–90%	Elastin, gelatine, collagen, myosin
Fish	80–90%	Actin, myosin, collagen
Soya Beans	74%	Glycinin
Rice	67%	Oryzenin
Wheat	53%	Gluten
Maize	40%	Zein
Gelatine	0%	

Supplementary role of protein

If a protein is deficient in one amino acid the deficiency can be overcome by eating a food rich in that amino acid at the same meal, e.g. beans on toast:

- beans are **high** in lysine and **low** in methionine
- toast is **low** in lysine and **high** in methionine

LINK

- Vegetarianism (p. 56)

The **complementary** role of proteins ensures that vegans and vegetarians can get all their essential amino acids from plant foods.

Properties of protein

1. Denaturation and coagulation	• Protein chain unfolds and its structure changes • Sequence of amino acids is the same *The change may be due to:* (a) **Agitation** – mechanical action, e.g. whipping or whisking an egg white (b) **Chemicals** – adding acids, alkalis, e.g. lemon juice causes milk to curdle (c) **Heat** – albumin (eggs) coagulates and sets (d) **Enzymes** – rennin coagulates casein in the stomach
2. Solubility	Most proteins are insoluble in water. *Exceptions:* (a) Collagen is soluble in hot water (b) Albumin is soluble in cold water
3. Maillard reaction (dry heat)	Non-enzymic browning results when an amino acid reacts with carbohydrate in dry heat, e.g. toasting
4. Elasticity	Gluten (wheat) is very elastic – it allows breads to rise during baking
5. Moist heat	During stewing, boiling and steaming, connective tissue changes to gelatine, making foods more digestible
6. Gel formation	A gel is a semi-solid viscous solution with a three-dimensional network in which molecules of water can become trapped. *Gel formation process:* (a) Gelatine absorbs cold water and swells to form a **gel**. (b) When heated the gel becomes liquid and forms a **sol**. (c) On cooling, the **sol sets** and becomes solid. *Uses:* soufflé, cheesecake
7. Foam formation	• Whisking egg whites causes protein chains to unfold and air bubbles to form, which trap air (foaming) • Whisking produces heat, which lightly sets the egg white. Foam will collapse unless heated. *Uses:* meringues

LINKS
- Food commodities (p. 70)
- Food preparation and cooking processes (p. 107)

Biological functions of protein

Type	Functions	Deficiency
Structural proteins	• Growth and repair • Production of cells, muscles and skin	• Stunted growth • Delayed healing of wounds
Physiologically active	• Production of antibodies, enzymes, hormones, blood proteins and nucleoproteins	• Illness and infections
Nutrient proteins	• Provide essential amino acids • Excess converted to energy	• Lack of energy • Marasmus and kwashiorkor

Energy value: 1 g protein = 4 kcal/17 kJ energy.

RDA – how much protein do I need?

1 g of protein a day is required for each 1 kg of body weight.

Group	RDA per day
Children	30–50 g
Adolescents	60–80 g
Adults	50–75 g
Pregnant women	70–85 g

Digestion of protein

Hydrolysis and digestion of protein – a summary

Proteins are hydrolysed with the help of protein-splitting enzymes.

DEAMINATION   HL

1. Excess proteins are deaminated by the liver.

2. The amino group (NH_2) of the amino acids is converted into ammonia and then urea. Urea is excreted from the body in urine.

3. The carboxyl group (COOH) is oxidised (used for heat and energy). Excess is stored in the body as glycogen (energy source).

Organ/Gland	Secretions	Enzymes	Substrates	Products
Stomach	Gastric juice	Pepsin Rennin	Protein Caseinogen	Peptones Casein
Pancreas	Pancreatic juice	Trypsin	Peptones	Peptides
Ileum (small intestine)	Intestinal juice	Peptidase	Peptides	Amino acids

Absorption of amino acids/proteins

Amino acids are absorbed by the blood vessels in the villi of the small intestine and transported to the liver via the hepatic portal vein.

Utilisation of amino acids

Amino acids in the liver are used to:

- repair and maintain liver cells.
- form new cells, repair damaged tissues and make antibodies, enzymes and hormones.
- excess amino acids are deaminated in the liver.

Exam questions and sample answers

Higher Level 2008, Section A, Q1 (6 marks)

In relation to protein, describe the formation of a peptide bond/link.

The carboxyl acidic group (COOH) of one amino acid reacts with the alkaline group (NH$_2$) of the other, with the elimination of water (H$_2$O).

Higher Level 2007, Section A, Q1 (6 marks)

Name **two** methods by which protein can be denatured and give an example in each case.

Method of denaturation	Example
1 Heat	Coagulation of eggs
2 Mechanical action	Whipping eggs to form a foam

Ordinary Level 2008, Section A, Q2 (6 marks)

Complete the following statement in relation to the digestion of protein using the words listed below:

enzyme, pancreas, casein (3 × 2 marks = 6 marks)

*In the stomach the **enzyme** rennin changes caseinogen to **casein**.*

*In the duodenum the enzyme trypsin from the **pancreas** changes peptones to peptides.*

Ordinary Level 2007, Section A, Q1   (6 marks)
Name **three** sources of protein under each of the following headings:

(6 × 1 marks = 6 marks)

High biological value protein (HBV)	Low biological value protein (LBV)
Meat/fish	Wheat
Milk	Rice
Eggs	Maize

Ordinary Level 2007, Section B, Q1 (c)   (30 marks) (part question)
(c) Give an account of protein under each of the following headings:

(i) Composition   (1 point × 6 marks = 6 marks)
  Carbon (C), hydrogen (H), oxygen (O), nitrogen (N), smaller amounts of
  phosphorus, sulphur and iron.

(ii) Functions in the body   (2 points × 6 marks = 12 marks)
  1. Supplies all essential amino acids needed for growth and repair of body cells.
  2. Aids the manufacture of antibodies, enzymes and hormones.

(iii) Properties   (2 points × 6 marks = 12 marks)
  1. Denatured by heat, chemicals, enzymes and agitation.
  2. Insoluble in water: exceptions are collagen and egg white.

Carbohydrates

Photosynthesis – formation of carbohydrates in plants

- Roots absorb water from the soil.
- Leaves absorb carbon dioxide from the air.
- Chlorophyll in leaves converts sunlight into energy.
- Sunlight reacts with water and carbon dioxide to produce glucose and oxygen.

$$6CO_2 \quad + \quad 6H_2O \quad + \quad \text{sunlight} \longrightarrow C_6H_{12}O_6 + \quad 6O_2$$

carbon dioxide	water	energy	glucose	oxygen
from air	from soil			

Elemental composition

Carbon (C), hydrogen (H) and oxygen (O).

Chemical structure of carbohydrates

- Monosaccharides.
- Disaccharides.
- Polysaccharides.

exam focus

Higher level students: practise drawing the chemical structures of carbohydrates and learn the explanations for each one.

1. Formation of a monosaccharide – hexagonal ring structure.

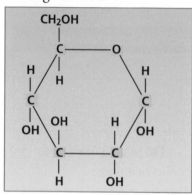

2. Formation of a disaccharide. (Higher level) HL

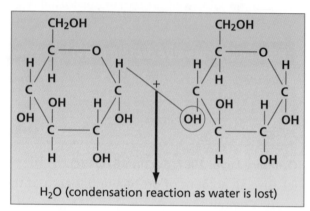

H_2O (condensation reaction as water is lost)

3. Formation of polysaccharides (condensation reaction).

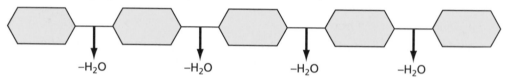

$-H_2O$ $-H_2O$ $-H_2O$ $-H_2O$

Condensation reaction (removal of water):

$$C_6H_{12}O_6 + C_6H_{12}O_6 = C_{12}H_{24}O_{12} - H_2O = C_{12}H_{22}O_{11} + H_2O$$

Classification, chemical formulae, properties and sources

Classification	Chemical formula	Characteristics	Examples and sources
Monosaccharides (*Mono* = one – single unit)	$C_6H_{12}O_6$	Simple sugar unit with a ring structure	Glucose ⟶ fruit Fructose ⟶ honey, fruit Galactose ⟶ milk
Disaccharides (*Di* = two)	$C_{12}H_{22}O_{11}$	Two simple sugars joined together with the removal of H_2O (condensation)	Maltose (glucose + glucose) ⟶ barley Sucrose (glucose + fructose) ⟶ table sugar Lactose (glucose + galactose) ⟶ milk
Polysaccharide (*Poly* = many)	$(C_6H_{10}O_5)n$	• Three or more sugar units joined together • Chains may be branched or straight	Starch ⟶ cereals, potatoes Glycogen ⟶ meat Cellulose ⟶ skins of fruit/vegetables Pectin ⟶ fruits
Non-starch polysaccharides (NSP)		• Indigestible • Absorb water • Aids waste removal	Soluble fibres (gums, pectins) Insoluble fibres (cellulose, lignins)

Properties of carbohydrates – a summary

LINK
- Food commodities (p. 70)

Sugars

1. Sweetness	Varying degrees of sweetness
2. Solubility	Sugar is soluble in water Solubility increases if water is heated
3. Maillard reaction	Causes browning
4. Assists aeration	Whisking or beating sugar with eggs denatures the protein and causes the egg to trap air, resulting in a light mixture *Uses:* egg sponges, cakes
5. Caramelisation	Happens between 104°C and 177°C in dry heat *Uses:* crème brûlée
6. Crystallisation	Occurs when excess sugar is added to a liquid already saturated with sugar and crystals form on cooling *Uses:* confectionery
7. Hydrolysis	Disaccharides react with water to produce monosaccharides
8. Inversion (or hydrolysis) of sugar	When sugar reacts with water in the presence of an acid *or* an enzyme (invertase) it converts disaccharides into monosaccharides *Uses:* jam-making
9. Reducing sugars	Acts as a reducing agent by removing oxygen from other substances *Examples:* glucose, fructose

LINK
- Protein (p. 8)

Starch

1. Solubility	Insoluble in cold water
2. Hygroscopic	Absorbs moisture from the air, e.g. biscuits go soft if left exposed
3. Flavour	Starches lack flavour
4. Gelatinisation	*Gelatinisation happens in stages:* (a) Moist heat causes starch grains to swell, burst, absorb moisture and thicken liquids, e.g. sauces (b) As the liquid is heated to initial temperatures of 55–70°C it is absorbed by the starch (c) The starch granules swell and join together to form a sticky paste (d) Temperatures greater than 85°C create a sol. *Examples:* sauces, soups (e) On cooling the mixture forms a gel

key point

Different starches gelatinise at different temperatures

5. Dry heat	Starch grains burst and absorb any fat present *Example:* popcorn
6. Dextrinisation	Heating starchy foods causes foods to brown and polysaccharide chains called pyrodextrins to form *Example:* toast
7. Gel formation	Heating pectin in the presence of an acid and sugar causes its long polysaccharide chains to form a three-dimensional network which traps water molecules. On cooling, this mixture forms a gel *Examples:* jams, jellies

Non-starch polysaccharides (NSP)

1. Gel formation	**Gums** absorb water to form gels
	Pectins form gels in presence of heat, acids and sugar
2. Solubility	**Cellulose** is insoluble in water. It absorbs water, creating bulk in the diet
3. Pectin extraction	Protopectin in under-ripe fruit cannot absorb water and form a gel. Adding acid (lemon juice) converts protopectin to pectin. *Examples:* jams, jellies

> ## LINKS
> - Food preservation (p. 158)
> - Sauces (Chapter 3, Extension 2, see www.moresuccess.ie)

Biological functions of carbohydrates

Class	Biological functions
Sugars	1. Source of heat and energy
	2. Excess is converted into **fat**: stored as adipose tissue; insulates the body
	3. Act as 'protein sparers'
Starch	Good source of heat and energy
Cellulose (NSP or dietary fibre)	1. Prevents bowel diseases by encouraging peristalsis and speeds up waste removal
	2. Produces a feeling of fullness, reduces over-eating

Culinary uses of carbohydrates

Sugar

1. **Preservative:** prevents microbial growth.
2. **Sweetener:** sweetens cakes, desserts, beverages.
3. **Caramelisation:** dry heat caramelises sugar (desserts, cakes).

4. **Fermentation:** activates yeast fermentation.

5. **Aeration:** strengthens whisked egg white proteins.

Starch

1. **Thickener:** gravies, sauce and soups.

2. **Hygroscopic:** extends shelf-life of cakes.

3. **Dextrinisation:** browning of foods.

Pectin

Gel formation: pectin acts as a setting agent in jam making.

Cellulose/fibre

1. Adds **texture** to dishes, e.g. stews.

2. Creates a feeling of **fullness.**

Energy value: 1 g carbohydrate = 17 kJ energy.

RDA of carbohydrates: none – deficiency is rare.

> ### LINKS
> - Food preparation and cooking processes (p. 107)
> - Sauces (Chapter 3, Extension 2, see www.moresuccess.ie)
> - Food commodities (p. 70)

Dietary targets for NSP intake

Intake of NSP should be approximately 25–35 g per day, drawn from a variety of grains, fruits, legumes and vegetables.

Achieving the targets – increasing fibre in the diet

1. Replace processed cereals with wholegrain varieties.

2. Eat high-fibre breakfast cereals, e.g. porridge.

3. Eat whole fruits/vegetables as well as drinking juices.

4. Use wholemeal flour for bread and cakes.

5. Eat skins of fruits and vegetables.

> ### LINK
> - The Irish diet (p. 64)

Digestion of carbohydrates

Organ/gland	Secretions	Enzymes	Act on/substrates	Products
Salivary glands (mouth)	Saliva	Salivary amylase	Starch	Maltose
Pancreas	Pancreatic juice in the duodenum	Amylase	Starch	Maltose
Ileum (small intestine)	Intestinal juice	(a) Maltase	(a) Maltose	Glucose
		(b) Lactase	(b) Lactose	Glucose + galactose
		(c) Sucrase	(c) Sucrose	Glucose + fructose

Absorption of carbohydrates

1. Monosaccharides are absorbed through the villi of the small intestine into the bloodstream.
2. They are transported to the liver via the portal vein.

Utilisation of carbohydrates

In the liver:

1. Glucose is oxidised for heat and energy.
2. Glucose is converted into glycogen (energy reserve).
3. Excess is converted to fat and stored as adipose tissue (insulation).

LINK

- Modified diets: diabetes (p. 59)

Exam questions and sample answers

Higher Level 2007, Section A, Q2 (6 marks)

Complete the following table in relation to the digestion of carbohydrates.

Secretion	Enzyme	Substrate	Product
Saliva	Salivary amylase	*Starch*	*Dextrin maltose*
Intestinal juice	Lactase	*Lactose*	*Glucose and galactose*

Ordinary Level 2007, Section A, Q2 (6 marks)

(a) List the **three** elements found in carbohydrates.

Carbon (C), hydrogen (H), oxygen (O) (3 × 1 = 3 marks)

(b) In relation to the digestion of carbohydrates, indicate with a tick (✔) whether each of the following statements is true or false.

Digestion of Carbohydrates	True	False
Starch is changed to maltose in the mouth	✔	
Carbohydrate digestion takes place in the stomach		✔
Intestinal juice contains sucrase	✔	

Higher Level 2005, Section B, Q1 (compulsory question) (a), (b) and (c)

Carbohydrates

A recent survey found the main sources of carbohydrates in the Irish diet are as illustrated below

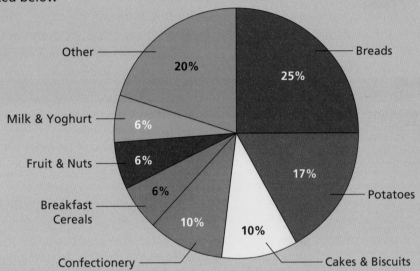

(a) Using the information provided in the chart and having regard to current healthy eating guidelines, suggest three ways that the food sources of carbohydrates in the diet should be adjusted. Give a reason for each suggestion.   (3 points × 6 marks = 18 marks)

Adjustments needed	Reasons for suggestion
1. Increase breakfast cereals and reduce intake of other cereals	• Breakfast cereals may be fortified with vitamins and minerals (check labels) • Good source of fibre, e.g. porridge
2. Increase intake of milk and yoghurt	• Good source of HBV protein • Good source of calcium
3. Reduce intake of cakes and biscuits and increase intake of bread	• Cakes and biscuits high in fats and sugars; low in fibre • Wholemeal bread high in fibre; low in fats and sugars

(b) Describe the chemical structure of **each** of the following. Give **one** example of each.   (3 structures × 6 marks = 18 marks)

   (i) Monosaccharides

       Formula: $C_6H_{12}O_6$

       Examples: glucose, fructose, galactose

   (ii) Disaccharides

       Formula: $C_{12}H_{22}O_{11}$

       Disaccharides form when two monosaccharides join together with the loss of water (H_2O).

       Examples: maltose, sucrose, lactose

(iii) Polysaccharides

Formula: $(C_6H_{10}O_5)_n$

Long chains of monosaccharides are linked together in straight or branched chains.

Examples: cellulose/fibre, glycogen, pectin, sugar

(c) Name and explain **three** properties of carbohydrates that are useful in food preparation. (3 properties × 6 marks = 18 marks)

Property	Explanation
Caramelisation (sugar)	When sugar is heated on its own it melts, forms syrup, and on further heating changes to a brown colour. Ten changes between melting and caramelisation occur between 104°C and 177°C. Example: crème caramel
Inversion (sugar)	Sucrose splits into glucose and fructose. In the presence of water and under slightly acidic conditions sucrose becomes invert sugar. Example: jam-making
Gelatinisation (starch)	When starch is heated in a liquid the grains swell, burst and absorb the liquid, forming a thick mixture. On further heating this forms a sol, in which the particles are evenly distributed in the liquid. On cooling it becomes a gel. Examples: sauces, soups

Ordinary Level 2009, Section B, Q1 (b) and (c)

(b) Give an account of carbohydrates under **each** of the following headings:

Functions in the Body (2 functions × 4 marks = 8 marks)

1. Provide heat and energy
2. Cellulose/fibre helps the movement of food in the digestive tract and prevents bowel problems, e.g. constipation

Sources in the Diet (3 sources × 4 marks = 12 marks)

Sources	Examples of sources
1. Sugars	Table sugar, cakes, biscuits, jam
2. Starch	Porridge, potatoes, pasta, rice
3. Fibre/cellulose	Skins of fruits and vegetables, brown bread, wholegrain breakfast cereals, bran

Properties of Carbohydrates (2 properties × 4 marks = 8 marks)

1. **Maillard reaction**: Dry heat causes sugars and amino acids to react, resulting in browning of food, e.g. roast potatoes.
2. **Solubility**: Sugars are soluble in water. Solubility increases on heating. Starch is insoluble in cold water.

(c) List **three** culinary uses of sugar.

1. As a preservative, e.g. prevents growth of microbes in jam.
2. As a sweetener, e.g. in cake making, desserts.
3. To activate yeast in bread making (fermentation). (3 uses × 3 marks = 9 marks)

Lipids

Elemental composition

Carbon (C), hydrogen (H) and oxygen (O).

Chemical structure of a triglyceride

- A triglyceride is formed when **one** molecule of glycerol combines with **three** fatty acids.
- Glycerol is an alcohol with three hydroxyl groups (OH).
- A fatty acid attaches itself to each OH group with the elimination of three molecules of water (condensation).

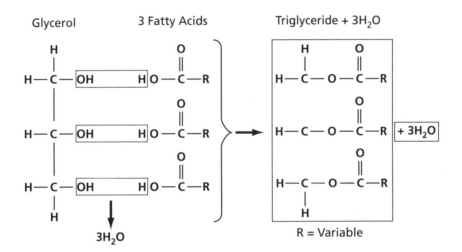

Classification of fatty acids

1. Saturated fatty acids.
2. Monounsaturated fatty acids.
3. Polyunsaturated fatty acids (PUFAs).

1. Saturated fatty acids

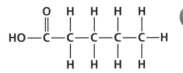

Structure	Properties	Sources and examples
• Saturated with hydrogen atoms • **No** double bonds, carbons linked by single bonds	• Solid at room temperature • High melting point	• *Sources:* dairy produce, egg yolk, meat, fats, some hard margarines • *Examples:* stearic acid (meat), butyric acid (butter)

2. Monounsaturated fatty acids (one double bond)

$$HO-\overset{\overset{\displaystyle O}{\|}}{C}-\overset{\overset{\displaystyle H}{|}}{\underset{\underset{\displaystyle H}{|}}{C}}-\overset{\displaystyle H}{C}=\overset{\displaystyle H}{C}-\overset{\overset{\displaystyle H}{|}}{\underset{\underset{\displaystyle H}{|}}{C}}-H$$

Structure	Properties	Sources and examples
• Carbon **not** saturated with hydrogen atoms • Bonds are incomplete • One double bond	• Liquid/soft at room temperature • Lower melting point • Prone to oxidative rancidity • Lowers cholesterol	• Plants • Olive oil (oleic acid)

3. Polyunsaturated fatty acids (two or more double bonds)

$$HO-\overset{\overset{\displaystyle O}{\|}}{C}=\overset{\overset{\displaystyle H}{|}}{\underset{\underset{\displaystyle H}{|}}{C}}-\overset{\overset{\displaystyle H}{|}}{C}-\overset{\displaystyle H}{C}=\overset{\displaystyle H}{C}-\overset{\overset{\displaystyle H}{|}}{\underset{\underset{\displaystyle H}{|}}{C}}-H$$

Structure	Properties	Sources and examples
• Carbon atoms **not** saturated with hydrogen atoms • **More than one** double bond	• Liquid/soft at room temperature • Lower melting point • Lowers cholesterol	• *Plant sources:* corn oil, vegetable oils, nuts, margarine • *Examples:* linoleic acid (two double bonds); linolenic acid (three double bonds); arachidonic acid (four double bonds)

Essential fatty acids

What are fatty acids?

1. Fatty acids are long chains of hydrocarbons.
2. A fatty acid has a **methyl group** (CH_3) at one end and a **carboxyl group** (COOH) at the other end.

Cis fatty acids: hydrogen atoms are located on the same side as a double bond.

Sources: foods containing some fat or oil.

Trans fatty acids: hydrogen atoms are located at opposite sides of the double bond.

Sources: hard margarines, fried foods, processed foods.

Significance of trans fatty acids in the diet:

1. May be involved in the increase in coronary heart disease.
2. May raise levels of **LDL** (bad cholesterol).
3. High levels reduce levels of **HDL** (good cholesterol).

Omega-3 polyunsaturated fatty acids:

1. Omega-3 is determined by the position of the double bond.
2. A double bond is between the third and fourth carbon atoms.
3. Help lower blood fat levels; reduce risk of blood clots, strokes and coronary heart disease (CHD); and improve brain function.
4. Main sources are oily fish, nuts, seeds and soya beans.

key point

LDL = low-density lipoprotein (bad cholesterol)

HDL = high-density lipoprotein (good cholesterol)

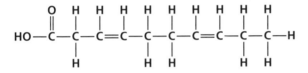

key point

Omega-3 fatty acids are known as EPA (eicosapentaenoic) and DHA (docosahexaenoic).

Functions of essential fatty acids

1. To build healthy cell membranes.
2. To reduce risk of CHD.
3. To counteract the effects of cholesterol in arteries.

Classification of lipids by source

Sources		Degree of saturation
Animal	Dairy produce, egg yolk, meat, meat fats	Mainly saturated
Plant/vegetable	Avocado, cereals, olive oil, nuts, soya bean	Unsaturated except for some margarines
Marine	*Oily fish:* salmon, mackerel, trout *Fish oils:* cod, halibut	Fish contain omega-3 polyunsaturated fatty acids (EPA and DHA)

HL Distribution of fatty acids in foods – some examples

	Saturated fatty acids	Monounsaturated fatty acids	Polyunsaturated fatty acids
Vegetable			
Olive oil	10%	20%	66%
Sunflower oil	13%	74%	8%
Soft tub margarine	17%	47%	31%
Block margarine	19%	59%	18%
Animal/marine			
Tuna	27%	26%	37%
Chicken fat	30%	45%	21%
Butter	62%	29%	4%

Properties of hard fats and oils

1. Fats are **solid** and oils are **liquid** at room temperature.
2. **Solubility:** insoluble in water, soluble in solvents.
3. **Absorb flavours** if left uncovered, e.g. from onions.
4. **Effects of heat:**
   - *melting point* – solid fats melt between 30°C and 40°C
   - *smoke point* – overheating causes glycerol to change to acrolein and a blue haze or smoke to rise (fats 200°C, oils 250°C)
   - *flash point*: can burst into flames (fats 310°C, oils 325°C).

5. **Rancidity:** spoilage of lipids happens in two ways:
   - *oxidative rancidity* occurs when oxygen in the air reacts with the carbon atoms of a double bond in an unsaturated carbon chain
   - *hydrolytic rancidity* is caused when enzymes or microbes react in a lipid, e.g. food in a freezer.

6. **Hydrogenation:** occurs when hydrogen is added to an unsaturated fatty acid in the presence of a nickel catalyst, e.g. margarine.

$$-\overset{\overset{\displaystyle H}{|}}{C}=\overset{\overset{\displaystyle H}{|}}{C}- \;\underset{H_2}{\Rightarrow}\; -\overset{\overset{\displaystyle H}{|}}{\underset{\underset{\displaystyle H}{|}}{C}}-\overset{\overset{\displaystyle H}{|}}{\underset{\underset{\displaystyle H}{|}}{C}}-$$

7. **Plasticity:** relates to whether the lipid is solid, liquid or spreadable. Allows for shape and structure and is determined by the degree of saturation: the more unsaturated fatty acids present, the softer the lipid.

8. **Emulsions:** form when two immiscible liquids are forced together to form a solution. There are two types of emulsion:
   - oil in water (mayonnaise)
   - water in oil (butter).

   Emulsions may be permanent or temporary:
   - *permanent emulsions* are formed in the presence of an emulsifier, e.g. lecithin in egg yolk in mayonnaise
   - *temporary emulsions* are formed when oil and vinegar are shaken together, e.g. French dressing.

   Working principle of an emulsifier:
   The hydrophilic end (water-loving) attaches itself to the water molecule. The hydrophobic (water-hating) end attaches itself to the fat/oil molecule. The mixture stabilises.

   Examples of emulsions in foods:
   (a) *lecithin* in mayonnaise (oil-in-water emulsion)
   (b) *casein* in butter (water-in-oil emulsion)
   (c) *casein, lecithin and GMS* in margarine.

9. **Stabilisers:** maintain the emulsions in cakes, ice cream and salad cream, preventing the ingredients separating out, e.g. gelatine, gum, pectin.

Biological functions of lipids

1. Concentrated source of heat and energy.
2. Excess forms adipose tissue, insulates the body.
3. Protect delicate organs, e.g. kidneys, heart.
4. Source of fat-soluble vitamins (A, D, E and K).
5. Source of essential fatty acids.

Energy value: 1 g lipid = 9 kcal/37 kJ energy.

Digestion of lipids – a summary

Organ/gland	Secretions	Enzymes	Acts on/ substrates	Products
Liver	Bile	Bile salts	Large fat globules	Emulsified fats
Pancreas	Pancreatic juice	Pancreatic lipase	Lipids	Glycerol and fatty acids
Ileum	Intestinal juice	Intestinal lipase	Lipids	Glycerol and fatty acids

Absorption of lipids

1. Glycerol and fatty acids are absorbed into the lacteals of the villi of the small intestine.
2. Digested lipids are transported to the bloodstream via the left subclavian vein.

HL ## Utilisation of lipids

1. Oxidised in the liver and muscles to produce energy.
2. Excess is stored as adipose tissue (insulation) or around delicate organs, e.g. kidneys, and as an energy reserve.

Exam questions and sample answers

HL **Higher Level 2005, Section A, Q2** (6 marks)

(a) State **two** functions of lipids in the body. (2 × 1 mark = 2 marks)
  (i) *Source of fat-soluble vitamins A, D, E and K.*
  (ii) *Concentrated source of energy.*

(b) Complete the following table in relation to the digestion of lipids. (4 marks)

Digestive gland	Secretion	Enzyme	Change
Pancreas	*Pancreatic juice*	Lipase	*Lipids to fatty acids and glycerol*

Ordinary Level 2009, Section A, Q2 (6 marks)

Complete the following statement in relation to the digestion of lipids (fats) using the words listed below. (3 words x 2 marks = 6 marks)

glycerol, lipase, fatty acids

The enzyme **_lipase_** converts lipids into **_fatty acids_** and **_glycerol_**.

HL *Long questions – Section B*

Higher Level 2008, Section B, Q1 (80 marks)

'Fat is an essential part of our diet. Fat has health benefits but it also has a lot of negative aspects. Consumers must make informed decisions on the amount and type of fat included in their daily diet.'

The following table provides information on three commonly used products. (Typical % values per 100g)

Constituents	Extra light spread	Original spread	Butter
Energy	188 kcal	531 kcal	744 kcal
Fat	18 g	59 g	82.2 g
Saturated fatty acids	5.1 g	12 g	52.1 g
Monounsaturated fatty acids	4.1 g	17 g	20.9 g
Polyunsaturated fatty acids	8.8 g	29.5 g	2.8 g
Omega-3 fatty acids	1.6 g	3.5 g	0.6 g
Trans fatty acids	0.3 g	0.5 g	2.9 g

(a) Using the information provided in the table, evaluate each of the three products described, having regard to current dietary advice on fat intake. (6 points × 4 marks = 24 marks)

> You must give **two** points on each of the three products.
>
> **Read, analyse** and **evaluate** the information given in the chart.
>
> Keep in mind the current dietary advice on fat intake.

Extra Light Spread

1. *Lowest energy value of the three products, therefore is lowest in calories and is suitable for those on weight-reducing diets.*
2. *Is lowest in saturated fats, which helps reduce risk of CHD, and raised total blood cholesterol and LDL levels.*

Original Spread

1. *Contains almost twice the saturated fat levels as the extra light spread but much less than the butter.*
2. *Contains four times as many monounsaturated fats as the extra light spread, which helps lower total blood cholesterol and LDL levels.*

Butter

1. *Has the highest energy value of the three products, highest calories and is unsuitable for those on weight-reducing diets.*
2. *Highest in saturated fats, which contribute to CHD, raised blood cholesterol and LDL levels.*

> Give **two** points of information under Structure for each fatty acid.

(b) Describe the **structure and** give **one** example of **each** of the following fatty acids:

(3 points × 8 marks = 24 marks)

Type	Structure	Example
Saturated	*Each carbon atom has its full complement of hydrogen. There are no carbon bonds. Solid at room temperature*	*Stearic acid*
Monounsaturated	*Contains one double bond. Liquid at room temperature*	*Oleic acid*
Polyunsaturated	*Has more than one double bond between the carbon atoms. Liquid or soft at room temperature*	*Linolenic acid*

(c) Write an explanatory note on **each** of the following properties of lipids:

(12 marks)

(i) Rancidity   (2 points × 3 marks = 6 marks)

(ii) Emulsification   (2 points × 3 marks = 6 marks)

> **LINK**
> • Go to page 22

(d) Explain how (i) advertising **and**
(ii) a person's health status might influence decision
making when purchasing dairy products.

(4 points × 5 marks = 20 marks)

> **LINK**
> • Go to page 23

(i) *Advertising*

     Advertising constantly draws attention to the health benefits of existing or new products using well-known individuals to highlight the product in magazines and TV programmes.

(ii) *Person's health status*

     People suffering from CHD choose dairy products low in saturated fats and high in polyunsaturated fatty acids, plant sterols and omega-3 fatty acids.

> Make **one** point on advertising and **one** point for health status, **plus any other two points.**

(iii) *People wanting to reduce weight tend to choose low-fat products.*

(iv) *An individual suffering from osteoporosis would choose calcium enriched dairy products e.g. Super Milk.*

Vitamins

Classification of vitamins

Fat-soluble vitamins	Water-soluble vitamins

Vitamin A (retinol; beta-carotene)
Vitamin D (cholecalciferol; ergocalciferol)
Vitamin E (tocopherol)
Vitamin K (naphthoquinone)
	Vitamin C (ascorbic acid)
	Vitamin B group:
	  • B_1 (thiamine)
	  • B_2 (riboflavin)
	  • B_6 (pyrodoxine)
	  • B_{12} (cobalamin)
	  • folic acid (folate)
	  • niacin

LINKS

• The Irish diet (p. 64)
• Fruit (p. 94)
• Vegetables (p. 97)
• Food processing (p. 126)
• Food additives (p. 139)

Fat-soluble vitamins

Vitamin A (retinol and beta-carotene)

Vitamin A is available in two forms:

	Sources	Examples
1. Retinol (pure vitamin A)	Animal	Fish, fish oils, butter, liver, fortified milk, margarine
2. Beta-carotene (pro-vitamin A converted to retinol in the body)	Fruit and vegetables (brightly coloured)	Dark green leafy vegetables, broccoli, apricots, carrots, tomatoes, peppers

Functions, deficiency, RDA and properties of vitamin A

Functions	• Produces rhodopsin to aid night vision • Essential for lining membranes • Aids growth and repair of cells • Needed for healthy hair and skin
Effects of Deficiency	• Night blindness • Xerophthalmia (dry eyes) • Retarded/stunted growth in children • Dry mucous membranes
RDA (µg per day)	• Children: 400–500µg • Adolescents: 600–700µg • Adults: 600–700µg • During pregnancy: 700µg • During lactation: 950µg
Properties	*Retinol:* • yellow fat-soluble alcohol • insoluble in water • heat stable • reduced by dehydration • powerful as an antioxidant • destroyed by exposure to oxygen *Beta-carotene:* • bright orange or yellow oil • insoluble in water • heat stable • sensitive to dehydration • powerful anti-oxidant

HL

Dangers of hypervitaminosis – excess vitamin A

Dry skin, enlarged liver, fatigue, hair loss, headaches, vomiting and even death, risk of birth defects and miscarriage.

Vitamin D – the sunshine vitamin

Vitamin D is available in two forms:

	Sources	Examples
1. **Cholecalciferols** (Vitamin D$_3$)	Sunlight	Sunlight converts 7-dehydrocholesterol in the skin to choleocalciferol
	Food	Oily fish, fish oils, eggs, milk, margarine
2. **Ergocalciferols** (Vitamin D$_2$)	Plants, fungi, yeasts	Made by the action of the sun

Functions, deficiency, RDA and properties of vitamin D

Functions	• Needed for strong bones and teeth • Aids absorption of calcium and phosphorus • Prevents rickets and osteomalacia • Regulates blood calcium levels
Effects of Deficiency	• Rickets in children • Osteomalacia (weakness of bones) • Osteoporosis (brittle bones) • Dental caries/decay
RDA (µg per day)	• Children: 10µg • Adolescents: 15µg • Adults: 10µg • During pregnancy/lactation: 10µg
Properties	• A fat-soluble vitamin • Insoluble in water • Stable to heat • Stable to acids, alkalis, oxygen • Some loss during dehydration

Dangers of hypervitaminosis – excess vitamin D

More common among young children than adults due to a high concentration of calcium in the blood.

Symptoms: nausea, mental confusion, a metallic taste, vomiting and thirst, loss of bone mass.

Vitamin E (tocopherols)

Sources	Margarine, egg yolk, wholegrain cereals, spinach, pulses, olive oils, wheat germ, nuts, avocados
Functions	<ul><li>Acts as an antioxidant</li><li>Destroys free radicals</li><li>Healthy blood cells</li></ul>
Deficiency	Rare
RDA (μg/per day)	None
Properties	<ul><li>Fat-soluble alcohol vitamin</li><li>Insoluble in water</li><li>Delays rancidity and oxidation</li><li>Damaged by alkalis, oxygen and light</li><li>Heat stable, stable in acids</li></ul>

Vitamin K (napthoquinones)

There are three forms of Vitamin K:

1. Phyllonapthoquinone (from plant sources) – K_1
2. Menanapthoquinone (made by bacteria in the intestine) – K_2
3. Menanapthone (a synthetic form) – K_3

Sources	*Plant*: green vegetables, cereals, liver, eggs *Body*: made by bacteria in the gut
Functions	<ul><li>For synthesis of prothrombin, essential for clotting of blood</li><li>Regulates calcium balance in bones</li></ul>
Effects of Deficiency	<ul><li>Delayed clotting of blood</li><li>Deficiency is rare but may occur in newborn babies</li></ul>
RDA (μg/per day)	None
Properties	<ul><li>Fat-soluble</li><li>Insoluble in water</li><li>Heat stable, unaffected by cooking</li><li>Destroyed when exposed to sunlight</li></ul>

Water-soluble vitamins

Vitamin C (ascorbic acid)

Sources	*Fruit:* blackcurrants, rosehips, strawberries, citrus fruits *Vegetables:* cabbages, tomatoes, potatoes, green peppers
Functions	<ul><li>Antioxidant, prevents CHD</li><li>Prevents scurvy</li><li>Essential for collagen formation</li><li>Necessary for strong bones/teeth</li><li>Essential for the absorption of non-haem iron</li><li>Helps white cells fight infections</li></ul>
Effects of Deficiency	<ul><li>Scurvy in severe cases</li><li>Anaemia (poor absorption of iron)</li><li>Slow healing of cuts and wounds</li><li>Bruising and bleeding</li></ul>
RDA (mg per day)	<ul><li>Children: 45mg</li><li>Adolescents: 50–60mg</li><li>Adults: 60mg</li><li>During pregnancy/lactation: 80mg</li></ul>
Properties	<ul><li>White, water-soluble acidic vitamin with a sharp flavour</li><li>Destroyed by alkalis, dry or moist heat and enzymes</li><li>Acts as an antioxidant</li><li>Destroyed by oxygen and light</li><li>Affected by metals, e.g. copper</li></ul>

Vitamin B complex or B group vitamins

Vitamin B$_1$ (thiamine)

Sources	Wholegrain cereals, fortified breakfast cereals, meats, offal, milk, eggs, yeast extract
Functions	<ul><li>Aids metabolism of carbohydrates and fats (release of energy)</li><li>Needed for a healthy nervous system</li><li>Promotes growth in children</li><li>Necessary for general good health</li></ul>
Deficiency	<ul><li>Beri-beri in severe cases</li><li>Lack of energy, depression, irritability</li><li>Tiredness and muscle cramps</li><li>Stunted growth in children</li></ul>
Properties	<ul><li>Water-soluble</li><li>Destroyed by high temperatures, dry heat and alkalis</li><li>70% destroyed during the milling process</li></ul>

Vitamin B$_2$ (riboflavin)

Sources	Milk, eggs, dark green leafy vegetables, offal, yeast extracts
Functions	<ul><li>Involved in the metabolism of nutrients</li><li>Necessary for healthy membranes</li><li>Needed for healthy skin</li><li>Promotes healthy growth</li></ul>
Deficiency	<ul><li>Sore mouth and swollen red tongue</li><li>Eye infections, sensitivity to light</li><li>Lack of energy, loss of appetite</li><li>Checked growth and poor health</li></ul>
Properties	<ul><li>Water-soluble, yellow-orange in colour</li><li>Destroyed by alkalis, sunlight</li><li>Unstable at high temperatures</li></ul>

Vitamin B$_6$ (pyridoxine)

Sources	Meat, fish, wheat germ, dark green leafy vegetables, bananas, cereals, yeast
Functions	<ul><li>Assists metabolism of protein, carbohydrates and fats by acting as a co-enzyme</li><li>Aids the formation of blood cells</li><li>Required for a healthy nervous system</li><li>Promotes healthy skin</li></ul>
Deficiency	<ul><li>Anaemia, tiredness and fatigue</li><li>Convulsions in infants</li><li>Pre-menstrual tension</li><li>Reduced immunity</li></ul>
Properties	<ul><li>Water-soluble</li><li>Generally stable at normal temperatures but destroyed by high temperatures</li><li>Destroyed by sunlight and oxygen</li></ul>

Vitamin B$_{12}$ (cobalamin)

Sources	Dairy produce, eggs, fish, offal, meats
Functions	<ul><li>Aids the formation of the myelin sheath surrounding nerve fibres</li><li>Needed for red blood cells</li><li>Aids the metabolism of fatty acids and folic acid</li></ul>
Effects of Deficiency	<ul><li>Fatigue, shortness of breath</li><li>Pernicious anaemia</li><li>Anxiety and irritability</li><li>Degeneration of nerve fibres</li></ul>

RDA (µg per day)	<ul><li>Children: 0.7–1µg</li><li>Adolescents: 1.4µg</li><li>Adults: 1.4µg</li><li>During pregnancy: 1.6µg</li><li>During lactation: 1.9µg</li></ul>
Properties	<ul><li>Water-soluble</li><li>Heat stable up to 100°C</li><li>Stable in light, strong acids and alkalis</li></ul>

Folic acid (folate)

Sources	Fortified foods, wholegrain cereals, green leafy vegetables, offal, milk, wheat germ
Functions	<ul><li>Essential for DNA and RNA</li><li>Protects against neural tube defects, e.g. spina bifida</li><li>Assists B_{12} in the formation of red blood cells</li><li>Assists protein metabolism</li><li>Supports the immune system</li></ul>
Effects of Deficiency	<ul><li>Tiredness and fatigue</li><li>Risk of neural tube defects</li></ul>
RDA (µg per day)	<ul><li>Children: 100–200µg</li><li>Adolescents: 300µg</li><li>Adults: 300µg</li><li>During pregnancy: 500µg</li><li>During lactation: 400µg</li></ul>
Properties	<ul><li>Water-soluble</li><li>Unaffected by acid environments</li><li>Sensitive to light and oxygen</li><li>Unstable in cooking, easily destroyed</li></ul>

Niacin (nicotinic acid)

Sources	Bread, fortified cereals, meat and meat products
Functions	<ul><li>Assists the metabolism of carbohydrates</li><li>Necessary for a healthy nervous system</li><li>Promotes growth and healthy skin</li><li>Prevents pellagra</li></ul>
Deficiency	<ul><li>Pellagra (symptoms are the five Ds)</li><li>Lack of energy, fatigue and weight loss</li></ul>
Properties	<ul><li>Water-soluble</li><li>Stable to heat, acids and alkalis</li><li>80%–90% lost in milling</li></ul>

Exam questions and sample answers

Higher Level 2009, Section A, Q2 (6 marks)

Identify a vitamin necessary for the absorption of each of the minerals listed
below. (2 × 3 marks = 6 marks)

Mineral	Vitamin
Calcium	*Vitamin D*
Iron	*Vitamin C*

Higher Level 2004, Section A, Q3

State **one** possible effect on the body of each of the following dietary deficiencies.
(3 × 2 marks = 6 marks)

Deficiency	Effect
Lack of Thiamine (B_1)	*Beri-beri*
Lack of Folic Acid	*Neural tube defects, e.g. spina bifida*
Lack of Cobalamin (B_{12})	*Pernicious anaemia*

Ordinary Level 2008, Section A, Q3

Name **two** classes of vitamins and state **one** example of each class. (6 marks)

Class	Example
Fat-soluble	*A,D,E,K*
Water-soluble	*B group and C*

Ordinary Level 2005, Section A, Q3

(a) State **one** function of folate (folic acid). (2 marks)

*Protects the foetus in the womb from developing neural tube defects, e.g.
spina bifida.*

(b) Name **two** good dietary sources of folate (folic acid).
(2 points × 2 marks = 4 marks)

1. *Leafy green vegetables.*
2. *Fortified foods, e.g. cereals.*

Higher Level 2009, Section B, Q1 (c)

'Vitamin B_{12} is sometimes lacking in the diet of vegetarians.'

Give an account of vitamin B_{12} (cobalamin) and refer to:

• Sources in the diet (3 × 3 marks = 9 marks)
• Properties (2 × 3 marks = 6 marks)

● Biological functions   (2 × 3 marks = 6 marks)

Sources	1. *Dairy products* 2. *Eggs* 3. *Offal*
Properties	1. *Water-soluble vitamin* 2. *Not affected by acids, alkalis and light*
Functions	1. *Needed for metabolism of fatty acids and folic acid* 2. *Needed for the manufacture of red blood cells*

Higher Level 2007, Section B, Q1 (c)   (28 marks)

Give an account of folic acid/folate and refer to:

(i) **Sources**   (2 sources × 4 marks = 8 marks)
     1. *Wholemeal bread.*
     2. *Fortified breakfast cereals.*

(ii) **Properties**   (2 properties × 4 marks = 8 marks)
     1. *Water-soluble vitamin.*
     2. *Destroyed by light.*

(iii) **Biological functions**   (2 functions × 4 marks = 8 marks)
     1. *Essential for the development of the brain and spinal cord.*
     2. *Prevents the foetus developing neural tube defects.*

(iv) **Recommended dietary allowance (RDA)**   (1 RDA × 4 marks)
     Children: 200µg per day

Higher Level 2004, Section B, Q1 (d)   (24 marks)

'Oily fish is a good source of vitamin D.'

Give an account of vitamin D and refer to (i) properties, (ii) biological functions and (iii) recommended dietary allowance.

(i) **Properties**   (3 points × 3 marks = 9 marks)
     1. *Fat-soluble vitamin, insoluble in water.*
     2. *Heat stable vitamin.*
     3. *Not affected by oxygen, acids or alkalis.*

(ii) **Biological functions**   (3 points × 3 marks = 9 marks)
     1. *Assists the absorption of calcium.*
     2. *Regulates calcium levels in the blood.*
     3. *Needed for strong bones and teeth.*

(iii) **Recommended dietary allowance (RDA)**   (RDA = 6 marks)
     Children = 10µg
     Teenagers = 15µg
     Adults = 10µg

Minerals

Major mineral elements	Trace mineral elements
Calcium (Ca)*	Iron (Fe)*
Chloride (Cl)	Chromium (Cr)
Magnesium (Mg)	Cobalt (Co)
Phosphorous (P)	Copper (Cu)
	Fluoride (F)
Potassium (K) **HL**	Iodine (I) **HL**
Sodium (Na)	
Sulphur (S)	Manganese (Mn)
	Nickel (Ni)
	Selenium (Se)
	Zinc (Zn) **HL**

*Important for Ordinary *and* Higher level.

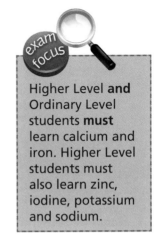

Higher Level **and** Ordinary Level students **must** learn calcium and iron. Higher Level students must also learn zinc, iodine, potassium and sodium.

LINKS
- Dietary and food requirements (p. 46)
- The Irish diet (p. 64)

Calcium

Sources	Calcium-fortified foods, dairy products, green leafy vegetables, tinned fish, hard water
Functions	• Aids formation of strong bones and teeth • Assists blood clotting • Aids functioning of nerves and muscles • Helps regulate metabolism in cells
Deficiency	• Poor quality teeth, tooth decay • Osteomalacia in adults • Osteoporosis in elderly people • Rickets in children • Muscular spasm/cramps • Abnormal clotting of blood
RDA (mg per day)	• Children: 800mg • Adolescents: 1200mg • Adults: 800mg • During pregnancy/lactation: 1200mg

Absorption of calcium

1. Absorption is **increased** by vitamin D, phosphorus, an acid environment, amino acids and parathormone.
2. Absorption is **inhibited** by saturated fatty acids, dietary fibre, oxalic acid, phytic acid, lack of acid, vitamin D deficiency and low oestrogen levels in post-menopausal women.

- **Phytic acid** binds to calcium and prevents its absorption. *Sources:* cereals and grains.
- **Oxalates** bind to calcium and prevent its absorption. *Sources:* rhubarb and spinach.

Iron

Iron is available in two forms:

1. **Haem** (ferrous iron, Fe_2+, organic): soluble and easily absorbed.
2. **Non-haem** (ferric iron, Fe_3+, inorganic): insoluble; must be reduced from ferric state to ferrous state in order to be absorbed.

Sources	Haem iron: chicken, liver, red meat
	Non-haem iron: fish, green vegetables, eggs, cereals, pulses
Functions	• Component of haemoglobin in red blood cells • Transports oxygen to the cells • Essential component of enzyme systems
Deficiency (mild/severe)	• Iron deficiency anaemia • Breathlessness, fatigue, paleness
RDA	• Children: 10mg • Adolescents: 13–14mg • Adults: 10–14mg (*females need higher intake*) • During pregnancy/lactation: 15mg

Absorption of Iron

Absorption of iron depends on its source:

1. **Haem iron:** more absorbable than non-haem iron; absorption is independent of meal composition.
2. **Non-haem iron:** strongly influenced by meal composition; boosted by the presence of vitamin C and meat in a meal, or inhibited by dietary factors.

Absorption is **increased** by:	Absorption is **inhibited** by:
1. **Combining** haem and non-haem iron sources 2. **Vitamin C** – converts non-haem into haem iron 3. **Hydrochloric acid** in the stomach aids non-haem absorption 4. The **MFP factor** (meat, fish and poultry)	1. **Oxalic acid** (rhubarb) 2. **Phytic acid** (cereals) 3. High **fibre** intake 4. **Tannins** (tea, coffee, cocoa)

key point

All these attach or bind to iron, making it insoluble.

Excess iron may result in:

- **haemochromatosis:** iron overload caused by a genetic disorder
- **haemosiderosis:** iron overload associated with nutritional overload.

Zinc

Sources	Meat, meat products, shellfish, bread
Functions	<ul><li>Enzyme and hormone activity</li><li>Helps in the healing of wounds</li><li>Promotes general good health</li><li>Protein and carbohydrate metabolism</li></ul>
Deficiency	<ul><li>Poor appetite</li><li>Slow healing of wounds</li><li>Increased risk of infections</li><li>Dry, flaky skin</li></ul>
RDA (mg per day)	<ul><li>Children: 4–7mg</li><li>Adolescents: 7–10mg</li><li>Adults: 7–10mg</li></ul>

Iodine

Sources	Fish, seaweed, iodised salt, meat, milk, eggs
Functions	<ul><li>Necessary for the production of thyroxine</li><li>Regulates metabolism</li><li>Growth and repair</li></ul>
Deficiency	<ul><li>Lethargy, tiredness, fatigue</li><li>Goitre, enlargement of the thyroid gland</li><li>Cretinism in children</li></ul>
RDAs (µg per day)	<ul><li>Children: 60–90µg</li><li>Adolescents: 125µg</li><li>Adults: 140µg</li></ul>

Potassium

Sources	Whole foods, fruits, vegetables, whole grains, fresh meat, fish, milk
Functions	<ul><li>Controls fluid balance in body tissues</li><li>Formation and functioning of body cells</li><li>Involved in protein metabolism</li><li>Regulates nerve and muscle activity</li></ul>
Deficiency	<ul><li>Deficiency is rare</li><li>Muscular weakness</li><li>Severe depletion can cause cardiac arrest</li></ul>
RDA (g per day)	Adults: 3.5g

HL Sodium

Sources	Bread, fish, butter, processed foods, soy sauce, table salt
Functions	• Regulates water balance in the body • Assists muscle functioning • Promotes healthy nerve activity
Deficiency	• Rare due to availability of salt in diet • Low blood pressure • Loss of appetite and weakness
RDA (g per day)	Adults: 1.6g

Exam questions and sample summary answers

Higher Level 2008, Section A, Q3 (6 marks)

(a) How does osteoporosis affect the body?

Osteoporosis causes loss of bone density/mass, brittle bones, loss in height and a curved back.

(b) State **two** possible causes of this condition.

(i) Hereditary factors, gender and age.

(ii) Deficiency in calcium, phosphorus and vitamin D.

Higher Level 2007, Section A, Q3 (6 marks)

(a) List **four** sources of calcium in the diet.

(i) Dairy products, e.g. milk, cheese.

(ii) Fish, e.g. sardines, tinned salmon.

(iii) Dark green vegetables, e.g. spinach.

(iv) Fortified flour.

(b) Identify **two** factors that inhibit the absorption of calcium.

(i) Oxalic acid.

(ii) Phytic acid.

Ordinary Level 2007, Section A, Q3 (6 marks)

(a) State **one** function of iron in the body. (2 marks)

Iron is essential for the formation of haemoglobin in red blood cells, which carries oxygen around the body.

(b) List **two** good dietary sources of iron. (2 × 2 = 4 marks)

(i) Offal, e.g. liver, kidneys.

(ii) Eggs.

Ordinary Level 2006, Section A, Q3

(a) State **two** functions of calcium in the body. (4 marks)

(i) Essential for formation of strong bones and teeth.

(ii) Needed for the clotting of blood.

(b) List **two** good dietary sources of calcium.   (2 marks)
    (i) *Dairy products, e.g. milk, cheese.*
    (ii) *Canned fish, e.g. salmon, sardines.*

Ordinary Level 2008, Section B, Q1

The table below shows the iron content, per average serving, of a range of different foods.

Food	Iron content (mg)
Calves' liver	12.2mg
Black pudding	9.2mg
Minced beef	3.1mg
Sardines	2.9mg
Bowl of cornflakes	2.0mg
Baked beans	1.9mg
Spinach	1.4mg
Broccoli	0.9mg
Egg	1.1mg

(a) State:
    (i) <u>Two</u> reasons why it is important to include iron in a teenager's daily diet:
                                (2 × 5 marks = 10 marks)

    1. *For the formation of haemoglobin in red blood cells.*
    2. *To form myoglobin, which carries oxygen to the muscles.*

    (ii) **One** ill-effect of a diet deficient (lacking) in iron.   (5 marks)
    Anaemia, particularly in young females.

(b) Name **one** nutrient that assists (helps) the absorption of iron in the body.
                                                        (5 marks)

    Vitamin C

(c) The RDA of iron for a teenager is 14mg. Using the information from the table given above, prepare a set of menus for one day (three meals) for a teenager which will provide an adequate supply of iron. (Other foods can be added.)
                                                        (20 marks)

Menus (3 × 6 marks = 18 marks + 2 marks for iron content)

Breakfast	Lunch	Dinner
Glass of apple juice	*Baked liver and bacon, baked beans, steamed broccoli*	*Lasagne, baby spinach salad*
***		*****
Bowl of cornflakes	*****	*Stewed prunes and yoghurt*
Poached egg, grilled black pudding, wholemeal bread	*Wholemeal roll*	
***	*****	*****
Milk	*Glass of orange juice*	*Milk/tea/coffee*

(d) State how the menus you have prepared take account of:
- the healthy eating guidelines   (2 points × 5 marks = 10 marks)
- the nutritional requirements of a teenager (2 points × 5 marks = 10 marks)

Healthy eating guidelines:

The menus provide for –

- *increased fibre from fruit, vegetables, wholegrain cereals*
- *recommended intake of fruit and vegetables (6 portions).*

Teenager's nutritional requirements:

The menus provide –

- *A good supply of iron in cereals, eggs, black puddings, liver, baked beans, prunes and minced beef with added vitamin C to help iron absorption.*
- *Protein, for growth and repair, in meat, baked beans, eggs and cereals.*

Other guidelines you could refer to:

- reduce intake of saturated fat, salt and sugar
- follow a balanced diet based on the food pyramid.

Ordinary Level 2004, Section B, Q1 (part question)
'Recent studies suggest that 36% of Irish women consume less than the average daily requirement of calcium.' (National Dairy Council)

(a) Why is it important to include calcium in the diet? (3 points × 4 marks = 12 marks)
   1. *For the formation and development of healthy bones and teeth.*
   2. *Necessary for normal functioning of muscles and nerves.*
   3. *Essential for blood clotting and regulating blood pressure.*

Other requirements you could mention:

- energy foods in the form of complex carbohydrates
- adequate calcium and vitamin D for strong bones and teeth.

(b) State **three** effects of a diet that is deficient in calcium.   (3 points × 4 marks = 12 marks)
   1. *Rickets in children.*
   2. *Osteoporosis in adults and the elderly.*
   3. *Muscular spasm.*

(c) Name **one** nutrient that is necessary for the absorption of calcium.   (6 marks)
   Vitamin D

(d) The RDA of calcium for a pregnant woman is 1200mg. Using the information from the table provided, prepare a set of menus for one day (three meals) for a pregnant woman to ensure an adequate supply of calcium. (Other foods can be added.)

Include the foods from the table that have the highest calcium content.

(18 marks)

Food	Calcium (mg per 100g/100ml)	Food	Calcium (mg per 100g/100ml)
Milk	115	Baked beans	53
Cheddar cheese	720	Broccoli	76
Cottage cheese	60	Stewed rhubarb	84
Fruit yoghurt	180	White bread	100
Canned sardines	550	Muesli	200
Canned salmon	98	Special K	42
Cabbage	57	Fortified orange juice	122

Breakfast	Lunch	Dinner
Fortified orange juice *** Muesli *** Welsh rarebit *** Tea	Sardines, mixed green salad, wholemeal roll *** Fruit yoghurt *** Glass of milk	Roast beef, baked potato, steamed broccoli, steamed spinach *** Stewed rhubarb and yoghurt *** Glass of water

(e) State how the menus you have prepared meet the general nutritional requirements of a pregnant woman. (3 × 4 marks = 12 marks)

1. The calcium content meets the RDA requirements.
2. Vitamins D and C in the foods helps the absorption of calcium and iron.
3. All the essential nutrients are included across the menus.
4. The four main food groups are represented.

Water

Composition: 2 hydrogen + 1 oxygen = H_2O (ratio 2:1).

Sources, properties, function and RDA

Sources	Most foods, beverages (milk, tea, coffee), tap and bottled water, fruit and vegetables
Properties	• Colourless, odourless and tasteless liquid • Boils at 100°C, freezes at 0°C • Neutral pH of 7, neither acid nor alkaline • Three states: solid (ice), liquid, gas (steam) • A solvent: substances dissolve readily in water • Water absorbs and retains heat
Functions	• Component of all body cells and fluids • Assists digestion (hydrolysis of nutrients) • Transports nutrients, oxygen, hormones, enzymes • Source of calcium and fluorine • Assists the removal of waste from the body • Regulates body temperature through perspiration • Refreshing to drink, quenches thirst
RDA (litres per day)	2–2·5 litres per day, with 2 litres coming from beverages and 0·5 litres from food

Exam questions and sample answers

Higher Level 2005, Section A, Q3

(a) State **two** biological functions of water. (4 marks)

   (i) *Necessary for transporting nutrients, oxygen, hormones and enzymes around the body to the cells.* (2 marks)

   (ii) *Assists the removal of waste from the body.* (2 marks)

(b) State **one** property of water. (2 marks)

   Water is a colourless, odourless and tasteless liquid.

aims To learn and revise:

- Energy
- Current dietary guidelines
- Dietary needs of individuals and special groups
- The Irish diet.

Energy

Energy is defined as 'the body's ability to do work'.
Sources of energy: proteins, lipids and carbohydrates.

MEASURING ENERGY
Proteins: 1 g = 4 kcal (17 kJ) energy
Lipids: 1 g = 9 kcal (37 kJ) energy
Carbohydrates: 1 g = 4 kcal (17 kJ) energy

exam focus

The topics in this chapter are examined in **Section A** and **integrated** with nutrients and food commodities in **Section B** of the exam paper.

Factors determining energy requirements

1. Age	Children/teenagers require more energy than adults
2. Body size	Larger bodies require more energy
3. Climate	Less energy is needed in warmer climates
4. Gender	Males have higher energy requirements
5. Occupation	Sedentary workers require less energy than more active people
6. Physical activity	The greater the physical activity, the higher the energy needs
7. Pregnancy and lactation	More energy required for the foetus to grow and when breast feeding
8. Illness	Less energy needed due to less activity

Role of energy in the body

Energy is needed for:

1. Chemical and metabolic reactions.
2. Physical activities, both voluntary and involuntary.
3. Growth, e.g. during pregnancy, adolescence, childhood.
4. Producing heat and maintaining body temperature.
5. Functioning of all internal organs.

LINK
- Dietary and food requirements (p. 46)

Metabolism is the total number of chemical reactions that take place in the body.
Basal metabolic rate (BMR):
- Is the minimum amount of energy needed to keep the body functioning.
- Is measured when a person is at rest, 10–12 hours after their last meal, during which time no physical activity has taken place.
- **BMR is highest** in growing babies and children, and decreases as one gets older.
- **BMR varies** between individuals due to a variety of factors, e.g. climate, after eating a meal.

Daily energy requirements

	Males (kcal per day)	Females (kcal per day)
Children	1,500	1,400
Adolescent	2,800	2,300
Sedentary adult	2,400	2,150
Active adult	2,800	2,450
Elderly	2,200	1,800
Pregnancy		2,400
Lactation		2,800

To maintain a constant **energy balance (intake/output):**

Energy intake = Energy output

LINKS
- Meal management and planning (p. 106)
- Energy value (protein, carbohydrates and lipids) (pp. 9, 15, 23, 43)

Factors controlling food intake

Physiological factors	• Hunger (desire to find food) • Satiety (fullness) • Hypothalamus (centre of control in the brain)
Psychological factors	• Appetite (desire to eat) • Dislike of a particular food • Stress • Mood
External factors	• Cultural preferences • Stimuli from food/foods • Social occasion • Time of day

Dietary guidelines

The health of the Irish population is monitored by Department of Health and Children supported by the HSE, National Nutritional Surveillance Centre, Health Promotion Unit and the Irish Nutrition and Dietetic Institute.

The purpose of the nutritional guidelines is to:

- encourage people to improve their eating habits
- encourage people to take more exercise
- reduce diet-related diseases in Ireland.

exam focus

Check for changes in the above departments and agencies.

Current nutritional guidelines

1. Eat the correct amount of food for your body size.
2. Use the Food Pyramid as a guide.
3. Eat more dietary fibre (whole grains, fruits, vegetables).
4. Choose calcium and iron-rich foods (especially important for females).
5. Eat five or more portions of fruit and vegetables daily.
6. Eat foods rich in starch (cereals, potatoes, rice, pasta).
7. Eat less saturated fat, sugar and salt.
8. Avoid processed foods (high in fat, salt and sugar).
9. Drink at least 6–8 glasses of water each day.
10. Keep within the recommended guidelines for alcohol.

LINKS
- The Irish diet (p. 64)
- Meal management and planning (p. 106)

Measuring nutrient intake

The term **Recommended Dietary Allowance (RDA)** corresponds to Reference Nutrient Intake (RNI) in Britain and Population Reference Intake (PRI) in the EU.

The **RDA** is the recommended daily intake of a nutrient that meets the nutritional needs of almost all the population (97–98% approx.) based on stage of life (age group) and gender.

Dietary Reference Values (DRV) refers to a range of specific types of value. These are:

- **Estimated Average Requirement** (EAR) – energy intake level
- **Lowest Threshold Intake** (LTI) – the least amount of a nutrient needed for health.
- **Lower Reference Nutrient Intake** (LRNI) – individuals with low nutritional needs.

Dietary and food requirements

Choosing a balanced diet

A well-balanced diet contains all the nutrients in the correct proportions for each individual, which is achieved by eating a wide variety of foods chosen from all the food groups the Food Pyramid.

Others (sparingly)

Meat, fish and alternatives (2 servings)

Milk and dairy group (3 servings)

Fruit and vegetable group (5+ servings)

Cereal, bread and potato group (6+ servings)

The healthy Food Pyramid

The food groups: servings and dietetic value

Food group	Servings per day	What is a single serving?	Dietetic value
Bread, cereals, potatoes, rice, pasta	6+	1 bowl porridge 25 g brown bread 1 potato 2 tbsps rice 2 tbsps pasta	● Main energy source ● NSP (fibre) ● B-group vitamins ● Low in lipids
Fruit and vegetables	5+	1 piece fresh fruit 1 bowl salad ½ glass fresh juice	● NSP (fibre) ● Vitamins ● Minerals ● Water ● Almost fat free
Milk, cheese, yoghurt (dairy sources)	3 Teenagers: 4 During pregnancy: 5	75 ml milk 25 g Cheddar cheese 1 small carton yoghurt	● Calcium ● Proteins ● Lipids ● Vitamin D (low-fat ranges)
Meat, fish, poultry, eggs, beans, peas	2 During pregnancy: 3	50 g cooked meat/poultry 75 g cooked fish 2 eggs 6 tbsps peas/beans 75 g nuts	● Protein ● Iron (rich supply) ● B-group vitamins ● Other minerals
Others (fats, oils, cakes, snacks, fizzy drinks, etc.)	Very small amounts		● Eat sparingly ● High in cholesterol, fats, salt and sugars

Individual dietary requirements

Babies

The early stages of life are a period of rapid growth and development. A baby can be bottle fed with formula feeds or breast fed.

Breast feeding is recommended because breast milk:

- contains all nutrients in the correct proportions
- provides antibodies to protect against infection
- is at the right temperature and sterile
- reduces risks of respiratory, gastrointestinal and other infections.
- assists bonding between baby and mother.

key point

We should aim to include three of the four main food groups in each meal for all individuals.

LINK
- Nutrients (p. 2)

If formula milk is used the manufacturer's instructions should be followed strictly. Do not over- or under-dilute.

Dietary guidelines

1. When weaning, introduce single foods at a time: choose soft, sieved/puréed foods, e.g. cereals, fruit, vegetables, potatoes, eggs, meat, chicken, etc.
2. Include a balance of foods from the food groups.
3. From six months, the baby needs foods rich in iron and vitamin C.
4. Sieving and puréeing make foods more digestible.
5. As the baby grows, include more protein and energy foods.
6. Exclude tea, coffee, fatty, fried and spicy foods, sugar and salt. Do not give honey to babies under one year old.

Children

1. 'Faddy' eating should be discouraged.
2. Regular mealtimes, without rushing, are recommended.
3. Provide healthy nutritious snacks and packed lunches.
4. Serve small, easy-to-manage portions.
5. Choose a balanced diet from the four main food groups.
6. Encourage children to eat breakfast every day.
7. Avoid sweets, sugary foods, salty snacks and fizzy drinks.

Specific dietary needs of children

Nutrient	Function	Main sources
Protein	Needed for repair and for rapid growth	Meat, poultry, fish, eggs, cheese
Carbohydrate	Energy production	Cereals, fruit, vegetables
Fibre	Prevents constipation	Cereals, fruit, vegetables
Calcium (aided by vitamin D)	Healthy bones and teeth	Milk, cheese, yoghurt
Vitamin D	Absorption of calcium	Eggs, milk, oily fish, sunlight
Iron (aided by vitamin C)	Prevents anaemia General good health	Meat, dark green vegetables
Vitamin C	Absorption of iron Healing of wounds	Fruit, vegetables
Water	Prevents dehydration	Beverages, tap water

Adolescents

Adolescence is a time of rapid growth and increased activity.

Specific dietary needs of adolescents

Nutrient	Function	Main sources
Protein	Rapid growth and hormone production	Meat, poultry, fish, eggs, cheese, soya products
Carbohydrate	Energy production	Cereals, fruit, vegetables
Fibre	Prevents bowel disorders and constipation	Whole cereals and products, brown rice, brown bread, fruit, vegetables
Calcium (aided by vitamin D)	• Healthy bones and teeth • Extra calcium for females to prevent osteoporosis	Milk, cheese, yoghurt
Vitamin D	Absorption of calcium	Eggs, milk, oily fish, sunlight
Iron (aided by vitamin C)	Prevents anaemia (especially in females)	Meat, dark green leafy vegetables (cabbage, spinach)
Vitamin C	• Absorption of iron • Healing of wounds	Fruit, juices, vegetables
Water	Healthy skin	Beverages, tap water, juices

Adults

1. Adults need a well-balanced, varied diet based on their lifestyle, gender and age.
2. In adulthood the rate of growth slows; energy needs may have reduced.
3. Reduce intake of salt to prevent high blood pressure.
4. Reduce saturated fats to prevent CHD (Coronary Heart Disease).
5. Give up smoking and reduce/eliminate alcohol consumption.

Specific dietary needs of adults

Nutrient	Function	Main sources
Protein	Growth and repair of body cells	Meat, fish, eggs, soya products
Carbohydrate	Energy production	Cereals, fruit, vegetables
Fibre	• Prevents constipation • Reduces risk of CHD	Wholegrain cereals, fruits, vegetables
Lipids – unsaturated	• Reduces risk of CHD • Reduces cholesterol build-up	Chicken, turkey, fish, lean meat
Calcium (aided by vitamin D)	• Healthy bones and teeth • to maintain bone mass	Milk, cheese, tinned fish
Vitamin D	Absorption of calcium	Oily fish, eggs, sunlight
Iron (aided by Vitamin C)	• Prevents anaemia • Healthy blood	Dark green leafy vegetables, meat
Vitamin C	• Absorption of iron • Healing of wounds	Fruits, juices, vegetables
Vitamin B group	Release of energy from foods/cell metabolism	A wide variety of foods
Water	Prevents dehydration	Beverages, tap/bottled water, juices

During pregnancy and lactation

1. Choose a well-balanced, varied diet.
2. Ensure adequate folic acid prior to and after conception to reduce risks of neural tube defects, e.g. Spina Bifida.
3. Eliminate risk of Listeria and Salmonella by avoiding raw eggs, unpasteurised cream cheeses and cook-chill products.
4. Limit salt intake to prevent Hypertension and Oedema.
5. Avoid fried, spicy or sugary foods and coffee.
6. Give up smoking and alcohol.

Specific dietary needs during pregnancy/lactation

Nutrient	Function	Main sources
Folate/folic acid	• Prevents/reduces neural tube defects • Essential for formation of new cells in foetus	Fortified cereals/bread, spinach, fortified milk, liver, kidneys
Protein	Foetal growth and development	Meat, fish, eggs, soya products
Carbohydrate	Energy production	Cereals, fruit, vegetables
Fibre	Prevents constipation – common during pregnancy	Wholemeal bread and pasta, brown rice, fruits, vegetables
Lipids – fatty acids	Development of foetus's healthy nervous system	Oily fish, eggs, liver
Calcium (aided by vitamin D)	Healthy bones and teeth	Milk, cheese, tinned fish
Vitamin D	Absorption of calcium	Eggs, sunlight
Iron (aided by vitamin C)	Prevents anaemia in mother and baby	Dark green leafy vegetables, meat
Vitamin C	Absorption of iron	Fruit, vegetables
Water	Prevents dehydration	Beverages, water, juices

Elderly people

Problems associated with ageing and related dietary issues:

1. **Reduced income** limits choice, changes priorities, can result in poverty and inadequate diet.
2. **Poor general health or physical disabilities**, e.g. dental problems (false teeth, gum disease), anaemia, etc.
3. **Difficulties when shopping**, e.g. less mobile, too far from shops, shopping bags too heavy to carry.
4. **Difficulties when preparing foods**, e.g. arthritis in hands.
5. **Loss of interest** in buying a variety of fresh foods.
6. **Loneliness and lack of interest** in cooking for one person, leading to malnutrition.

Specific dietary needs of older people

Nutrient	Function	Main sources
Protein (concentrated and easy to digest)	Replacement or repair of worn cells	Fish, chicken, turkey, eggs
Carbohydrate	Energy production	Cereals, fruit, vegetables
Fibre	Prevents constipation and bowel disease	Wholegrain cereals, fruits, vegetables

Calcium (aided by vitamin D)	• Strong bones • Prevents osteoporosis	Milk, cheese, tinned fish
Vitamin D	Absorption of calcium	Milk, yoghurt, eggs, sunlight
Iron (aided by vitamin C)	Prevents anaemia	Offal, dark green vegetables
Vitamin C	Absorption of iron Healing of wounds	Fruit, vegetables
Vitamin A	Healthy eyes and skin	Carrots, butter, eggs, liver, fish liver oils
Water	Prevents dehydration	Beverages, water, juices

Older people should:

1. Choose a varied, well-balanced diet.
2. Serve smaller portions and eat more regular meals.
3. Reduce intake of cholesterol and saturated fats.
4. Reduce salt/salty foods to prevent hypertension.
5. Reduce sugars to prevent diabetes mellitus.
6. Avoid spicy foods to prevent indigestion.

Convalescents

When someone is recovering from illness serve:

1. Concentrated protein foods.
2. Foods that are easy to digest.
3. Small portions that are easy to eat.

Meals should be prepared under strict hygienic conditions.

key point

Avoid spicy foods, coffee and fast foods.

Dietary needs of convalescents

Nutrient	Function	Main sources
Protein	Repairs damaged cells	Fish, chicken, eggs
Carbohydrate	Energy production	Fruit, steamed vegetables
Fibre	Prevents constipation	Fruits, vegetables
Calcium (aided by vitamin D)	Promotes recovery	Milk
Vitamin D	Absorption of calcium	Milk, yoghurt, eggs
Iron (aided by vitamin C)	Prevents anaemia	Offal, dark green vegetables
Vitamin C	Absorption of iron Healing of wounds	Fruit, vegetables
Vitamins/minerals	Promote healing	Variety of foods
Water (increase intake)	Prevents dehydration	Water, fruits, juices

Dietary needs for diet-related health problems

Bowel disorders

Main bowel disorders

Disorder	Symptoms	Dietary deficiency or other reasons
Constipation	• Faeces hard and painful to pass • Irregular bowel movements	Low-fibre diet
Haemorrhoids (piles)	• Enlarged veins in anus and rectum • Severe itching • Passing blood	Low-fibre diet Obesity Straining
Irritable bowel syndrome (IBS)	• Bloating • Abdominal cramps • Constipation • Diarrhoea	Low-fibre diet Stress
Bowel cancer	Can be blood loss via the colon	Lack of fibre (fruit, vegetables) Diet high in saturated fat
Diverticulitis	Formation of pouches in intestinal walls containing food waste; bacteria, acids and gases form, which leads to pain	Low-fibre diet Low fluid intake

Guidelines for preventing bowel disorders – a high-fibre diet

1. Use wholegrain cereals and cereal products.
2. Eat more fruit, vegetables and pulses.
3. Use fruits and vegetables with skins where possible.
4. Choose high-fibre breakfast cereals.
5. Drink plenty of water (at least eight glasses a day).
6. Take regular exercise.

Benefits of a high-fibre diet:
1. less saturated fat is consumed
2. gives a feeling of fullness
3. prevents bowel disorders.

Osteoporosis

Osteoporosis occurs when bones become thinner and less dense. The bones break easily.
Who is affected?

• Elderly people, especially women. Osteoporosis is common among women, whose peak bone mass is reached on average between 25 and 35 years of age.

What are the main causes (of osteoporosis)?

- A lack of calcium during the bone developmental stage.
- Hormonal changes.

Main risk factors

Specific dietary guidelines

1. Eat a well-balanced diet.

1. Age	Risk increases with age, especially for post-menopausal women, due to a lack of the hormone oestrogen which maintains calcium levels
2. Genetic	Heredity or family history of osteoporosis
3. Gender	Females are more at risk than males
4. Hormonal	Menopausal hormonal changes hasten calcium loss
5. Dietary	Inadequate intake of calcium, vitamin D and phosphorus
6. Exercise	Lack of exercise results in weak bones

2. Increase intake of vitamin D, calcium-rich and phosphorus-rich foods.
3. Take regular exercise, **daily**.
4. Avoid smoking and reduce alcohol consumption.
5. Reduce salt and caffeine (decreases bone density).

Obesity

When an individual's weight is 20 per cent above the recommended weight for their height, they are considered obese or overweight.

Main causes of obesity

1. Energy intake is greater than energy output.
2. Diet is high in refined, convenience and fast foods.
3. Increase in consumption of saturated fats and sugar.
4. Hormonal imbalance, e.g. thyroid problems.
5. Lack of exercise, a sedentary lifestyle.
6. Certain medications.
7. Depression, low self-esteem, boredom.

key point

Factors increasing the risk of obesity may be behavioural, environmental or genetic.

Health risks associated with obesity

1. CHD, high blood pressure, varicose veins.
2. Respiratory/breathing difficulties.
3. Diabetes, especially non-insulin-dependent.
4. Gallstones form due to high cholesterol.
5. Infertility or difficulties in childbirth.

6. Psychological problems (depression).

7. Arthritis, joint problems due to excess weight.

Treatments for obesity include: dietary changes to reduce weight, changing eating patterns, exercising regularly, surgical procedures and drug treatments.

Specific dietary requirements/guidelines

1. Consult a doctor before starting a weight-reducing diet.

2. Balance a weight-reducing diet with an exercise programme.

3. Eat balanced regular meals, avoid snacking between meals.

4. Increase intake of high-fibre foods.

5. Avoid convenience foods, fast foods and takeaways.

6. Avoid high sugar and sugary foods, e.g. biscuits.

Cardiovascular disease

LINKS
• Dietary fibre (pp. 14–15)
• Carbohydrates (p.11)

- **Examples:** aneurisms (blood clots), coronary heart disease (CHD), strokes.
- **Main cause:** atherosclerosis.
- **Locations of atherosclerosis in the body:** aorta, cerebral arteries, coronary arteries and femoral arteries.

Coronary heart disease (CHD)

CHD occurs when the coronary arteries become blocked or narrowed due to a build-up of cholesterol. Blood pressure may rise and the restriction of blood flow can lead to heart attack, angina or death.

Fixed risk factors

- **Age:** women over 55 years and men over 45 are most at risk.
- **Gender:** women generally have lower rates of CHD than men, but *after menopause* the rate is the same.
- **Genetics:** individuals are likely to develop CHD if their parents have CHD.

Dietary and lifestyle risk factors

1. Overweight and obesity.

2. Diets high in saturated fats and salt.

3. High blood cholesterol levels.

4. High blood pressure levels.

5. Diabetes mellitus.

6. High stress levels.

7. Lack of exercise.

8. Smoking and excess alcohol.

Dietary and lifestyle measures to reduce CHD

Dietary	1. Reduce intake of saturated fats 2. Choose low-fat alternatives 3. Increase use of polyunsaturated fats 4. Increase fibre (fruit and vegetables) 5. Reduce salt, avoid processed foods 6. Use fat-free cooking, e.g. steaming, poaching 7. Avoid refined carbohydrates (sugar), processed foods and takeaways
Lifestyle	1. Exercise regularly to increase levels of HDL (see below) 2. Do not smoke and avoid alcohol 3. Manage stress 4. Reduce weight or maintain correct body weight

Cholesterol

Functions of cholesterol:

- Involved in the production of hormones.
- Essential component in the production of cell walls.
- Necessary component of bile salts (produced in the liver).

Types of blood cholesterol:

- low-density lipoproteins (LDL = 'bad')
- high-density lipoproteins (HDL = 'good').
    1. **LDL** carries cholesterol from the liver to body tissues, delivering triglycerides. High levels of LDL are a risk factor for heart disease.
    2. **HDL** picks up excess cholesterol and transfers it to other lipoproteins, which return it to the liver for recycling or excretion. High levels of HDL reduce the risk of heart disease.

Factors that improve the LDL to HDL ratio are antioxidants, polyunsaturated fats, soluble fibres, weight control and exercise.

> **LINKS**
> - Lipids (p. 19)
> - Carbohydrates (dietary fibre) (pp. 14–15)

Reducing cholesterol levels

Reduce intake of:

- Saturated fats (butter, cheese, red meat).
- High-cholesterol foods (eggs).

Increase intake of polyunsaturated fats (oily fish, olive oil, nuts).

Eating disorders

Anorexia nervosa

Anorexia is a psychological condition in which fear of becoming fat is accompanied by some of the following behaviour:

- abuse of laxatives
- over-exercising
- self-induced vomiting and starvation.

Symptoms include:

- periods stop (amenorrhoea).
- increased facial and body hair.
- hair loss.
- death.

Recovery may be short- or long-term. Psychotherapy and special dietary treatment are required to help recovery.

Bulimia nervosa

Bulimia is an eating disorder in which binge eating is followed by self-induced vomiting in order to avoid gaining weight.

Symptoms include:

- mottling/decay of teeth.
- dehydration.
- irritation of throat.
- inflammation of oesophagus.
- swollen salivary glands.

Modified diets

Vegetarianism

Definition: a vegetarian is a person whose diet consists mainly of plant food and who does not eat meat or, in some cases, any animal products.

Reasons for vegetarianism

1. **Cultural:** The accepted diet among a family group or community.
2. **Health:** A diet without saturated animal fat and high in fibre is considered healthier.
3. **Moral/ethical:** Killing, harming or intensively rearing animals is believed to be wrong.
4. **Religious:** Some religions do not allow the eating of meat.
5. **Aesthetic:** Individuals may not like the look, smell or taste of meat.
6. **Economic:** Meat is too expensive for some families.

Types of vegetarian

Lacto-ovo vegetarian	Eat eggs and dairy products, do not eat meat
Vegan	Live on plant foods; do not eat meat or any animal products
Ovo vegetarian	Eat eggs, do not eat meat
Pesco vegetarian	Eat fish, do not eat meat
Pollo vegetarian	Eat chicken only, no other meat

Benefits of a vegetarian diet

1. Low in saturated fats – reduces risk of obesity and CHD.
2. Low in cholesterol – reduces high blood pressure and CHD.
3. High in fibre – reduces risk of/prevents bowel disorders.
4. Low in salt – lower levels of high blood pressure.
5. Contains less sugar – fewer vegetarians develop diabetes.
6. More fresh foods eaten – contain fewer additives.
7. High intake of fruit/vegetables – reduces risk of obesity.

Main food groups for *lacto-vegetarians*

Food group	Recommended servings per day
Whole grains and nuts	6+ (bread, rice, pasta, almonds, etc.)
Vegetables	3+ (carrots, onions, peppers, broccoli, spinach, etc.)
Fruits	2+ (oranges, apples, bananas)
Legumes or pulse vegetables	2+ (peas, beans, lentils)
Milk and dairy products	2+ (milk, cheese, yoghurt)

Nutrient intake for vegetarians

The **lacto-vegetarian diet** provides sufficient amounts of protein, carbohydrates, dietary fibre, calcium, B-group vitamins, vitamins A, D, E and C, folate, and trace minerals for their dietary needs.

The **vegan diet**, because of the absence of all animal products, may lack HBV protein, vitamins B_{12} and D, calcium, iron and zinc.

Nutrients and sources

Nutrients	Sources
HBV protein	Soya protein, seeds, nuts
Fibre	Wholemeal breads, fruits, vegetables, whole cereals
Vitamin B_2 (riboflavin)	Wholegrain cereals, green leafy vegetables, seeds, nuts
Vitamin B_{12} (cobalamin)	TVP, fortified cereals, fortified soya milk, supplements
Vitamin D	Fortified cereals, fortified margarine, sunlight
Calcium	Fortified soya milk, tofu, green vegetables
Iron	Dark green vegetables, whole grains, dried fruit, beans
Zinc	Whole grains, beans, lentils, seeds, nuts

Dietary guidelines for vegetarians/vegans

1. Include all food groups in each meal.
2. Check food labels for hidden animal products.
3. Replace meat with alternatives (TVP, tofu).
4. Use vegetable stocks in soups and sauces.
5. Use vegetable oils and margarine instead of animal fats.
6. For **lacto-vegetarians**: include milk, cheese and yoghurt for HBV protein and calcium.
7. For **vegans**: choose soya products as alternatives to dairy products.

Make sure that the **nutritional needs** of the individual are met.

Ingredients suitable for vegetarian cookery

Ingredients	Examples
Grains	Wheat, oats, millet, couscous, bulgur wheat, rice, buckwheat, corn (maize), barley, rye
Pulses	*Beans*: butter, adzuki, haricot, kidney, soya, chickpeas *Peas*: green, split green/yellow, chick *Lentils*: brown, green, red
Nuts	Almonds, brazils, cashews, hazelnuts, pecans, peanuts, pistachios, walnuts
Seeds	Linseed, pumpkin, sesame, sunflower
Dried fruit	Apricots, dates, figs, prunes, raisins, sultanas
Sea vegetables	Carrageen moss, dulse (Ireland); laver (Wales)

Vegetarian dishes include: vegetarian lasagne, quiche (modify the ingredients), omelette, mixed vegetable or mixed bean curry and vegetable cobbler.

Vegan dishes include: vegetarian curry, pasta dishes, rice dishes, vegetable stir-fry, vegetarian risotto and stuffed vegetables (tomatoes, aubergines, peppers).

Coeliac disease

LINK
- Supplementary role of protein (p. 8)

Exam questions and sample answers
Higher Level 2006, Section A, Q3 (6 marks)
(a) Define coeliac condition. (3 marks)

Coeliac disease occurs in individuals who are unable to break down gluten, the protein found in wheat/wheat products. It damages the lining of the small intestine, the villi become inflamed and are unable to absorb adequate nutrients from food.

(b) Name **three** foods which should be avoided by a person with coeliac condition. (3 marks)

1. Processed foods, e.g. sausages, some soups and sauces.
2. Breads and cakes.
3. Pastries and pies.

Other sources of gluten: batters, biscuits, some breakfast cereals, pasta, pizza, lasagne, stuffing, coated foods.

Symptoms of coeliac disease:

- **Adults**: anaemia, diarrhoea, reduced body weight, abdominal pain, mouth ulcers, tiredness.
- **Children**: slow growth, weight loss.

Dietary guidelines

1. Follow the doctor's instructions.
2. Stick to a gluten-free diet.
3. Look for the gluten-free symbol on foods.
4. Read food labels, e.g. on processed foods.
5. Avoid all hidden sources of gluten.

Gluten-free symbol

Suitable foods: dairy products, eggs, unprocessed fresh meat, fish (uncoated), poultry, fruit, vegetables, soya products, rice, breakfast cereals made from maize or rice, soups and sauces made with cornflour, gluten-free products.

Diabetes

Diabetes is a disorder of the endocrine system which is caused by:

- a deficiency/lack of insulin; **or**
- not enough insulin being produced.

Symptoms: blurred vision, glaucoma, increased thirst, increased urination, tiredness/fatigue, weight loss.

key point

Insulin, a hormone produced by the pancreas, controls the level of glucose in the blood, which is used to produce energy.

Types of diabetes

TYPE 1: insulin-dependent diabetes (juvenile onset)

- The pancreas does not manufacture insulin.
- Found in young children and adolescents.
- Controlled by insulin injections.

Dietary guidelines for **Type 1** diabetes:

1. Co-ordinate times of meals and injections.
2. Eat regular meals: **never** miss meals.
3. Reduce intake of saturated fat (risk of CHD).
4. Reduce intake of salt (risk of high blood pressure).
5. Eat a high-fibre diet.

TYPE 2: non-insulin-dependent diabetes (maturity onset)

- Occurs in older people.
- Is associated with being overweight.
- The pancreas produces insulin, but it is not effective.
- Can be controlled by diet and sometimes medication.

Treatment: balanced diet, reduction of sugar intake, exercise.

Dietary guidelines for **Type 2** diabetes:

1. Eat regular meals; **never** miss meals.
2. Reduce intake of saturated fat (risk of CHD).
3. Reduce intake of salt (risk of high blood pressure).
4. Replace sugary snacks with low-sugar fruit.
5. Eat high-fibre starches in fixed amounts at regular times each day.
6. Replace sugar-rich jams with low-sugar varieties.
7. Keep alcohol consumption low.
8. **Always** follow the doctor's advice.

Compiling menus

Learn to devise a day's menus for all modified diets, using the correct menu format and keeping in mind the specific needs for a balanced diet.

LINKS

- Nutrients (p. 2)
- Meal management and planning (p. 106)

Exam questions and sample answers

Higher Level 2004, Section A, Q8 (6 marks)

In relation to each nutrient listed, recommend **two** good sources for a vegan diet.

(6 sources × 1 mark = 6 marks)

Nutrient	Sources for a Vegan Diet
Protein	*Soya beans, textured vegetable protein (TVP)*
Calcium	*Fortified soya milk, leafy green vegetables*
Iron	*Prunes, whole grains (sources of non-haem iron)*

Ordinary Level 2009, Section A, Q5 (6 marks)

(a) List **two** factors that influence the amount of energy required by the body.
    1. Body size and weight.
    2. Climate.

(b) Explain the term Basal Metabolic Rate (BMR).

LINK

- BMR (p. 44)

Ordinary Level 2008, Section A, Q6 (2 points × 3 marks = 6 marks)

(a) Name **one** diet-related condition that commonly affects elderly people.

  Osteoporosis

(b) State **one** cause of this condition.

Age, e.g. post-menopausal women lack oestrogen which maintains calcium levels.

Higher Level 2009, Section B, Q1 (a)

Vegetarian diet

The following table provides information on the nutritive value of minced beef and Quorn mince.

	Energy	Protein	Fat	CHO	Fibre	Vitamins	Minerals
Minced Beef (raw)	225 kcal	19.7 g	16.2 g	0	0	B Group	Iron 1.4 mg Sodium 80 mg
Quorn Mince	94 kcal	14.5 g	2.0 g	4.5 g	5.5 g	0	Sodium 100 mg

(Nutritional information per 100 g.)

Using the information provided in the table, evaluate the contribution of Quorn mince to the diet of vegetarians. (6 points × 4 marks = 24 marks)

  1. *Lower energy value, useful for low-calorie diets.*
  2. *Lower in protein than minced beef. Contains mycoprotein, a high quality protein, which is a good meat alternative.*
  3. *Low in fat, which reduces risk of CHD, stroke, etc.*
  4. *Fibre present aids peristalsis and removal of waste.*
  5. *Lacks vitamins, must be served with vitamin-rich foods.*
  6. *Lacks iron, must be served with iron-rich foods.*

Higher Level 2007, Section B, Q2

'Coronary heart disease remains the leading cause of death in Ireland, accounting for over 7,000 deaths annually.'

(CHAIR – Coronary Heart Attack Ireland Register)

(a) Identify and elaborate on (i) the lifestyle changes **and** (ii) dietary guidelines you would recommend in order to reduce the incidence of coronary heart disease. (4 points × 4 marks = 16 marks)

(i) **Lifestyle Changes** – *A Summary*

  1. *Maintain a healthy weight for body size and activity.*
  2. *Do not smoke and reduce or eliminate alcohol.*
  3. *Exercise on a regular basis, walk instead of driving.*
  4. *Reduce stress.*

(ii) **Dietary Guidelines** – *A Summary*

    1. *Reduce intake of saturated fats.*

    2. *Choose oily fish, poultry and very lean meat.*

    3. *Increase dietary fibre, e.g. fruits, vegetables, cereals.*

    4. *Reduce intake of salt in the diet, avoid processed foods*

(b) Plan a day's menu for an individual suffering from CHD. Include **one** functional food in the menu and suggest a reason for its inclusion. (22 marks)

Breakfast	Lunch	Dinner
Cinnamon and raisin porridge	Mixed vegetable, goat's cheese and wholegrain rice salad	Poached lemon and dill salmon
Poached omega-3 eggs	***	Steamed broccoli and carrots
Wholewheat toast	Probiotic yoghurt	Boiled potatoes
***	****	****
Fresh juice/tea	Glass of water	Fresh berry salad
		****
		Glass of fresh juice

Functional food	Reasons for inclusion
Omega-3 eggs	To reduce risks of heart disease
Probiotic yoghurt	To improve the digestive system

(c) Write an account of **cholesterol**. (3 points × 4 marks = 12 marks)

    1. *Cholesterol is a wax–like substance manufactured by the liver and is present in animal foods.*

    2. *It is an essential component of cell walls, bile and some hormones.*

    3. *There are* **two** *types:*

       • **Low-density lipoproteins** *('bad cholesterol'). It is deposited on the walls of arteries and increases risks of CHD. Eating saturated and trans-fats increases levels of LDP.*

       • **High-density lipoproteins** *('good cholesterol'). It removes loose cholesterol from the arteries and help to reduce risks of heart disease. Eating mono-unsaturated and polyunsaturated fats raise the levels of HDP.*

Ordinary Level 2009, Section B, Q2

Case Study

John (25) is a builder with a local firm and works from 8.00 a.m. to 5.30 p.m. each day. He likes to watch football on television most evenings. He plays squash once a week. The following is a typical example of his daily intake.

Breakfast	Lunch	Dinner
Breakfast roll ½ litre milk	Brown bread ham sandwich Apple Packet of crisps Bar of chocolate Can of Coke	Fried steak and chips Tinned peas and beans Bowl of ice cream A doughnut Coffee

(a) Evaluate John's daily menu under each of the following headings:

   (i) **Healthy Eating Guidelines**   (any 2 points × 4 marks = 8 marks)

- *Not getting the recommended 5+ servings of fruit and vegetables (only three – apple, peas, beans).*
- *Eating too many processed foods (ham, crisps, chocolate, ice cream, doughnut).*
- *Eating too many sugary foods (chocolate, Coke, ice cream, doughnut).*
- *Breakfast roll and steak are high in saturated fats.*
- *Menus not balanced according to healthy eating guidelines.*
- *No water included in any meal.*

   (ii) **Nutritional Value**   (any 2 points × 4 marks = 8 marks)

- *HBV protein in steak, beans and peas (animal/vegetable).*
- *Calcium in milk.*
- *Dietary fibre in brown bread, apples, peas and beans.*
- *Lacking in essential vitamins and minerals.*
- *Carbohydrates in breakfast roll, bread and chips provide energy.*

   (iii) **Energy Value**   (1 point × 8 marks)

- *John needs high-energy foods as he is a manual worker.*
- *Energy is provided in the breakfast roll, brown bread, steak and chocolate.*

(b) Suggest some changes John could make to (i) his lifestyle and (ii) his diet.

      (4 points × 4 marks = 16 marks)

   (i) **Lifestyle Changes** (2 points × 4 marks = 8 marks)

    1. *Reduce the amount of time watching television each day.*

    2. *Get more involved in sports, e.g. play squash more often.*

   (ii) **Dietary Changes** (2 points × 4 marks = 8 marks)

    1. *Increase intake of fruit and vegetables.*

    2. *Reduce intake of sugar, salt and fat.*

exam focus

Make **one** reference to lifestyle, **one** reference to diet and any **two other** changes.

(c) Explain the importance of including water in the diet.

      (2 points × 5 marks = 10 marks)

   1. *Assists the removal of waste from the body.*

   2. *Prevents dehydration and quenches thirst.*

Past exam questions to check out
Ordinary Level 2007, Section B, Q2: obesity, energy.
Ordinary Level 2006, Section B, Q1: children and fibre.
Ordinary Level 2005, Section B, Q2: teenagers' diet – case study.

The Irish diet

Sources of information on Irish eating patterns

- National Nutrition Survey 1946–48
- National Nutrition Survey 1990
- National Nutrition Surveillance Centre (set up in 1992)
- Slán Surveys of Lifestyle, Attitude and Nutrition (1998, 2002, 2007).

Factors influencing changes in the Irish diet

1. Developments in agricultural practices.
2. Developments in food distribution systems.
3. Improvements in food processing and retailing.
4. Improved dietary guidelines.
5. World War I and World War II.
6. Influx of people from other countries.
7. Irish people travelling abroad.
8. Consumer demand.

> **LINKS**
> - Food choices (p. 2)
> - Social, economic and technological changes affecting the family (p. 236)

Irish food and eating patterns since 1900

1900–1950

1. Active lifestyle – manual work was common.
2. Rural dwellers used homemade produce.
3. Home-made bread and porridge were staple foods.
4. Good supply of cereals, dairy produce and potatoes.
5. Meat and poultry were served only on special occasions.
6. Few processed foods were available.
7. Increase in food prices during World Wars I and II.
8. Food shortages during World War II led to rationing.

Nutritional significance:
1. High intake of carbohydrates.
2. Low intake of iron – anaemia was common.

3. Low intake of saturated fats.

4. Adequate supply of calcium from milk.

5. Fruit and vegetable intake increased after 1930.

Effects of World Wars I and II:

1. Rise in unemployment.

2. Higher food prices.

3. Insufficient supplies of basic foods.

4. Diets limited; deficiency diseases became common.

5. Diets were low in iron, vitamins and minerals.

> **key point**
> - Little knowledge of nutrition.
> - High levels of anaemia in women.
> - Food choices were based on economic status of family.

Post-World War II (1950–1990)

1. Increased availability of white bread, tea and processed foods.

2. Meat and dairy produce consumption increased.

3. Diets higher in fat and lower in carbohydrates.

4. Anaemia common among females.

5. Decreased intake of fruit, vegetables, porridge, potatoes and homemade foods.

6. Food imports increased, greater variety available.

7. Improvement in food storage, e.g. refrigeration, freezing.

8. Consumer demands for processed foods, new foods.

Nutritional significance:

1. Decreased intake of fibre, vitamins and minerals.

2. Increase in saturated fats.

3. Increase in sugar and salt.

4. Dramatic increase in the use of additives.

1990–present day

1. Increase in convenience/processed/takeaway foods.

2. Good range of foods (meats, breads, fruits, vegetables).

3. Increase in pre-prepared family meals.

4. Families eating out more (economic improvement).

5. Individuals becoming aware of nutritional needs.

6. Individuals becoming more health conscious.

7. Sedentary lifestyle and irregular eating patterns.

Nutritional significance:

1. Increase in saturated fats, salt and sugar.

2. Increase in HBV protein and iron.

3. Diet low in fibre (fruit, vegetables).

> **LINKS**
> - Nutrients (p. 2)
> - Food processing (p. 126)
> - Food labelling (p. 135)

4. Further increase in additives and preservatives.
5. Consuming more energy than is needed, increase in obesity.
6. Increase in alcohol consumption.
7. Increase in range of nutritional supplements on market.

Recent trends: 2000 onwards

- Establishment of farmers' markets.
- Availability of organic produce.
- Consumer demands for organic/free range produce.
- Traceability of meat, poultry, eggs, etc.

The Irish diet 1998–2007

The table below *compares the results from three Slán Surveys (1998, 2002, 2007) by the National Nutritional Surveillance Centre.*

The results show the percentage of respondents who consumed the recommended number of servings for each shelf on the food pyramid.

key point

1. Improvements in knowledge of nutrition.
2. Development of low-fat foods, gluten-free foods.
3. By 1990, vegetable intake reduced to half that of 1948.

LINKS
- Food choices (p. 2)
- Social, economic and technological changes affecting the family (p. 236)

LINK
- Dietary guidelines (p. 45)

Food groups	1998	2002	2007
Others	14%	17%	18%
Meat, fish, eggs	38%	39%	39%
Milk, cheese, yoghurt	22%	29%	20%
Fruit, vegetables	61%	69%	65%
Cereal, bread, potatoes	40%	34%	26%

Comparing the Irish diet with current dietary guidelines

Dietary guidelines	Current situation
1. Reduce salt	People consume too much salt
2. Reduce sugar	Intake is one of the highest in Europe – more than recommended
3. Reduce fat	Consumption of saturated fat is declining. There has been an increase in use of polyunsaturated fats and functional foods
4. Increase fibre	Irish people are not meeting the RDA of 25–35 g/day
5. Fruit/vegetables	65% are eating 5+ servings
6. Milk, cheese, yoghurt	Irish people are not reaching the recommended targets

Major concerns about the current Irish diet

1. High in saturated fats.
2. High in salt.
3. High in sugar.
4. Low in dietary fibre.
5. Low in iron.
6. Low in calcium.

LINK

- Dietary needs for diet-related health problems (p. 52)

Aspects of malnutrition

Low dietary fibre intake

Causes	Effects on body	Corrective measures
• Insufficient fibre-rich foods • Over-use of processed foods	• Bowel disorders, constipation, IBS • Gallstones • Piles	• Eat more fibre • Avoid processed foods • Eat more fruit and vegetables • Drink more water

LINKS

- Carbohydrates (p. 11)
- Fruit and vegetables (pp. 94–9)

LINKS

- Lipids (p. 19)
- Obesity (p. 53)
- CHD (p. 54)
- Methods of cooking (Chapter 3, Extension 1, see www.moresuccess.ie)

High saturated fat intake

Causes	Effects on body	Corrective measures
• Increased intake of foods high in saturated fats • Eating too many processed foods, takeaways and fast foods	• Diabetes • CHD • Obesity • High cholesterol	• Reduce saturated fat • Increase intake of polyunsaturated fats • Remove visible fats on meat, select lean cuts • Grill, poach or steam; do not fry • Use low-fat foods • Avoid convenience foods

Low iron intake

Causes	Effects on body	Corrective measures
• Lack of iron-rich foods • Inadequate vitamin C • Lack of variety in type of iron (haem, non-haem) • Inhibiting factors (phytic acid, fibre) • Menstruation	• Anaemia • Tiredness • Fatigue • Feeling 'run down' • Breathlessness	• Eat iron-rich foods • Include adequate vitamin C for iron absorption • Reduce intake of inhibiting factors

LINKS

- Iron (p. 36)
- Vitamin C (p. 30)

LINKS

- Calcium (p. 35)
- Vitamin D (p. 28)
- Functional foods (p. 130)

Low calcium intake

Causes	Effects on body	Corrective measures
Insufficient vitamin D	Rickets	Increase intake of calcium-rich foods
Insufficient calcium-rich foods	Osteomalacia	Increase intake of vitamin D
	Osteoporosis	Increase intake of protein-rich foods
Inhibiting factors (phytates, oxalates and dietary fibre)	Dental decay	Use fortified foods
		Avoid sugar

Exam questions and sample answers

Higher Level 2009, Section A, Q3 (6 marks)

Outline **three** changes that have taken place in Irish eating habits from the beginning of the twentieth century.

1. *Increased consumption of prepared, convenience, processed and takeaway foods and meals.*
2. *People are more aware of healthy eating guidelines, nutritional needs and special diets.*
3. *Decrease in consumption of potatoes and bread, increase in use of pasta and rice.*

Ordinary Level 2008, Section B, Q2(a) (linked to CHD)

'Studies show that we are eating more and more food away from home and that this trend is set to increase in the future. An Irish Heart Foundation study found that 72% of people surveyed eat out at least once a week with 32% saying that they eat out several times per week'. (*Consumer Choice*, January 2003)

Statements given in the questions in **Section B** frequently outline concerns about current dietary habits. **Read** statements carefully. If a table is given, **analyse** it thoroughly and **use** the information when answering the question.

(a) Comment on the above statement **and** explain what is meant by '**eating food away from home**'. (10 marks)

   Comment (5 marks)

   People are eating out more because:
   - *Less time to prepare and cook at home due to work/lifestyle commitments.*
   - *Greater lifestyle choices.*
   - *Poorer culinary skills than previous generations.*
   - *A lack of interest in cooking, not wanting to eat alone.*

'Eating food away from home' (5 marks)

This refers to the following:

- *Eating in hotels, restaurants, cafés, coffee shops.*
- *Availability of food in bars and pubs.*
- *Availability of food in clubs, e.g. golf clubs.*
- *Eating in the workplace canteen (at reduced cost).*
- *Takeaway food from fast food outlets, delicatessens.*

Higher Level 2006, Section B, Q2(c) (linked to calcium)

Outline the measures taken by the dairy industry to meet the current trends in eating patterns and lifestyle of the Irish consumer. (4 points × 3 marks = 12 marks)

1. Introduction of fortified food, e.g. folic acid in cereals.

2. Development of functional foods, e.g. probiotic yoghurt.

3. Introduction of prepared foods, e.g. grated/sliced cheese.

4. Development of low-fat foods, e.g. milk, cheese, yoghurt.

3 Food Studies: Part One

aims To learn and revise:

- Food commodities
- Meal management and planning
- Food preparation and cooking processes
- Recipe balance
- Aesthetic awareness
- Sensory analysis
- The Irish food industry.

exam focus

This section is examined in **Section A** and in **Section B**.

Food commodities

exam focus

Check Food Composition Tables in a Home Economics textbook for the composition of foods.

LINKS

- Properties of nutrients (Chapter 1)
- Food preparation and cooking processes (p. 107)
- Food processing (p. 126)
- Consumer choice (p. 218)

exam focus

Remember:

- **Nutritive value** = the nutrients in the food.
- **Dietetic value** = the contribution each of those nutrients makes to the diet.

Meat and poultry

Classification of meat

Carcass meat, game, offal, poultry.

Nutritive value/nutritional significance

Nutrient	Value in the diet
Protein	• HBV protein • Actin, myosin and globulin in meat fibres • Collagen and elastin in connective tissue
Fat/lipid	• Saturated fats (visible and invisible) • Amount depends on the cut of meat
Carbohydrate	• None present
Vitamins	• B group vitamins (B_1, B_2, B_6, B_{12}) • Traces of vitamins A and D in offal
Minerals	• Good source of haem iron • Zinc, phosphorus, potassium, sulphur
Water	• Leaner meat has higher water content • Fat meat has lower water content

Dietetic value/contribution to the diet

Protein	Needed for cell growth and repair (children, adolescents, pregnant women)
Fat	Provides heat and energy. People at risk of CHD and high cholesterol should avoid/reduce intake of saturated fat
Iron	Haem iron is easily absorbed and prevents anaemia (females, children, teenagers, adults)
Nutrients lacking	Carbohydrates, calcium, vitamin C. Serve with foods rich in these nutrients

Structure of meat

LINKS
• Protein (p. 3)
• Lipids (p. 19)
• Vitamins (p. 26)
• Minerals (p. 35)

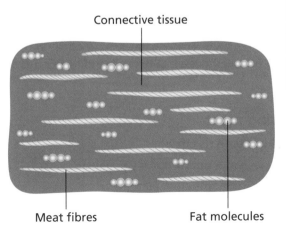

Connective tissue

Meat fibres   Fat molecules

Rules for buying meat

Buy meat from a reputable shop where:

1. Surfaces and equipment are clean and hygienic.
2. Staff wear protective clothing and follow hygienic procedures.
3. Raw and cooked meats are stored and handled separately.
4. The meat supplied is produced under the Bord Bia
   Quality Assured Programme (traceability, quality and safety
   standards).

QUALITY
ASSURANCE SCHEME
BORD BIA
ORIGIN-IRELAND

Rules for choosing meat

When choosing meat:

1. Buy fresh meat in small quantities.
2. Choose meat which has a good bright colour, is firm, moist and free of odours.
3. Avoid meats with gristle or a lot of fat.
4. Match the cut of meat to the cooking method.
5. Cheaper cuts are as nutritious as expensive cuts.

Rules for storing meat

1. Store fresh meat quickly after purchase, below 5°C.
2. Unwrap, put on a clean plate, cover, store in a refrigerator below cooked foods.
3. Store raw and cooked meats separately, never on the same plate or shelf. Use within 2–3 days.
4. Leave vacuum-packed meat in wrapping until needed.

Causes of toughness in meat

1. Age	Older animals have longer fibres and produce tougher meat; meat from younger animals is tender
2. Activity	Less active parts of animals are tender, active parts are tougher
3. Conditioning of animals	• Resting before slaughter allows glycogen to build up in muscles • Hanging after slaughter changes glycogen to lactic acid – tenderises meat
4. Cooking method	• Slow, moist methods tenderise tougher cuts of meat, e.g. stewing • Fast methods are better suited to tender cuts of meat

Methods of tenderising meat

1. Injecting animals with proteolytic enzymes.
2. Sprinkling tenderising enzymes on raw meat e.g. papain.
3. Mechanical methods (beating, mincing, piercing).
4. Slow, moist methods of cooking, e.g. stewing.
5. Marinating in acids, spices and herbs.

Effects of heat/cooking on meat

Protein	Coagulates, meat shrinks, becomes firmer, collagen changes to gelatine, fibres become tender and digestible
Fat/lipid	Melts and improves flavour
Vitamins	Some B group vitamins are destroyed
Minerals	Some lost during cooking
Extractives	Are released, flavours improve
Bacteria	Are destroyed
Colour	Changes from red to brown

> **LINK**
> ● Food preservation (pp. 126, 158)

Methods of preserving and processing meat

Process	Method	Effects
1. Canning	Ingredients heated to high temperatures, canned and sealed *Examples*: meat stews, corned beef	● Loss of B group vitamins ● Colour, flavour and texture changes ● Increase in fat content
2. Curing	Brine solution injected into meat; meat soaked for 5 days and hung May be smoked *Examples:* bacon, ham	● Changes in colour and flavour ● Increase in salt content
3. Drying	Removal of water from small pieces of meat: accelerated freeze drying (AFD) *Examples:* packet soups, sauces	● Loss of moisture ● Loss of B group vitamins ● Colour, flavour and texture changes
4. Freezing	Commercial blast freezing at −30°C *Examples:* most meats	Loss of B group vitamins
5. Vacuuming	Meat is placed in polythene, air is removed and edges are heat-sealed *Examples:* rashers, gammon	● Little change in food value ● No change in colour, flavour and texture

Offal

Offal is the edible internal organs of animals, e.g. heart, kidney, liver, sweetbreads and tongue. It is cheap and nutritious.

Nutritional value/nutritional significance

Protein	HBV protein
Fat/lipid	Most low in fat
Carbohydrates	None present
Vitamins	● B group vitamins ● Vitamin C ● Vitamins A and D (liver, kidney)
Minerals	Good source of iron (liver, kidney)

exam
Q

Exam question and sample answer

Ordinary Level 2005, Section A, Q8   (6 marks)
Explain **three** effects of cooking on meat.
  1. *Collagen changes to gelatine.*
  2. *Fat melts and flavours develop.*
  3. *Micro-organisms are destroyed, meat is safe to eat.*

Ordinary Level 2005, Section B, Q1   (80 marks)
A local restaurant has a choice of three meats to add to a pasta dish. The main
nutrients present in each of the three meats are listed in the table.

Nutritional Comparison of Ingredients per 100 g

	Minced beef	Chicken fillet	Bacon
Energy (kcals)	221	116	428
Protein (g)	18.8	21.8	14.2
Lipids (g)	16.2	3.2	41.2
Carbohydrate (g)	0	0	0
Iron (mg)	2.7	0.5	1.0

(a) Using the information provided in the table and bearing in mind current
    healthy eating guidelines, recommend **one** meat for use in the pasta dish.
    Give **three** reasons for your choice.   (16 marks)

Name of meat (4 marks)	Reasons for choice (3 × 4 marks)
Minced beef	*1. HBV protein supplies essential amino acids for growth and repair* *2. Haem iron in meat is easily absorbed* *3. Provides B$_{12}$ for making red blood cells*

(b) Suggest a suitable accompaniment for the pasta dish referred to above. Give
    two reasons for your choice.   (12 marks)

Accompaniment	Reasons for choice
Mixed green salad	*Provides vitamin C and minerals* *Adds colour, flavour and texture*

(c) Give an account of lipids (fats) and refer to:
    (i) **Functions in the body**   (3 × 4 marks = 12 marks)
      1. *Concentrated source of energy, provides heat.*
      2. *Source of essential fatty acids.*
      3. *Source of fat-soluble vitamins A, D, E, and K.*

(ii) **Sources in the diet** (4 × 2 marks = 8 marks)

Animal: meat, milk

Vegetable: nuts, olive oil

Marine: oily fish (salmon), fish oils (cod)

(iii) **Properties** (2 points × 4 marks = 8 marks)

1. Oils can form emulsions, e.g. mayonnaise

2. Lipids are insoluble in water but soluble in solvents, e.g. benzene

(iv) **Energy Value** (4 marks)

1g fat = 9 kilocalories or 37 kilojoules

(d) Summarise **five** factors that consumers should consider when buying meat and meat products. (5 × 4 marks = 20 marks)

> **LINK**
> ● Fat p. 21.

Poultry

Classification

Domestic (chicken, duck, goose, turkey), game (duck, pheasant).

Nutritive value/nutritional significance

Nutrient	Value in the diet
Protein	HBV proteins
Fat/lipid	● Small amount of saturated fat ● Amount depends on the type of bird
Carbohydrate	None present
Vitamins	B group vitamins (B_1, B_2, niacin)
Minerals	● Iron (less than in meat) ● Traces of calcium, phosphorus, zinc
Water	Significant amount: 50–70%

Dietetic value/contribution to the diet

Protein	HBV protein for growth and repair (children, convalescents)
Fat/lipid	Lower fat content, good alternative for low-cholesterol and low-calorie diets
Carbohydrate	Serve with carbohydrate-rich foods
Digestibility	Easy to digest, suitable for invalids and the elderly
Economic value	Inexpensive and versatile

Rules for buying poultry

1. Buy from a reliable source that is clean and hygienic.
2. Check origin and 'use by' or 'best before' label.
3. Check for signs of freshness – firm, plump flesh.

> **LINKS**
> ● Protein (p. 3)
> ● Lipids (p. 19)

4. Avoid poultry with a bad smell and poor colour.

5. Frozen poultry should be frozen solid.

Rules for storing poultry

- **Frozen poultry:** place in a freezer as soon as possible after purchase.
- **Fresh poultry:** store as for fresh meat.

Fish

Classification of fish

Fish may be classified according to:

- habitat
- shape: flat (e.g. plaice, sole); or round (e.g. salmon, trout)
- nutritive value.

key point

Poultry can be free range, organic or factory reared. Bord Bia operates the **Poultry Products Quality Assurance Scheme.**

LINK

- Methods of cooking (Chapter 3, Extension 1, see www.moresuccess.ie)

Habitat

Freshwater	Saltwater	Farmed
Rivers, lakes	**Demersal:** on the seabed	Aquaculture
Examples: salmon, trout, pike, eel	*Examples:* cod, plaice, sole	*Examples:* oysters, mussels, salmon, trout
	Pelagic: in shoals near the surface	
	Examples: herring, mackerel	

Nutritive value (based on fat content)

White fish	Oily fish	Shellfish
Low in fat, fat stored in liver	High in unsaturated fatty acids in flesh	Lower in fat, higher in cholesterol
Examples: cod, haddock, plaice	*Examples:* herring, mackerel, salmon, tuna	**(a) Molluscs:** shells
		Examples: mussels, oysters
		(b) Crustaceans: claws
		Examples: prawns, crabs, lobsters

Nutritive value/nutritional significance

Nutrients	Nutritive value
Protein	HBV protein
	Actin, myosin and collagen
Fat/lipid	Oily fish – polyunsaturated fatty acids (PUFA), omega-3
	Traces in liver of white fish
Carbohydrates	None present
Vitamins	B group in all fish
	Vitamins A and D in oily fish
Minerals	Iodine, phosphorus and potassium
	Calcium in canned fish
Water	65–80% water
	Highest in white fish

Dietetic value/contribution to the diet

Protein	HBV protein for growth (children, teenagers, pregnant women)
Fat/lipid	Omega-3 fatty acids useful in low-cholesterol diets and low-calorie diets
Carbohydrates	Serve with carbohydrate-rich foods
Digestibility	Easy to digest, ideal for invalids and the elderly
Economic value	Most are cheaper when in season; some are expensive
Availability	Widely available in a variety of forms
Cooking	Easy and quick to prepare and cook; versatile; short cooking time

Structure of fish

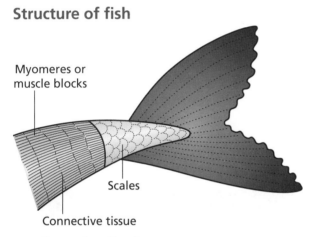

Myomeres or muscle blocks

Scales

Connective tissue

LINKS
- Protein (p. 3)
- Lipids (p. 19)
- Vitamins (p. 26)
- Minerals (p. 35)

key point

Polluted waters may contaminate shellfish.

Spoilage (staling)

Fish is perishable and spoils because of:

1. **Oxidative rancidity:** reacts with oxygen in the air.
2. **Enzymes:** spoil fish even at low temperatures.
3. **Bacteria:** when caught, fish struggle and use up glycogen stored in muscles and liver. Lactic acid is not formed, fish stales quickly, bacteria multiply rapidly and fish begins to 'go off', producing tri-methylamine.

Rules for buying fish

Fresh fish:

1. Choose fish in season.
2. Eyes should be fresh, bright and bulging.
3. Flesh should be firm, shiny and moist, gills bright red or pink in colour.
4. Colour should be characteristic of species.
5. Smoked fish should have a glossy skin and smoky smell.
6. Shellfish should be clean: *molluscs* should not be open; *crustaceans* should be active and alive.

Frozen and pre-packed fish:

1. Check the sell-by date.
2. Ensure the fish is frozen solid.
3. Packaging must not be damaged.
4. Place in the freezer soon after purchase.

Rules for storing fish

Place in the fridge or freezer immediately.

Fresh fish:

1. Remove wrapping, rinse and cover.
2. Place on a bed of ice in the fridge.
3. Store away from other foods.

Tinned fish: use immediately after opening.

Effects of cooking on fish

1. Bacteria and parasites are destroyed.
2. Protein coagulates.
3. Collagen changes to gelatine, fish flakes easily.
4. Fish shrinks, flesh becomes opaque.
5. Loss of B group vitamins and minerals.

Commercial fish processing

Method	Effects	Examples
Canning	● Softens bones ● Increase in calcium ● Loss of B vitamins ● Bacteria are destroyed	Sardines, tuna, salmon
Freezing	● Inactivates micro-organisms ● No change in colour, flavour and texture unless breaded, etc.	Whole, steaks, fish fingers, pies
Smoking	● Change in colour and flavour ● Increase in salt content ● Bacteria are destroyed	Mackerel, salmon, eel

Exam questions and sample answers

Higher Level 2006, Section A, Q4   (2 points × 3 marks = 6 marks)
Explain **two** factors that contribute to the spoilage of fish.
1. *Oxidative rancidity: fish reacts with oxygen in the air.*
2. *Enzymic activity: spoils fish flesh even at low temperatures.*

Ordinary Level 2005, Section A, Q7   (6 marks)
Classify fresh fish and give **one** example of each class.

Classification	Example (1 per class)
Oily fish	*Mackerel*
White fish	*Haddock*
Shell fish	*Prawns*

Higher Level 2004, Section B, Q1 – fish (summary answer)
'Fish and other seafood is becoming a more popular choice as an alternative to meat.' (*Consumer Choice*, June 2001)
Estimated Consumption of Seafood in Ireland, 1997–2001 (live weight, tonnes).

Fish type	1997	1999	2001
Salmon and trout	7,500	11,500	12,500
White fish	36,850	34,500	33,125
Tuna	4,100	6,200	7,100
Shellfish	3,490	4,050	4,565

(Bord Iascaigh Mhara)

(a) Using the information provided in the table, comment on consumer trends in fish consumption. Suggest reasons for such trends.   (4 points × 5 marks = 20 marks)

Salmon and trout consumption increased due to:
1. *Increased awareness of the health benefits of fish oils.*
2. *Improved availability of salmon due to commercial fish farming.*

White fish consumption decreased due to:
1. *Depletion of white fish stocks off Ireland due to over-fishing.*
2. *EU determining quotas and affecting availability.*

Tuna consumption increased due to:
1. *Affordability and convenience of tinned tuna*
2. *Fresh tuna has become more available*

Shellfish – there was a small increase due to:
1. *Shellfish becoming more affordable and available.*
2. *Versatility in cooking, e.g. starters, main courses.*

(b) Give a detailed account of the nutritive value of fish.

(4 points × 3 marks = 12 marks)

Choose any four nutrients from the table below.

Nutrient	Nutritive value
Protein	HBV protein, actin, myosin, collagen
Fats	Polyunsaturated fatty acid (omega-3) in oily fish. Low in white fish
Carbohydrates	None
Vitamins	B group in all fish. Vitamins A and D in oily fish
Minerals	Iodine, potassium, phosphorus. Calcium in bones of canned fish
Water	Varies with class of fish

(c) State why oily fish is recommended for the diet of a person with coronary heart disease. (6 marks)

Oily fish contain polyunsaturated fatty acids (PUFAs), e.g. omega-3, which reduce cholesterol and risk of heart disease.

(d) Oily fish is a good source of Vitamin D. Give an account of Vitamin D and refer to (i) properties, (ii) biological functions and (iii) recommended dietary allowance (RDA). (24 marks)

> **LINK**
> - Nutrients (p. 28)

(e) Give an account of **six** key factors that consumers should consider when **buying** fresh fish and fish products. (6 points × 3 marks = 18 marks)

> **LINK**
> - Buying fish (p. 77)

Ordinary Level 2006, Section B, Q2 – fish, nutrition and preservation

(a) Describe (i) the nutritive value and (ii) the dietetic value of fish. (20 marks)

(i) **Nutritive Value** (10 marks)

1. *Protein: high biological value (HBV).*
2. *Lipids: polyunsaturated fatty acids (PUFAs), omega-3.*
3. *Carbohydrates: none.*
4. *Vitamins: some B-group, A and D in oily fish.*
5. *Minerals: excellent source of iodine, good source of phosphorus and potassium; canned fish contains calcium.*

4 points × 5 marks = 20 marks

Give **one** point on nutritive value **and one** point on dietetic value **plus two** other points.

(ii) **Dietetic Value** (10 marks)

1. *HBV protein in fish is a good alternative to meat.*
2. *Excellent source of omega-3, reduces risk of CHD, ideal for those on low-cholesterol diets.*
3. *Easy to digest, useful for children and the elderly.*

(b) Name **three** different types of processed fish products and state why these products are popular. (14 marks)

Name of product (3 × 2 marks)	Reasons for popularity (4 × 2 marks)
1. Canned: tuna, salmon, sardines	No preparation needed
2. Frozen: fillets, fingers, cakes	Easy to cook and serve
3. Ready fish meals: fish pies, chowders	No waste, good value Ready to use

(c) Freezing is one method of storing fish for a period of time. Outline the general rules to be followed when freezing fresh fish. (4 points × 4 marks = 16 marks)

1. Set fast-freeze button at −25°C for 3–4 hours beforehand.
2. Freeze in useable quantities/portions.
3. Use no more than one-tenth of freezer capacity in any 24-hour period.
4. Cool all foods before freezing.

exam focus

Other rules are also acceptable.

Eggs

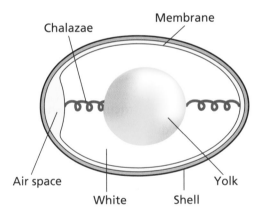

Chalazae   Membrane

Air space   Yolk

White   Shell

Nutritive value/nutritional significance

Protein	• Rich source of 100% HBV protein • *White*: ovalbumin and globulin • *Yolk*: vitelin and livetin
Fat/lipid	• Saturated fat • Cholesterol present • Contain lecithin, a natural emulsifier
Carbohydrates	None
Vitamins	• B_1, B_2, B_{12}, niacin (water-soluble) • A, D and E (fat-soluble)
Minerals	Calcium, iron, phosphorus, zinc, sulphur, selenium
Water	High content: 74% in whole egg

Dietetic value

Protein	• Contains all the essential amino acids • Ideal for children, adolescents, lacto-ovo vegetarians • Good alternative to meat
Fat/lipid	• Restrict in low-cholesterol diet • Easy to digest, ideal for elderly people
Carbohydrate	Serve with carbohydrate-rich foods
Vitamins and minerals	Useful source of vitamins B_1, B_{12}, iron, phosphorus and zinc
Digestibility	Easy to digest, ideal for elderly people, children, convalescents
Water	High water content (74%)
Versatility	Used in a variety of dishes, economical, cooks quickly

Rules for buying eggs

1. Buy from a clean shop with a good turnover.
2. Check for the Quality Assurance logo (Bord Bia)
3. Check shells are not broken/cracked.
4. Check best before date.
5. Check that eggs are heavy for their size.

LINKS
• Protein (p. 3)
• Lipids (p. 19)
• Vitamins (p. 26)
• Minerals (p. 35)

Egg Quality Assurance Scheme (EQAS)

- Implemented by the Department of Agriculture, Fisheries and Food.
- Strict regulations cover hygiene, disease control, flock welfare and environmental protection of poultry.
- Hens are tested and certified salmonella-free.
- Feed is heat-treated.
- Farms are inspected and monitored.

LINK
• Bord Bia (p. 119)

Grading and labelling of eggs

Weight/size	Quality/class
XL (very large) = 73 g L (large) = 63–73 g M (medium) = 53–63 g S (small) = under 53 g	A = top quality B = suitable for baking C = sold to industry only

Egg boxes must carry the following information:

- packing centre code/registration
- name and address of packer
- country of origin
- number of eggs
- laying date or period (weeks 1–52)
- quality/class
- weight grading
- use-by date (minimum durability)
- storage instructions
- Quality Assurance mark/logo.

Eggs must carry the following codes:
- Farming method code: 0 = organic;
  1 = free range; 2 = barn; 3 = cage
- Country of origin (e.g. IR = Ireland)
- County and farm code/ID
- Best before date.

Rules for storing eggs

1. Store in a fridge with the pointed end down.
2. Do not store near strong-smelling foods.
3. Use eggs in rotation.
4. Egg whites and yolks can be frozen separately.
5. Remove eggs from the fridge one hour before use.

Effects of heat and cooking on eggs

1. Bacteria are destroyed.
2. Proteins are denatured and coagulate.
3. Albumin becomes insoluble, changes colour and becomes opaque.
4. Overcooking causes curdling, eggs become indigestible.
5. Sulphide ring forms if overcooked.
6. Some loss of vitamin B.

> **LINK**
> - Properties of protein (p. 8)

Properties of eggs

Method	Effects	Application
Aeration	1. Whisking unfolds the structure of protein 2. Whisking traps and holds air, creates foam 3. Beating creates heat, which coagulates the foam 4. Cooking sets the foam	Sponge cakes, meringues, soufflés
Coagulation	1. Eggs coagulate or set when heated (white at 60°C and yolk at 68°C) 2. Overheating causes curdling/denaturation – protein tightens, shrinks, water escapes	• Boiling, poaching • Coating food • Glazing food • Thickening sauces • Binding ingredients
Emulsifying	Lecithin is an emulsifier in egg yolk: 1. Enables two immiscible liquids to mix together and form an emulsion 2. Mixture becomes stable and does not separate	• Mayonnaise (oil/vinegar) • Cakes (fat/sugar) • Hollandaise sauce (butter/vinegar)

Culinary uses of eggs	Examples
Binding	Burgers, omelettes, potato cakes, rissoles
Coating	Batters, coating sweet or savoury fried foods
Garnishing	Halved, sieved or sliced for savoury dishes
Glazing	Pastry flans, pies, scones, tarts
Thickening	Custards, quiches, sauces, soups

Exam questions and sample answers

Higher Level 2009, Section A, Q4   (6 marks)

Listed below are **three** properties associated with eggs and food preparation. Give **one** practical application of each property.   (3 examples × 2 marks = 6 marks)

Property	Application in food preparation
Coagulation	*Poached eggs*
Aeration	*Meringue*
Emulsification	*Mayonnaise*

Ordinary Level 2006, Section A, Q5   (6 marks)

(a) Name **four** nutrients found in eggs   (4 × 1 = 4 marks)

   (i) HBV proteins, e.g. albumin.

   (ii) Lipids: saturated fat in egg yolk.

   (iii) Minerals: calcium, iron, phosphorus, sulphur.

   (iv) Vitamins: B group, D and E. Yolk is good source of A.

(b) List **two** effects of heat on eggs.   (2 × 1 = 2 marks)

   (i) Protein coagulates or sets.

   (ii) Bacteria are destroyed.

Alternative protein foods – novel proteins

Novel proteins are derived from two non-animal sources:

- **processed plant foods:** soya beans, wheat
- **micro-organisms:** fungi, yeast and bacteria

Soya foods

Examples of soya foods:

- textured vegetable protein (TVP)
- tofu (soya bean curd)
- tempeh (fermented soya bean plant)

- miso (soya bean paste)
- soy sauce, soya oil, soya flour
- soya margarine, milk and yoghurt.

Nutritive value/nutritional significance

Protein	HBV protein (74%)
Fat/lipid	Unsaturated fat, polyunsaturated fatty acid (linoleic acid)
Carbohydrates	Starch and fibre
Vitamins	B group vitamins (soya beans)
Minerals	Calcium, non-haem iron
Water	Low amount (14%)

Dietetic value

Protein	HBV protein, useful for all groups including vegetarians
Fat/lipid	• Polyunsaturated fat, which helps to reduce cholesterol • Suitable for low-cholesterol and low-calorie diets
Carbohydrate	Fibre helps prevent bowel disorders
Versatility	• Versatile, available in a variety of forms, easy to use • Good alternative to meat in the diet

Textured vegetable protein (TVP)

Manufacture:

1. Oil is extracted from soya beans.
2. Beans are ground into flour.
3. Carbohydrates are removed, leaving only protein.
4. Oil, additives and flavouring are added.
5. Mixture is heated and extruded to create specific textures.
6. It is dried, fortified, weighed and packed.

Learn TVP as a food profile.

Advantages and disadvantages of TVP:

Advantages	Disadvantages
• Nutritious and cheap substitute for meat	• Inferior flavour to meat, tends to be bland
• Low in saturated fat	• Extra flavouring is usually required
• Source of dietary fibre	• Inferior texture
• Little waste, very versatile	• Limited range of forms/shapes

Culinary uses of TVP: burgers, casseroles, curry, lasagne, stews.

Rules for storing TVP:

1. Store in a dry, well-ventilated press.
2. Once rehydrated, use as for raw meat.

Mycoprotein

Nutritive value/nutritional significance

Protein	HBV protein, low in methionine
Fat/lipid	Low in saturated fat, cholesterol free
Carbohydrate	Source of dietary fibre
Vitamins	B group vitamins
Minerals	Zinc, non-haem iron
Water	Low water content

Manufacture of mycoprotein (Quorn)

1. Produced from a fungus, *Fusarium graminearum*.
2. Fungus cells are grown in a fermenter at 65°C.
3. Oxygen, glucose, nitrogen and minerals are added.
4. Mixture is harvested and filtered.
5. Flavourings and colourings are added.
6. Mixture is textured to resemble meat.
7. It is shredded, diced or sliced.

Main uses of Quorn

Pies, curries, casseroles, stews.

Milk

Nutritive value/nutritional significance

Protein	• HBV protein • Caseinogen, Lacto-albumin, Lacto-globulin
Fat/lipid	• Mainly saturated fat • An emulsion stabilised by lecithin
Carbohydrate	• Milk sugar, lactose, a disaccharide
Vitamins	• Fat-soluble vitamins A and D in milk fat • Water-soluble B_1, B_2 and niacin • Lacks vitamin C (due to processing)
Minerals	• Rich source of calcium • Phosphorus, potassium, iodine • Lacks iron
Water	• High water content (87%)

Dietetic value/contribution to the diet

Protein	• HBV protein for growth (babies, children, adolescents, pregnant/nursing mothers) • For repair of cells (invalids and the elderly)
Fat/lipid	• Easily digested form of fat • Low-fat milk is suitable for low-cholesterol or low-kilocalorie diets. • Omega-3 fatty acids added to milk reduces CHD, suits those with high cholesterol
Carbohydrate, vitamins and minerals	Serve with foods rich in fibre, starch, vitamin C and iron
Digestibility	Easy to digest, ideal for all groups
Versatility	Many uses (savoury and sweet dishes)
Economic value	An economical, balanced food, widely available. Some milks are fortified

Culinary uses of milk

1. As a beverage on it own, in milk shakes, smoothies.
2. As a main ingredient, e.g. batters, puddings, desserts.
3. In sauces, e.g. parsley sauce, custard sauce.
4. In soups, e.g. cream of vegetable soup.
5. Enriching dishes/increasing nutritive value.
6. Glazing scones, tarts, breads.

LINKS

• Protein (p. 3)
• Lipids (p. 19)
• Vitamins (p. 26)
• Minerals (p. 35)

Types of milk

Whole milk (full fat milk)	Minimum of 3.5% fat
Semi-skimmed milk	2% fat (low fat or light milk)
Skimmed milk	0.2% fat, fewer fat-soluble vitamins
Fortified milk	Fortified with vitamins and minerals (calcium, folic acid, vitamin A + D, etc.), made from whole or low-fat milk
Organic milk	From cows grazed on pasture on which no chemical fertilisers or pesticides have been used
Buttermilk	Soured milk used in bread making
Flavoured milk	Chocolate, strawberry, banana
Dried milk	Water is removed from milk
Evaporated milk	Canned milk with 60% water removed
Condensed milk	Evaporated milk with added sugar
Soya milk	Milk substitute from soya beans

Reasons for processing milk:

- to destroy micro-organisms
- to increase shelf life
- to improve flavour.

Methods and effects of processing on milk:

LINKS

- Protein (p. 3)
- Dietary guidelines (p. 45)
- Food pyramid (p. 46)

Method	Effects
Homogenisation	• Uniform consistency • No nutrients lost
Pasteurisation	• Destroys pathogens • Some loss of vitamins B_1 and C • Extends shelf life
Sterilisation (whole, semi-skimmed and skimmed)	• Destroys bacteria • Loss of vitamin B_1, folic acid and vitamin C • Changes in flavour and colour • Longer shelf life (unopened)
Ultra-heat treated (UHT)	• Destroys pathogens • Longer shelf life (unopened) • Little change in colour and flavour
Evaporated milk	• Destroys bacteria • Shelf life of one year or more • Has a cooked flavour • Colour changes
Condensed milk	• Destroys bacteria • Change in colour and flavour • Increase in sugar • Loss of vitamins • Long shelf life
Dehydrated milk Spray dried Roller dried	• Destroys bacteria • Loss of vitamins – B group, C • Reduced fat content • *Spray dried:* reconstitutes easily, uniform in shape • *Roller dried:* has cooked flavour, tends to form lumps when mixed with water

Effects of heat/cooking on milk

Learn the information on milk processing in the table above.

Buying and storing milk

1. Check 'best before' date.
2. Store fresh milk in its own container in a fridge.

LINK

- Food profile – milk (pp. 128–129)

3. Never mix new and old milk; use in rotation.

4. Store away from strong-smelling foods.

Exam questions and sample answers

Higher Level 2009, Section A, Q5   (6 marks)
State the function of **each** of the following in relation to the processing of milk.

(a) **Homogenisation**   (3 marks)
   Fat globules are broken up into droplets and distributed evenly in the milk, making it creamier and more digestible.

(b) **Sterilisation**   (3 marks)
   All pathogenic micro-organisms are killed and the milk will last for several weeks unopened.

Ordinary Level 2008, Section A, Q5 (a)   (3 marks)
Name **three** different methods of processing milk to make it safe for consumption.
   (i) Sterilisation
   (ii) Pasteurisation
   (iii) Dehydration

Dairy products

Yoghurt
Classification of yoghurt:

- full-fat
- low-fat/fat-free
- set
- live/bio-yoghurt

- drinking
- frozen
- Greek.

Production of yoghurt:

1. Milk is homogenised and pasteurised for 15–30 minutes at 85–95°C.

2. Milk is cooled and inoculated with a starter culture.

3. Mixture is incubated at 37°C for 6–8 hours.

4. Lactose changes to lactic acid, protein coagulates, mixture thickens and flavour develops.

5. Yoghurt is cooled to 4.5°C.

6. Fruits, nuts, cereals, colourings, sweeteners or flavourings are added.

7. Yoghurt is packaged, labelled and refrigerated.

Nutritive value/nutritional significance

Protein	HBV protein, similar value to milk
Fat/lipid	Saturated animal fat: amount depends on type of milk
Carbohydrates	Milk sugar, lactose Sugar increased with fruit and sweeteners, contains fibre
Vitamins	Fat-soluble A and D Water-soluble B_1, B_2, niacin
Minerals	Calcium Potassium and phosphorus (trace)
Water	Varies depending on fat content (type)

Dietetic value

1. A nutritious, inexpensive food.
2. Provides HBV protein for growth and development in children, adolescents, pregnant and nursing mothers.
3. Excellent source of calcium for healthy bones and teeth.
4. Easy to digest, ideal for babies, elderly people and invalids.
5. Ideal snack food, for packed lunches and desserts.
6. Low-fat varieties are useful in low-kilocalorie diets.

Culinary uses

- On its own, as a dessert or snack.
- On breakfast cereals.
- Dips, salad dressings, marinades, smoothies.
- In sauces and savoury dishes.

— FAMILY POT —

• LIVE • NO ADDED SUGAR • LOW FAT

NATURAL YOGHURT

FUNCTIONAL PROBIOTIC

Exam question and sample answer

Ordinary Level 2008, Section A, Q5(b) (3 marks)

State the benefit to the consumer of adding bacterial cultures, such as acidophilus, to bio yoghurt.

Acidophilus aids digestion.

Cheese

Classification of cheese

Hard	Semi-hard	Soft	Others
Cheddar	Edam	Brie	Cottage
Emmenthal	Port Salut	Camembert	Processed
Parmesan	Stilton	Mozzarella	Farmhouse

Nutritive value/nutritional significance

Protein	HBV protein, casein is present
Fat/lipid	Saturated animal fat, higher in hard cheese
Carbohydrates	None – lactose is drained away in the whey
Vitamins	B_2, A and D, lacks vitamin C
Minerals	Excellent source of calcium, low in iron
Water	Varies with the type of cheese: hard cheese has less water than soft cheese

Dietetic value

1. A concentrated source of HBV protein and calcium, which are essential for growth.
2. Its saturated fat content makes it a high-energy food.
3. Serve with foods rich in carbohydrates.
4. A good alternative to meat, fish and poultry.
5. Suitable for snacks and packed lunches.
6. Quick, convenient, economical and versatile.

LINKS
- Nutrients (p. 2)
- Food pyramid (p. 46)

Exam question and sample answer

This question integrates the manufacture of cheese with the food industry.

Higher Level 2009, Section B, Q2 (50 marks)

'There can be no compromise on food safety and consumers' health has to be protected. Small businesses can produce safe food of high quality but their viability is threatened by a very competitive market place, not the cost of compliance with food safety regulations alone.' (FSAI)

(a) Discuss the role of small businesses and home enterprises within the Irish food industry. (4 points × 4 marks = 16 marks)

 1. Create new employment in rural areas, allowing individuals to remain locally rather than emigrating or migrating to cities and towns.
 2. Promote Ireland's reputation for quality foods by developing exclusive ranges of foods.

3. Cater to changing markets and consumer demands.

4. Promote the use of quality local ingredients.

(b) Write a **profile** of an 'added value' food you have studied. Give details of **each** of the following: (26 marks)

- Name of food
- Stages of production
- Packaging
- Labelling

Name of food: (2 marks)

Cheese

Stages of production: (4 × 4 marks = 16)

1. Milk is pasteurised, a starter culture (lactic acid bacteria) is added, lactose changes to lactic acid.

2. Milk is warmed to 30°C. Rennet is added and converts milk protein (caseinogen) to casein. The mixture is left for 30 to 45 minutes until it changes to 'curds and whey'. Whey is drained off and curds are chopped up.

3. Curds are heated to 40°C to release more whey (scalding). Curds are cut into blocks and piled on top of each other and the remaining whey drains away (cheddaring).

4. Curds are cut again, 2% salt is added to improve flavour and keeping properties. Salted curds are put in moulds, pressed and sprayed with hot water. The cheese is removed from moulds, date stamped and stored for three to 12 months to ripen.

Packaging: (1 × 4 marks = 4 marks)

Cheese is graded and packaged with a use before date.

Labelling: (1 × 4 marks = 4 marks)

Provides name of cheese, nutritional information and suggestions for storage and use.

(c) Give a brief account of the role of the Food Safety Authority of Ireland (FSAI). (2 points × 4 marks = 8 marks)

1. The FSAI is the Irish national agency with responsibility for enforcing food safety legislation.

2. It advises government ministers, regulators, the food industry and consumers about food safety and takes action when regulations are not implemented.

Buying and storing cheese

1. Buy in small amounts from a clean shop.
2. Check use-by date.
3. Ensure seals are not damaged on pre-packed cheese.
4. Store cheese in a covered container in a fridge.

Processed Cheddar **Cheese**   Best Before   03.05.11 11:24

Using cheese

- Use fresh cheese within 2–3 days.
- Remove from fridge 30 minutes before use.
- Serve cheese at room temperature.
- Grate leftover hard cheese and use as a garnish.

Culinary uses of cheese:

Snacks	Cheese sandwich
Main dish	Quiche Lorraine, cheese fondue
End of meal	Cheese board
Sauces	Lasagne, cauliflower cheese
Fillings	Omelettes, baked potato, toasted sandwiches
Toppings	Lasagne, macaroni cheese, pizza
Accompaniment	Dips, spreads, salads, grated on salads
Dessert	Cheesecakes, tiramisu
Baking	Scones, pastry and biscuits

Effects of heat/cooking on cheese:

1. Protein coagulates, shrinks and denatures.
2. Fat melts at high temperatures.
3. Overcooking causes fat to separate, become stringy.
4. Dry heat causes cheese to brown.
5. Overheating causes cheese to become indigestible.

Exam question and sample answer

Ordinary Level 2006, Section A, Q8 (6 marks)

Name **three** classes of cheese and give one example of each class.

Class (3 classes × 1 mark)	Example (3 examples × 1 mark)
Hard	Cheddar
Semi-hard	Gouda
Soft	Cottage cheese

Fruit

Classification of fruit

Berries	Blackcurrants, blueberries, cranberries, gooseberries, raspberries, strawberries
Citrus	Grapefruit, lemons, limes, oranges
Dried	Apricots, dates, raisins, prunes, sultanas
Hard	Apples, pears
Stone	Cherries, nectarines, peaches, plums
Tropical	Bananas, kiwis, passion fruit, pineapples
Other	Rhubarb

Nutritive value/nutritional significance

Protein	Traces of LBV protein
Fat/lipid	None except avocadoes (polyunsaturated fat)
Carbohydrates	<ul><li>Starch in unripe fruit</li><li>Glucose and fructose in ripe fruit</li><li>Dried fruit high in sugar</li><li>Source of dietary fibre (NSP) and pectin</li></ul>
Vitamins	<ul><li>Rich supply of vitamin C</li><li>Beta-carotene in apricots, peaches</li></ul>
Minerals	<ul><li>Calcium in some fruits</li><li>Traces of iron (non-haem)</li></ul>
Water	High in fresh fruit, low in dried fruit

Dietetic value

1. Rich in vitamin C, which aids absorption of iron.
2. Vitamins and minerals protect against disease.
3. Excellent source of dietary fibre (NSP).
4. Ideal in low-kilocalorie and high-fibre diets.

LINKS

- Nutrients (p. 2)
- Food pyramid (p. 46)

Rules for buying, storing and using fruit/vegetables

Buying	1. Buy in season when cheapest
	2. Choose young fresh produce free from blemishes
	3. Buy loose or netted
	4. Check the use-by date
	5. Buy in useable quantities
Storing	1. Remove from plastic wrapping
	2. Store in a cool area with good air circulation to slow down the action of enzymes and moulds
Using	1. Wash to remove residues of sprays
	2. Use quickly

Effects of cooking on fruit/vegetables

1. Enzymes and micro-organisms are destroyed.
2. Texture softens, fruits become digestible.
3. Colours and flavours change.
4. Vitamin C is destroyed (greatest nutrient loss).
5. Loss of water-soluble vitamins and minerals.

LINK

- Food preparation and cooking processes (p. 107)

Culinary uses of fruits

- decoration on flans, pies, tarts
- garnishes, e.g. lemon wedges with fish
- starters, e.g. grapefruit and snacks (whole fruit)
- beverages, e.g. milk shakes, smoothies
- main courses, e.g. pineapple on pizza
- desserts, e.g. Pavlova, fruit salad
- cheeseboard
- preserves: jams, jellies, chutneys, pickles.

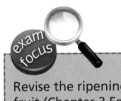

exam focus

Revise the ripening of fruit (Chapter 3 Food Studies: Part Two).

Effects of processing on fruit/vegetables

Method	Examples	Effects
Canning	Pears, strawberries Beans, peas, sweetcorn	• Loss of B group and C vitamins • Changes in colour, flavour and texture • Bacteria are destroyed • Increased sugar content
Drying	Apricots, raisins, sultanas Peas, beans, lentils	• Reduced water content • Loss of B group vitamins • Enzymes and bacteria are inactivated • Changes in colour, flavour and texture • Increased sugar content • Iron is concentrated
Freezing	Apples, berries, rhubarb Carrots, peas, broccoli	• Little loss of nutrients • Change in texture • Enzymes and bacteria are inactivated
Irradiation	Strawberries Onions, potatoes	• Destroys enzymes and micro-organisms • Extends shelf life • Prevents sprouting • Some vitamin loss • No change in appearance

Irradiation

Irradiation involves exposing food to ionising radiation. The purpose of irradiation is to:

- control damage by insects
- reduce pathogenic micro-organisms
- delay ripening, germination or sprouting

In many countries irradiated foods carry the word 'irradiated' and they may also carry the Radura symbol.

> **LINK**
> Food preservation (p. 158)

Radura symbol

> **LINK**
> • Food labelling (p. 135)

Organic symbols

Vegetables

Classification of vegetables

Class/type	Examples
Leafy greens	Cabbage, kale, spinach
Flowers	Broccoli, cauliflower
Pulses (legumes)	Peas, beans, lentils
Fungi	Mushrooms, truffles
Stems	Asparagus, celery, leeks
Fruit	Aubergines, courgettes, cucumbers
Bulbs	Garlic, leeks, onions, shallots
Roots	Beetroot, carrots, parsnips
Tubers	Potatoes, sweet potatoes

Nutritive value/nutritional significance

Protein	Low in LBV protein *except* soya beans
Fat/lipid	• Low except in soya beans • Polyunsaturated oil in olives, seeds and nuts
Carbohydrate	• High in starch (potatoes) • Sugar in carrots, onions, tomatoes • Fibre in outer skins, flesh and husks
Vitamins	• Excellent supply of beta-carotene (vitamin A) • Water-soluble B group and C
Minerals	• Iron in dark green leafy vegetables • Calcium and potassium • Iodine in vegetables grown near the sea
Water	High % of water unless dried

LINKS
- Nutrients (p. 2)
- Vegetarianism (p. 56)

Revise carbohydrates (p. 11); vegetarian/ vegan diets (pp. 56–8).

Dietetic value

1. Provide a rich supply of nutrients for all age groups.
2. Important sources of dietary fibre.
3. Contain anti-oxidant vitamins A, C and E.
4. Useful in low-calorie and low-cholesterol diets.
5. Pulses are important for vegans (substitute for meat).
6. Versatile, used in a variety of dishes, raw/cooked.

Rules for buying vegetables

1. Buy in season in useable quantities.
2. Choose fresh, medium-sized vegetables that are even in colour.
3. Select crisp fresh greens, avoid wilted greens.
4. Choose roots and tubers heavy for their size.
5. Check grade/quality and best before dates.
6. Check pre-packed vegetables for bruising and wilting.

Rules for storing vegetables

1. Store potatoes in a dark place to prevent greening and sprouting.
2. Store salad vegetables/greens in the fridge.
3. Place frozen vegetables in freezer.
4. Store dried pulses in airtight jars.

Rules for preparing vegetables

1. Use raw or prepare just before cooking.
2. Avoid early preparation and steeping.
3. Wash, scrub and peel, trim sparingly.
4. Use a sharp knife to prevent nutrient loss, tear leafy green vegetables.
5. Wash under cold running water to remove dirt, prepare according to kind.

Rules for cooking vegetables

1. Cook in a small amount of boiling water, for the shortest possible time.
2. Keep a lid on the saucepan; never use copper pans.
3. Cook vegetables *al dente*.
4. Using bread soda and overcooking destroys vitamin C.
5. Use leftover cooking liquid for stocks, sauces, soups.

Effects of cooking on vegetables

See under Fruit, page 95.

Spoilage

1. Browning/bruising due to oxidation.
2. Leafy vegetables go limp and yellow.

LINK
- Food preparation and cooking processes (p. 107)

3. Root vegetables go woody and limp and develop soft patches.

4. Vegetables shrivel and reduce in size.

Methods of processing vegetables

- **Home:** dehydration (herbs), freezing, pickling.
- **Commercial:** bottling, canning, dehydration, freezing, pickling, irradiation.

Grading of fruit/vegetables

Class	Explanation
Extra Class	Top quality, no defects in colour, shape, size
Class 1	Good quality, free from bruising, cracking
Class 2	Marketable, some blemishes, defects in colour and shape
Class 3	Inferior quality but marketable, slight blemishes

Exam questions and sample answers

Higher Level 2006, Section A, Q5 (6 marks) **HL**

(a) Identify and explain **two** EU grading classes used for fruit and vegetables.

(4 marks)

  (i) Extra class: superior quality, free from defects in shape, size and colour.

  (ii) Class 1: good quality, no bruising or defects.

(b) What does this symbol convey to the consumer? (2 marks)

  *The **Radura symbol** indicates that the food has undergone irradiation.*

Ordinary Level 2007, Section A, Q7 (3 points × 2 marks = 6 marks)

Name a **different method** of preservation suitable for **each** of the following vegetables:

Vegetable	Method of preservation
Carrots	*Freezing*
Whole Tomatoes	*Canning*
Onions	*Pickling*

Higher Level 2008, Section B, Q2 (summary answer) **HL**

'Fruit and vegetables are highly nutritious and an essential part of the diet, however, only 21% of adult men and 19% of women in Ireland are meeting the current World Health Organisation target, with young children eating even less.'

(a) Discuss (i) nutritional significance and (ii) the contribution to the diet of fruit and vegetables. (5 points × 4 marks = 20 marks)

(i) **Nutritional significance:**

1. *Contain anti-oxidant vitamins A, C, E.*
2. *Protein is found in pulse vegetables.*
3. *Iron is found in dark green leafy vegetables, e.g. spinach.*

(ii) **Contribution to the diet:**

Fruit and vegetables are –

1. *Excellent sources of vitamins and minerals.*
2. *Virtually fat-free, ideal in low-calorie and low-cholesterol diets.*
3. *Useful for sweet and savoury dishes.*

(b) Suggest **one** method of food preservation which could be used to preserve a surplus of home-grown fruit or vegetables. Explain the underlying principle of the method of preservation you have selected. **(15 marks)**

Method (3 marks)	Underlying principle (3 points × 4 marks = 12 marks)
Jam-making	1. *High temperatures to destroy enzymes and micro-organisms (100°C)* 2. *Correct proportion of sugar acts as a preservative and prevents growth of micro-organisms* 3. *Correct proportions of pectin and acid helps jam set*

(c) Write an informative note on food irradiation. (3 points × 5 marks = 15 marks)

1. *Food is exposed to a specific dose of ionising radiation.*
2. *Irradiation destroys micro-organisms.*
3. *Irradiation delays the ripening and sprouting of fruit and vegetables.*

Ordinary Level 2004, Section B, Q2 **(50 marks)**

'An increasing number of adults are eating four or more portions of fruit and vegetables each day, but consumption of vegetables among young people is still lower than the recommended intake.'

(a) Suggest some interesting ways of including fruit and vegetables in the diet of young people. **(4 points × 2 marks = 8 marks)**

1. *Adding chopped fresh fruit to yoghurts.*
2. *Stir-frying vegetables.*
3. *Use smoothies as mid-morning snacks.*
4. *Add colourful berries to breakfast cereals.*

exam focus

(b) Classify vegetables and give **one** example of each class. **(12 marks)**

Three classes are required in your answer to question (b).

Classes (3 classes × 2 marks each)	Example (3 examples × 2 marks each)
Roots	Carrots (beetroot, parsnips)
Leafy greens	Cabbage (spinach, kale)
Pulses	Peas (beans, lentils)

(c) Discuss **four** reasons why it is important to include an adequate amount of fruit and vegetables in diet. **(4 points × 4 marks = 16 marks)**

1. Essential part of a balanced diet.
2. Excellent source of dietary fibre, which helps prevent bowel problems, e.g. constipation, diverticulitis, cancer.
3. Low in fat, suits low-calorie and low-cholesterol diets.
4. Good source of vitamins: C, B group and pro-vitamin A.

(d)(i) Name **two** types of food additives used in processed fruit/vegetables.
(2 points × 3 marks = 6 marks)

1. Preservatives used in jam making, e.g. sugar.
2. Colourings used in canned vegetables, e.g. chlorophyll.

(ii) Explain why food additives are used in the manufacture of food.
(2 points × 4 marks = 8 marks)

1. To enhance colour, flavour, taste, texture and keeping qualities of food.
2. To improve the nutritive value or to replace nutrients which were lost during processing.

Cereals

The **main sources** of cereals are the grains of cultivated grasses, e.g. barley, oats, maize, millet, rice, rye and wheat.

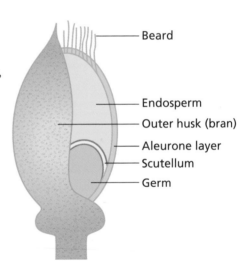

Beard

Endosperm

Outer husk (bran)

Aleurone layer

Scutellum

Germ

Structure of wheat grain

Bran layer or outer husk	13%	Contains cellulose, rich in fibre, B-group vitamins (especially niacin), calcium, iron, phosphate
Endosperm	85%	Contains the energy store of the grain (mainly starch), protein and B-group vitamins Aleurone is the outer layer of the endosperm; contains protein
Germ or embryo	2%	Rich in protein, fat, vitamins (B group, E), iron and the nutrients for the germination of a new plant, mainly essential fatty acids
Scutellum		A thin layer between germ and endosperm

Nutritive value/nutritional significance of wheat

Protein	• LBV proteins, higher in wholemeal flour than in white flour
	• Gluten, lysine, threonine, tryptophan
	• Lacks some amino acids
Fat/lipid	Polyunsaturated fats in the germ
Carbohydrates	• High in starch
	• Rich in cellulose (outer husk/bran)
Vitamins	• Rich in B group vitamins (niacin and thiamine)
	• Vitamin E in germ
Minerals	Useful amounts of calcium, non-haem iron, traces of phosphorus
Water	Low water content, about 13%

Dietetic value of cereals

1. A cheap, nutritious and versatile food.
2. Ideal energy food.
3. Suited to low-calorie, high-fibre diets.
4. Whole grains provide B group vitamins, non-haem iron and calcium.
5. Coeliacs should avoid cereals with high gluten content.

LINKS
- Carbohydrates (p. 11)
- Vitamins (p. 26)
- Minerals (p. 35)

Flour

Classes of flour

- strong flour – high in gluten
- weak flour – lower gluten content
- plain flour – mixture of weak and strong flour.

LINK
- Coeliac disease – dietary guidelines (p. 59)

LINK
- Food profile – flour (p. 128)

Types of flour

Types of flour	Extraction rates	Key points
Wholemeal	100%	Whole grain
Wheatmeal/brown	85%	Some bran removed
White (cream)	70–75%	Bran and germ removed
Self-raising	75%	Raising agent added
Strong		High-gluten flour, suits yeast baking
High-ratio	> 50%	A 'soft' finely milled high quality flour, low in gluten
Gluten-free		Gluten is removed, flour lacks elasticity

Effects of heat/cooking on cereals/cereal products

1. Protein coagulates, dry heat sets bread/cakes.
2. Moist heat causes gelatinisation and liquids to thicken.

3. Dry heat causes starch grains to swell, burst and absorb oils/fats, e.g. popcorn.
4. Dextrinisation and caramelisation occur.
5. Starch becomes digestible.
6. B group vitamins are destroyed.

Revise rice and pasta.

Exam questions and sample answers

Ordinary Level 2007, Section A, Q5   (2 points × 3 marks = 6 marks)
In relation to the wheat grain, explain **two** of the following:

(i) **Endosperm**
85% of grain, inner part of grain, mainly starch and the protein gluten. White flour is made from it.

(ii) **Germ**
2% of grain, rich source of protein, vitamins B and E present, contains unsaturated fats.

(iii) **Bran**
13% of grain, outer covering of grain, composed mainly of cellulose, some B vitamins, calcium and non-haem iron.

Ordinary Level 2006, Section B, Q1 (a) and (b)   (24 marks)
'Children are not eating enough fibre and are eating more fat and salt than is recommended.' (National Children's Food Survey – UCC and TCD)
The label on a packet of 'Jumbo Porridge Oats' has the following information:

Typical composition	Per 100 g	Per 40 g serving
Energy	1613 kJ 386.6 kcal	645.3 kJ 154.6 kcal
Protein	11.1 g	4.4 g
Carbohydrates	73 g	29.2 g
Fat	5.5 g	2.2 g
Fibre	6.1 g	2.5 g
Sodium	Trace	Trace
Thiamine	0.85 mg	0.35 mg
Iron	4.1 mg	1.64 mg

(a) Comment on the dietetic value of 'Jumbo Porridge Oats'.
            (3 points × 4 marks = 12 marks)

1. *Porridge is an important energy food.*
2. *It is low in salt/sodium, which helps to reduce the risk of high blood pressure.*

> 3. *It is a good source of fibre, which prevents bowel disorders, e.g. constipation.*
>
> (b) Suggest **two** foods (other than milk) you could serve with porridge to increase the nutritional value. Give **one** reason for your choice of each food. (12 marks)
>
>
>
> **exam focus**
>
> **Read** and **analyse** the information given in the table.
>
> | Foods (2 foods × 3 marks each) | Reason for choice (2 points × 3 marks) |
> |---|---|
> | Chopped apples | Adds extra dietary fibre |
> | Yoghurt | Increases calcium content |
>
> **Higher Level 2008, Section A, Q5** (6 marks)
>
> Name **three** cereals grown for food production and give **one** example of a different product manufactured from each cereal. (6 points × 1 mark = 6 marks)
>
> | Cereal | Products |
> |---|---|
> | Wheat | Flour |
> | Rice | Rice cakes |
> | Maize | Cornflakes |

Fats and oils

Main characteristics:

- **fats:** mainly saturated, solid at room temperature
- **oils:** mainly polyunsaturated, liquid at room temperature.

Sources of fats and oils

Animal fat	Marine oils	Vegetable oils
Saturated fat: • milk fat (butter, cheese) • meat and meat fat	Polyunsaturates: • fish liver oils (cod) • oily fish (herring)	Polyunsaturates: nuts, seeds, vegetables, olive

Nutritive value/nutritional significance of fats/oils

Protein	Insignificant levels of HBV protein (<1%)
Fat/lipid	Content ranges from 82% in butter to 90% in cooking oil; suet has 99% fat
Carbohydrates	Trace
Vitamins	• Fat-soluble vitamin A • Traces of B group, no vitamin C • Margarines fortified with A and D
Minerals	Traces of calcium in butter and margarine
Water	Depends on the amount of fat present

Dietetic value

1. Provide heat and energy.
2. Provide fat-soluble vitamins A, D, E and K.
3. Source of essential fatty acids.
4. Polyunsaturates help reduce cholesterol build-up.

exam focus

Revise the production of vegetable oil.

Margarine

Production of margarine

Oil Extraction
(from vegetable sources)
↓
Hydrogenation
Hydrogen gas is forced through oil, in the presence of a catalyst, to harden the mixture
↓
Blending
(of fats and oils)
↓
Ingredients Added
Colourings, emulsifiers, flavourings, nutrients, other oils, salt, skimmed milk and vitamins are added
↓
Emulsification
Ingredients are churned with a rotator machine to regulate consistency, and stabilisers are added
The temperature is lowered and the margarine kneaded, moulded and shaped
↓
Margarine is weighed, wrapped, labelled and packed

Types of margarine and dairy spreads

- **Block margarine:** made mainly from vegetable oils, high in saturated fats. *Uses:* frying, baking.
- **Soft margarine:** made from vegetable oils, packed in plastic tubs, high in saturated fats. *Uses:* in sandwiches, baking.
- **Low-fat dairy spreads:** not suitable for baking, high water content. *Uses:* in sandwiches, on toast.

Culinary uses of fats and oils

1. Creaming, flavouring, shortening and spreading.
2. As anti-staling agents, preventing food drying out.

3. In emulsions, e.g. mayonnaise, salad dressings.

4. Basting food e.g. meat; sautéing foods, e.g. onions.

5. Frying foods (shallow/deep-fat).

Rules for storing fats and oils

1. Store fats in a fridge to prevent rancidity.

2. Cover fats to prevent absorption of odours, e.g. garlic.

3. Store oils in a cool, dark, place.

4. Check the best before date.

LINKS
- Functional foods and spreads (p. 130)
- Food processing (p. 126)

Meal management and planning

When planning meals, consider:

- Current dietary guidelines
- Special dietary needs
- Life cycle stage of the individual
- Knowledge/skills of cook
- Resources available
- Time of year/season
- Occasion/number of people
- Aesthetics
- Religious beliefs.

exam focus

Make sure you can elaborate on these points in the exam.

Guidelines for meal planning

1. Plan ahead: make a shopping list for a week's menus.

2. Plan to use all leftovers.

3. Buy foods in season (when they are cheapest).

4. Vary cooking methods.

5. Serve hot dishes in winter, chilled dishes in summer.

6. Choose fast methods of cooking if time is limited.

7. Plan accompaniments, garnishes/decorations to suit dishes.

LINKS
- Dietary guidelines (p. 45)
- Food choices (p. 2)
- The Irish diet (p. 64)
- Family resource management (p. 179)
- Household technology (p. 201)

exam focus

In the exam you will be expected to demonstrate knowledge of current nutritional guidelines, balanced meal planning and correct menu formats.

Exam question and sample answer

Ordinary Level 2008, Section B, Q1 (e)

Discuss how the following factors influence the planning and management of family meals. (4 points × 5 marks = 20 marks)

Money available

Menus must be prepared within the budget available, e.g. use cheaper meats (which are just as nutritious as expensive meats), buy foods in season, when they are cheaper and better quality.

Equipment

- *Choose recipes/dishes that suit the equipment available.*
- *Use food processors and pressure cookers to save time or cook complete family meals in the oven to save energy and money.*

Knowledge and skills

- *Skill of cook will influence the dishes cooked – unskilled cooks might be over-reliant on convenience foods (tins and packages).*
- *Skilled cooks will have the knowledge needed to plan meals for every day and special occasions.*

Dietary considerations

- *Special diets will affect the choice of foods for a menu, e.g. lacto-vegetarians – no meat; coeliacs – no gluten; high cholesterol – no saturated fat.*
- *Consideration needs to be given to the age group and to current healthy eating guidelines, e.g. reduce salt and sugar, increase fibre.*

Food preparation and cooking processes

Reasons for cooking food

1. To destroy micro-organisms and enzymes.
2. To make foods look appetising.
3. To improve the flavour of food.
4. To stimulate the appetite.
5. To make food more digestible.
6. To preserve some foods.

> **LINK**
> - Cooking methods (Chapter 3: Extension 1, see www.moresuccess.ie)

Changes during food preparation – some examples

Physical changes	• *Tenderising meat:* using meat hammer • *Nutrient loss:* vitamin C is lost when food is cut, steeped or comes in contact with air • *Increase in size:* pulses absorb water
Chemical changes	• *Enzymic browning occurs:* cut apples turn brown when enzymes react with oxygen in air • *Increase in size:* yeast dough expands *Tenderising meat:* using marinades

Changes during cooking – some examples

Physical changes	• Colour changes • Micro-organisms are destroyed • Texture changes: food becomes digestible • Improved flavours, food is tastier • Loss of nutrients: at high temperatures or into cooking liquid • Decrease in size: meat shrinks • Increase in size: introduction of air in bread and cake-making • Thickening: adding flour to a sauce • Setting: gelatine sets desserts
Chemical changes	• Non-enzymic browning: Maillard reaction • Dextrinisation: toast • Caramelisation: sugar changes to a golden brown colour

Preventing nutrient loss during cooking

1. Prepare food just before cooking.
2. Use a sharp knife when cutting fruit/vegetables.
3. Use the minimum amount of cooking liquid.
4. Never steep overnight.
5. Cook vegetables for the shortest possible time.
6. Use cooking liquids for soups, stocks and gravies.

> **LINK**
> • Nutrients: properties (pp. 2–38)

Principles underlying cooking methods

Heat is transferred in three ways:

1. **Conduction:** heat passes from an area of high temperature to an area of lower temperature. *Example*: frying.
2. **Convection:** transfer of heat in currents. *Examples*: boiling, stewing, roasting.
3. **Radiation:** heat travels in straight lines from the heat source in the form of rays to the food. *Examples*: grilling, toasting, barbecuing.

Factors influencing cooking methods

- Composition of food: light or dense.
- Shape and size of food: joint, thin slices.
- Type of food: dense meat, spongy cake mixture.
- Personal taste: raw, medium or well done.

Methods of cooking

Method	Examples	Effects of cooking
Dry heat	Grilling Barbecuing Baking Roasting	● Loss of B group vitamins and vitamin C ● Fat melts, sugar caramelises ● Protein foods shrink ● Maillard reaction ● Foods become crisper
Moist heat	Boiling Braising Poaching Steaming Stewing Pressure cooking	● Loss of B-group and vitamin C ● Collagen changes to gelatine ● Cellulose softens ● Food becomes more digestible ● Overcooking causes food to fall apart
Using fat	Deep-fat frying Shallow frying Stir-frying Dry frying	● Increases fat content of food ● Loss of vitamin A ● Texture becomes crisper ● Fried food can be soggy and greasy ● More difficult to digest

Microwave cooking

LINK

● Microwave ovens, p. 208

LINKS

● Maillard reaction (p. 8)
● Dietary guidelines (p. 45)
● Guidelines for meal planning (p. 106)
● Food safety and hygiene (p. 170)

Pressure cooking

Similar to steaming, but temperatures are higher than 100°C because of the pressure build-up in the appliance.

exam focus

Learn the changes to the nutritive value and the palatability of foods when using different cooking methods.

Application of principle	● By increasing pressure, food cooks at higher temperatures ● Steam cannot escape, food cooks quickly
Advantages	● Saves time and energy ● Little loss of nutrients ● Little change in colour and flavour ● Complete meal can be cooked in one pot
Disadvantages	● Danger of overcooking food ● Needs constant attention ● Danger of scalding from steam
Suitable foods	Meat, poultry, preserves, vegetables, rice, complete meals, puddings

Basic structure of a pressure cooker

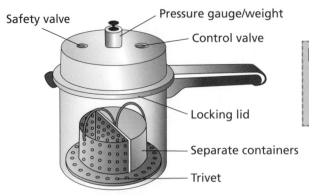

Safety valve

Pressure gauge/weight

Control valve

Locking lid

Separate containers

Trivet

LINK
- Cooking methods – moist heat (Chapter 3: Extension 1, see www.moresuccess.ie)

Rules for using a basic pressure cooker

1. Follow the manufacturer's instructions.
2. Never overfill with liquids or solids.
3. Ensure a steady stream of steam before adding weights.
4. Time the cooking carefully.
5. Turn off heat, lift pressure cooker off hob.
6. Allow pressure to reduce to normal.
7. Remove lid carefully to avoid a burst of steam.

Revise cooking methods, soups, sauces and pastry.

Raising agents and yeast cookery

Raising agents are used to introduce air into breads, cakes and pastries.

Classification of raising agents:

1. natural/mechanical
2. chemical
3. biological.

Natural raising agents

1. **Air:** introduced by beating, creaming, folding, rolling, rubbing-in, sieving and whisking.
2. **Steam:** acts as a raising agent in batters and choux pastry.

Chemical raising agents

A chemical reaction occurs between an acid and an alkali in the presence of a liquid to produce CO_2, which raises the dough.

1. **Baking powder**

$$\text{Acid} + \text{Alkali} + \text{Liquid} \rightarrow CO_2$$
$$\text{Baking Powder} + \text{Milk/Eggs} \rightarrow CO_2$$

2. **Bread soda**

$$\text{Acid} + \text{Alkali} + \text{Liquid} \rightarrow CO_2$$
$$\text{Buttermilk} + \text{Bread Soda} + \text{Buttermilk} \rightarrow CO_2$$

3. **Self-raising flour:** raising agent has been added.

Yeast – a biological raising agent

Yeast is a living organism which produces CO_2 due to fermentation. It needs warmth, moisture and food to multiply.

$$\text{Yeast} + C_6H_{12}O_6 + \text{Moisture} + \text{Warmth} \longrightarrow 2C_2H_5OH + CO_2 + \text{Energy}$$

| | Glucose | | | Alcohol | Carbon dioxide |

Glucose — Alcohol — Carbon dioxide

FERMENTATION

The actions involved in fermentation are:

Enzyme		Acts on		Produces
Diastase (flour)	→	Starch	→	Maltose
Maltase (yeast)	→	Maltose	→	Glucose
Invertase (yeast)	→	Sucrose	→	Glucose and Fructose
Zymase (yeast)	→	Glucose and Fructose	→	CO_2 + Alcohol

- Gluten becomes elastic and holds the CO_2 produced during fermentation.
- CO_2 in the dough expands and raises the dough until double in size (happens outside the oven).
- Yeast is killed in the oven, dough stops rising and dough crust sets.
- Alcohol produced evaporates.

LINK

- Try this exam question: 2009 Higher Level, Section A, Q6 (www.examinations.ie).

Exam questions and sample answers

Higher Level 2009, Section A, Q7   (6 marks)

List **two** physical changes that occur during the cooking of food and give one example of each.

Physical change	Example
Loss of nutrients	Loss of water-soluble vitamins into cooking liquid when cooking food
Coagulation	Protein in eggs and milk coagulate when making custards

Ordinary Level 2007, Section A, Q6 (6 marks)

Explain **each** of the following methods of cooking:

 (i) **Poaching:** *Cooking food in liquid just below simmering point (85°C).*

 (ii) **Pot Roasting:** *Cooking food in a little fat in a covered pot on the hob.*

Higher Level 2009, Section A, Q6 (6 marks)

(a) Define fermentation.

 Fermentation involves the breakdown of carbohydrates and sugars in food as a result of the action of micro-organisms (yeast and bacteria) and enzymes. Example: bread making, brewing

(b) Name **two** by-products of fermentation.

 (i) Carbon dioxide

 (ii) Alcohol

Food preparation and cooking equipment

Preparation equipment	Cooking equipment
Chopping board	Cooker
Sharp knives	Microwave oven
Food mixer	Deep-fat fryer
Food processor	Sandwich toaster
Liquidiser	Doughnut maker
Hand blender	Bread maker
Juice extractor	Kettle
Carving knives	Contact grill

Selecting food preparation and cooking equipment

Consider:

1. frequency of use
2. quality of the product
3. budget available
4. energy rating
5. storage space needed
6. guarantee and after-sales service.

Small electrical appliances

Examples: blenders (hand), food mixers, food processors and liquidisers.

Guidelines for safe use of small appliances

1. Follow the manufacturer's instructions.
2. Ensure hands are dry before operating appliance.
3. Remove/insert blades carefully, e.g. in a blender.
4. Fill to the recommended level.

5. Do not overfill small attachments: note level of contents.

6. Turn off and unplug electrical appliances after use.

Care of small appliances

1. Unplug appliance before cleaning.

2. Wash according to the manufacturer's instructions.

3. Never wash the motor part, never immerse it in water.

4. Wipe outer casing with a hot soapy cloth.

5. Take care when cleaning blades, graters and discs.

6. Dry well before storing.

7. Wind flexes loosely to avoid damage.

8. Store appliance unplugged with its attachments.

> **LINKS**
> - Household technology (p. 201)
> - Consumer choice (pp. 202, 218)

Recipe balance and adaptation

Recipes are adapted or modified to:
- improve nutritive value
- suit special dietary requirements
- alter the number of portions
- introduce variety in colour, flavour and texture
- implement current healthy eating guidelines
- make dishes/meals more economical
- use up leftovers and avoid waste.

> **LINKS**
> - Coeliac diets (p. 58)
> - Vegetarian diets (p. 56)
> - Dietary guidelines (p. 45)
> - Coronary heart disease (p. 54)
> - Special diets (pp. 52–60)

Modifications and some examples

Eat less salt	Reduce/omit salt in dishes
	Avoid processed/convenience foods
	Replace salt with herbs/spices
Eat less sugar	Reduce sugar in dishes
	Use artificial sweeteners
	Use dried fruits and fruit juices
Eat less fat	Remove visible fat from meat
	Use poultry and lean cuts of meat
	Choose low-fat polyunsaturated spreads
	Use low-fat products
	Use low-fat methods of cooking
Eat more fibre	Choose wholegrain products, e.g. pasta
	Increase intake of fresh fruit/vegetables
	Eat fruit/vegetables with skin on
	Add pulses to stews and casseroles

Exam questions – practising 'balancing menu' questions

Devise the menus asked for in the following questions:

- **Higher Level 2009, Section B, Q1** – A menu for a three-course meal for a vegan (using Quorn mince).
- **Higher Level 2007, Section B, Q2** – A day's menu for a person with coronary heart disease.
- **Ordinary Level 2009, Section B, Q2** – A menu for a manual worker.
- **Ordinary Level 2008, Section B, Q1** – Menus for one day for a teenager to provide adequate iron.
- **Ordinary Level 2007, Section B, Q2** – A day's menu for a family with young children.
- **Ordinary Level 2008, Section B, Q1** – A day's menu for a family with young children to increase their fibre intake.
- **Ordinary Level 2005, Section B, Q2** – Mid-morning snack and lunch for a school-going teenager.
- **Ordinary Level 2004, Section B, Q1** – A day's meals for a pregnant woman to provide adequate calcium.

Aesthetic awareness of food

The **main aesthetic factors** which influence the **choice** of food are:

- colour → sight
- flavour → taste
- aroma → smell
- texture → touch
- 'sound' → hearing.

Aesthetic awareness in food preparation

Appearance and **colour** are key indications of the freshness and quality of foods.

Colour (sight)

1. Choose naturally brightly coloured foods.
2. Add a variety of colours across the different courses.
3. Prepare simple garnishes, e.g. a twist of lemon.
4. Overcooking destroys colour.

> **key point**
>
> Foods are expected to have certain colours. Natural and artificial colours are used to replace colours lost during processing.

Flavour (taste)

Flavour involves a combination of taste and aroma.

To enhance flavour during food preparation:

1. Choose a variety of flavours for each menu.
2. Arrange flavours to suit the course: savoury to sweet.

3. Avoid strong overpowering flavours in every course.

4. Use only one strong flavour in the meal.

Aroma (smell)

The smell of food is an indication of quality, freshness, staleness. Smell receptors in the nose identify aroma.

To enhance the aroma of foods:

1. Add herbs/spices to improve aroma of bland ingredients.

2. Cook foods with aromas that stimulate the taste buds.

3. Overcooking foods produces 'burnt' aromas.

4. Prevent cross-flavours developing during preparation.

5. Avoid undercooking, which makes food bland.

Texture (touch)

Texture is registered by sight and the taste/feel of food in the mouth, or consistency.

1. Add interest to menus by using a variety of textures.

2. Individual foods produce expectations of what the textures will be, e.g. mayonnaise is smooth, apples are crunchy.

3. Texture of foods changes during cooking, e.g. roast potatoes.

4. Overcooking affects the texture of dishes, e.g. lumpy white sauces, curdled custards.

Sound (hearing)

The sounds made by food during preparation (e.g. popping, sizzling, fizzing) enhance our appreciation of individual foods, e.g. rashers frying, fizzy drinks, breaking a biscuit in two.

Aesthetic awareness in food presentation

The sight of food well presented is pleasing to the eye, and stimulates digestive juices and taste buds.

1. Foods should look attractive and be neatly arranged.

2. Serve cold or chilled food on cold plates.

3. Serve hot food piping hot on warmed plates.

4. Use plain plates for serving savoury foods.

5. Choose fancy plates and dishes for sweet foods.

6. Serve meats towards the centre or to the side of the plate.

7. Serve sauces in a sauce boat or around meat/fish.

8. Garnish/decorate lightly, in keeping with the food.

LINK

• Meal management and planning (p. 106)

Word bank for describing/evaluating food

Colour (sight)	Colourful, pale, fresh, greasy, cloudy, overcooked, undercooked, burnt
Flavour (taste)	Sweet, sour, bitter, tasteless, bland, spicy, salty, smoky, creamy
Aroma (smell)	Sweet, sour, smoky, burnt, fresh, spicy
Texture (touch)	Crisp, crunchy, hard, soft, nutty, brittle, smooth, chewy, lumpy, greasy
Sound (hearing)	Popping, sizzling, fizzing, crackling

HL Sensory analysis

Sensory analysis is used to determine the acceptability of a food product to consumers by measuring, analysing and explaining the characteristics of a food using the five senses: taste, smell, touch, sight and sound.

Sensory analysis is used to:

- develop new products
- modify products, e.g. by reducing fat
- evaluate food products.

Types of sensory analysis tests

1. Preference tests

Purpose: to determine the acceptability of a food or food products.
Techniques:

- **Paired preference tests** (which product is preferred)
- **Hedonic test** (the degree of liking).

2. Difference tests

Purpose: to identify differences in taste between two food samples.
Techniques:

- **Simple paired test**
- **Paired comparison test**
- **Triangle test.**

3. Grading or quality tests

Purpose: to rank specific organoleptic characteristics of food products, e.g. intensity of flavour, texture, odour.
Techniques:

- **Ranking test**
- **Rating test.**

Controlling test conditions

1. Timing of tests – mid-morning or mid-afternoon is best.
2. Avoid strong foods for 30 minutes before test.
3. Provide rinsing water for taster/s.
4. Temperature of food samples should be the same.
5. Same quantities of food in each sample.
6. Containers of same size, shape and colour – white or colourless.
7. Coding of samples (must not give information).
8. Sequence of samples (random, balanced or a combination).

Presenting results

Results are presented using pie charts, histograms or star diagrams, in order to determine the changes required.

Exam questions and sample answers

Higher Level 2009, Section A, Q8   (6 marks)

Outline **two** uses of sensory analysis in the food industry.

   (i) To evaluate new products or value-added products.

   (ii) To modify products, e.g. reduce salt/sugar.

Higher Level 2005, Section A, Q5   (6 marks)

(a) Give **one** reason why a food manufacturer might use sensory
     analysis.   (2 marks)

    To evaluate new products during product development.

(b) Name **two** categories of sensory analysis tests. List one test from each category.
                                                                  (4 marks)

Category of test	Example of test
Preference test	*Hedonic rating scale*
Descriptive test	*Descriptive rating scale*

Higher Level 2007, Section B, Q3   (50 marks)

'Sensory analysis is a scientific discipline used to evoke,
measure, analyse and interpret reactions to those
characteristics as they are perceived by the senses of
sight, smell, taste, touch and hearing.' (Institute of
Food Technologists, 1981)

(a) Discuss the influence of any **three** of the senses
    when choosing, buying or eating food.
               (3 × 5 marks = 15 marks)

Read the statement at
the start of the question
very carefully.

1. *Sight (Appearance)*

- *Sight (our eyes) evaluates visual appearance, colours, shape, size and surface appearance (smooth, dull, cloudy) of food.*

- *Choices are made based on what we see (acceptable appearance, freshness, quality), e.g. bright red tomatoes look fresh, red strawberries look of good quality.*

- *Mould is acceptable on blue-veined cheese but not on oranges.*

> Words for **evaluating appearance**: appetising, bright, clear, cloudy, colourful, dull, dry, fresh, greasy, mouth-watering, soggy, wilted, medium-sized, uneven.

2. *Smell (Aroma)*

- *Smell evaluates aroma: receptors are located in the nasal cavity.*
- *Receptors identify the type of food.*
- *Aroma is an indication of quality, freshness, staleness.*
- *Cooking aromas make food appetising, e.g. freshly baked scones, chilli chicken.*

- *Acceptable aromas make foods appetising to consumers.*
- *Cooking smells stimulate our appetite, e.g. spices.*
- *Burnt food has an unacceptable and unpleasant smell.*

> Words for **evaluating smell** (aroma): baked, burnt, coffee, floral, fruity, roasted, sour, spicy, sweet.

3. *Touch (Texture)*

- *Texture evaluates food consistency*
- *Texture is mainly evaluated by mouth feel but also by sight, touch and hearing*
- *Mouth 'feel' registers texture in the mouth, e.g. apples have a crunchy texture, ice cream has a smooth texture.*

> Words used **to evaluate texture:** chewy, coarse, greasy, creamy, crumbly, juicy.

- *Overcooking affects texture, e.g. vegetables become soggy and soft.*
- *Texture may be appropriate, e.g. a crisp apple.*
- *Texture can also be a sign that the food is not safe to eat, e.g. slimy meat.*

(b) Name **three** categories of sensory analysis tests and list **one** test from each category. (15 marks)

Categories of test (3 × 3 marks = 9 marks)	Example of test (3 × 2 marks)
Preference tests	Paired preference test
Difference tests	Triangle test
Descriptive tests	Ranking test

(c) Set out the conditions necessary for conducting sensory analysis testing to ensure accurate results.   (5 conditions × 4 marks = 20 marks)

1. *Timing of tests: mid-morning or mid-afternoon is best as tasters will be more sensitive to what they taste.*
2. *Tasters should not eat strongly flavoured foods for at least 30 minutes before the test.*
3. *Provide water for each taster to rinse out their mouth.*
4. *Foods should be of the same temperature, the same quantity and uniformity.*
5. *Containers, coding and sequencing of samples should not give any information about the test to tasters:*
   - *never use 1, 2, 3 or A, B, C*
   - *sequence samples randomly (for large numbers) or in a balanced manner (for triangle tests)*
   - *use a combination of random and balanced sequences.*

The Irish food industry

Structure of the Irish food industry: government departments and food agencies

Department of Agriculture, Fisheries and Food

Functions are to:
- develop and provide support services
- monitor and control aspects of food safety
- monitor and control animal health, plant health and animal welfare.

Department of Health and Children

Functions are to:
- monitor the Food Safety Authority of Ireland
- develop and implement food safety policies and health promotion in co-operation with the HSE.

Bord Bia (Irish Food Board)

Functions are to:
- promote Irish food, drink and horticulture nationally and globally
- provide quality assurance schemes for meat, eggs and horticulture
- provide consumer information via leaflets and website.

Bord Bia
Irish Food Board
www.foodisland.com

The **Bord Bia Quality Mark** can be found on pre-packed bacon, beef, chicken, cooked ham, duck, pork, rashers, eggs, fruit and vegetables.

Bord Iascaigh Mhara

Bord Iascaigh Mhara
Irish Sea Fisheries Board

Functions are to:

- promote Irish mariculture
- encourage the consumption of fish in Ireland
- provide information to consumers.

Teagasc (Agriculture and Food Development Authority)

Functions are to:

AGRICULTURE AND FOOD DEVELOPMENT AUTHORITY

- provide research, advice and training on all aspects of the agri-food industry
- provide services in partnership with various sectors of the agricultural and food industry
- advise farmers on the Rural Environmental Protection Scheme (REPS) and on all aspects of farming.

Food Safety Authority of Ireland (FSAI)

Functions are to:

- co-ordinate the enforcement of food safety legislation or recognised codes of good practice
- provide advice on food safety issues to ministers, the food industry and consumers

- work with the food industry to ensure the highest standards of food safety and hygiene in production, distribution and sale.

Enterprise Ireland

Functions are to:

- promote research and innovation in Irish industry
- provide finance and support for Irish-owned food industries.

Food exports

The pie chart shows the distribution of Ireland's food and drink exports in 2008.

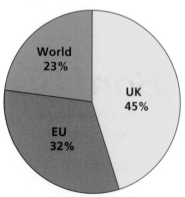

World 23%

UK 45%

EU 32%

exam focus

Data for exports/imports are constantly changing. Check the latest data before the exams.

Breakdown of Irish food exports 2008

Category	Export (%)	Examples
Dairy products and ingredients	29%	Milk powder, butter, cheese, ice cream, yoghurt
Beef	21%	Beef and live cattle
Sheepmeat/lamb	2%	France is the main market
Pigmeat	4%	Main market is the UK
Poultry	2%	Small market outside Ireland
Edible horticulture	3%	UK is the main importer of Irish mushrooms
Seafood	4%	Salmon, oysters, mussels – main market is France
Beverages	15%	Whiskey, cream liqueurs, spring water
Prepared foods	18%	Speciality foods: chocolates Convenience foods: frozen, chilled and dried foods

Food imports

Food	Examples
Fruit	Apples, citrus, melons, pineapples, strawberries (in fresh, frozen and dried forms)
Vegetables	Beans, garlic, lentils, mange tout, peas, peppers
Fish	Canned, dried, smoked, fresh
Drinks	Beers, wines, spirits, juices, soft drinks
Dairy	Milk, milk products, cheese, yoghurt
Cereals	Barley, rice, pasta, maize, flour
Others	Bottled water, tinned products, tea, coffee, soya products, sauces, soups, pâté, speciality foods

exam focus

Hint: visit your local supermarket around Easter time to check the countries of origin of produce on sale.

Small businesses and home enterprises

- Involve small numbers of people (some are family run).
- Produce speciality foods, e.g. cheese.
- Must implement EU hygiene and safety standards.

Reasons for growth of small businesses and home enterprises

1. Innovation, new ideas, desire to work for oneself.
2. Reduction in farm incomes and enforcement of farm quotas.
3. Potential for processing using new technology and skills.
4. State supports for new businesses and enterprises.
5. Recent unemployment, redundancy.

Benefits of small businesses and home enterprises

1. Create new employment opportunities.
2. Meet consumer demands for product variety.
3. Offer new exclusive ranges of food items.
4. Promote the use of quality local ingredients.
5. Identify and link into key markets.

Speciality food sectors

1. Bakery (bread, biscuits, flour).
2. Beverages (beers, apple juice).
3. Condiments (dressings, sauces, mustards).
4. Confectionery (chocolate, sweets, desserts).
5. Dairy (cheese, yoghurt, cheesecakes).
6. Prepared foods (fruits, vegetables, frozen meals).
7. Preserves (chutneys, relishes, jams, marmalade, jellies).
8. Speciality meats and fish (smoked fish, puddings, sausages, ham).

Investigating a local food industry

Sample investigation: a local chocolate producer.
Name of producer: Gartan Chocolate Company Ltd, Ireland.

exam focus

Investigate and write up a food industry in your local area using the following model.

When was it set up?	1999
Why was it set up?	1. Owner became redundant from a food-related business 2. Owner wanted to start a small family-owned and run business
Are the suppliers local?	No. Some products, which are specific to the business, are imported
Does the business contribute to the area?	Ten local families benefited from direct full-time employment
How many people are employed?	The company employs 15 people, 12 of whom are not family members
Do they have plans for expansion?	Not at present – it would involve too much financial investment in new technology
Do they have plans to increase employment?	No. Last year they increased the workforce by three people
Have there been any changes in any area since the industry was established?	1. In 2006 they set up a coffee shop close to the factory unit where customers sample products along with coffee/tea and homemade cakes 2. The owner modified the business plan and production so that specific products can be made at key times of the year to coincide with events, e.g. St Valentine's Day 3. All staff are trained in Hazard Analysis and Critical Control Point (HACCP) 4. Owner did a course in marketing

Where are their markets?	1. Local and county stockists
	2. A supermarket chain in Ireland and UK
	3. Export to Europe, USA and Australia using on-line ordering system
How do they market their product?	1. In-store marketing
	2. Marketing to retailers
What type of quality control do they use?	HACCP in accordance with EU regulations

Career opportunities in food and related industries

Certificates, diplomas and degrees are offered by:

- agricultural colleges
- Teagasc
- universities and institutes of technology
- colleges of education
- Fáilte Ireland.

LINKS

- Consumer responsibilities (p. 221)
- Food safety and hygiene (p. 170)
- HACCP (p. 172)

Career opportunities

- Creating new foods.
- Manufacturing/preparation in the food industry.
- Management and administration.
- Food technologists, biotechnologists, microbiologists.
- Non-designated crafts: bakers, butchers.
- Designated crafts: fitters, electricians, mechanics.
- Marketing and retailing.
- Product distribution and transport logistics.
- Suppliers of services and raw materials.

Careers in food production include: farming, fishing, horticulture and milling.

Careers in the catering/retail industry include:

- chefs, bakers, butchers, confectioners, caterers
- deli counter staff
- hospitality assistants
- managers (hotel, restaurants, catering)
- administrative staff (accountants, receptionists).

LINK

- Check the careers guidance board/file in your school to see if there are new food courses/careers available.

Exam questions and sample answers

Higher Level 2008, Section A, Q6 (6 marks)

(a) Name **two** major Irish food exports and **two** major foods imported into Ireland.

Food exports	Food imports
Beef	Fruits
Fish	Cheese

(b) State **one** function of the Food Hygiene Regulations Acts (1950–89).

To ensure that food premises are safe and hygienic and that food handlers follow the correct hygiene rules.

Higher Level 2007, Section A, Q7 (6 marks)

List **two** different functions of An Bord Bia (Irish Food Board) in the Irish food industry.

(i) To promote Irish food, drink and horticulture nationally and internationally, and to develop markets for Irish food.

(ii) To implement quality assurance schemes for meat, eggs and horticultural products.

Higher Level 2005, Section A, Q7 (6 marks)

(a) List **two** career opportunities in the food industry. (2 marks)

1. Farmer

2. Environmental Health Officer

(b) State **two** ways that the Food Safety Authority of Ireland (FSAI) support the work of the food industry. (4 marks)

1. By enforcing food safety and hygiene legislation

2. By establishing standards of hygiene at all stages of production, supply and point of sale

Ordinary Level 2006, Section A, Q6 (b) (2 marks)

Name **one** organisation that promotes the sale of Irish food products.

List any **one** of the following: An Bord Bia, Bord Iascaigh Mhara, Teagasc.

(5 points × 4 marks = 20 marks)

Higher Level 2009, Section B, Q1 (d) (20 marks)

Describe some of the measures taken by food manufacturers/retailers in order to meet the needs of consumers who have specific dietary requirements.

Choose any five points from the seven listed below.

Manufacturers:
1. Production of wider range of food for specific modified diets, e.g. vegetarian, gluten-free, diabetic.
2. Smaller portions catering for individuals.
3. Detailed labelling of products.
4. Suggestions for recipes to make the products tastier.

Retailers:
1. Specialised shelving in supermarkets.
2. Cookery courses for special diets.
3. A wider range of products available.

aims To learn and revise:
- Food processing
- Food profiles
- Functional foods
- Packaging
- Labelling
- Additives
- Microbiology
- Preservation
- Safety and hygiene legislation.

Food processing and food profiles

Reasons for processing food:

1. To extend shelf life, provide variety and choice.
2. To improve nutritive value by fortifying food.
3. To create new food products and flavours.
4. To provide variety and choice all year round.
5. To make food safe to eat.

Categories of processing

Primary: processing of basic foods, e.g. milling.
Secondary: using processed foods to create new products, e.g. margarine.

LINKS
- The Irish food industry (p. 119)
- Food commodities (p. 70)

Types of processed/convenience foods

1. Bottled/canned foods

Examples	Preparation	Cooking
Beans, beetroot, pears, jams	None	• Heating required • Saves time

2. Cook-chill products

Examples	Preparation	Cooking
Lasagne, fresh pastas, cartons of soup	None	Reheat until piping hot

3. Dehydrated foods

Examples	Preparation	Cooking
Bread/cake mixes, soups, sauces, custard, stock cubes	• Some needed • Takes less time than making from scratch • Add a liquid (eggs, milk, water)	Cook as normal

4. Frozen foods

Examples	Preparation	Cooking
Meats, poultry, fish, vegetables, cooked meals, prepared meals	None	• Cook from frozen • **But!** *Poultry should be fully thawed before cooking*

5. Instant/ready-to-serve foods

Examples	Preparation	Cooking
Takeaway foods, salads, pastries, cakes	None	None required Serve as normal

Advantages and disadvantages of convenience foods

Advantages	1. Save time and energy
	2. Less waste, easy to store and use
	3. May be fortified with nutrients
	4. Low-fat varieties available
	5. Some have longer shelf life
	6. Good variety available
Disadvantages	1. Some inferior to home-made varieties
	2. Expensive
	3. High in salt, sugar and fat
	4. Low in fibre
	5. Many contain artificial additives

LINKS
• Food choices (p. 2)
• The Irish diet (p. 64)

LINKS
• Food commodities (p. 70)
• Small businesses and home enterprises (p. 121)

Food profiles

Food profile 1. A food that undergoes extensive processing – Flour

Flour may be made from wheat, barley, rice, rye, etc.

Uses: baking, thickening sauces, coating food.

THE MILLING PROCESS

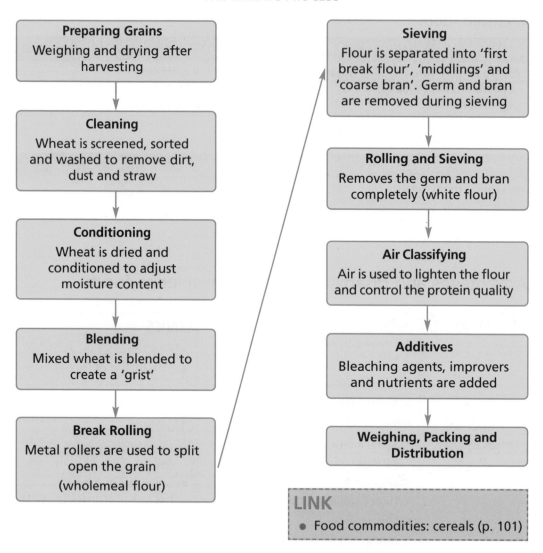

Preparing Grains
Weighing and drying after harvesting

Cleaning
Wheat is screened, sorted and washed to remove dirt, dust and straw

Conditioning
Wheat is dried and conditioned to adjust moisture content

Blending
Mixed wheat is blended to create a 'grist'

Break Rolling
Metal rollers are used to split open the grain (wholemeal flour)

Sieving
Flour is separated into 'first break flour', 'middlings' and 'coarse bran'. Germ and bran are removed during sieving

Rolling and Sieving
Removes the germ and bran completely (white flour)

Air Classifying
Air is used to lighten the flour and control the protein quality

Additives
Bleaching agents, improvers and nutrients are added

Weighing, Packing and Distribution

LINK
- Food commodities: cereals (p. 101)

Food profile 2. A food that undergoes processing to extend shelf life – Milk

Milk is a perfect medium for microbial growth. Processing delays spoilage and extends shelf life. Processing is carried out in two stages:

1. **Homogenisation** develops a uniform consistency.
2. **Heat treatments** destroy pathogenic bacteria and increase shelf life.

Homogenisation distributes fat globules evenly throughout the milk. Milk is heated to 60°C, forced through holes to make the fat globules smaller and to suspend them evenly in the milk. Homogenised milk then undergoes a heat treatment.

Heat treatments to extend shelf life:

1. **Pasteurisation:** milk is heated to 72°C for 25 seconds (HRST), cooled rapidly to below 10°C and sealed in sterilised containers. All pathogenic and some souring bacteria are destroyed.

2. **Sterilisation:** homogenised milk is bottled and sealed, heat-treated to 110°C for 30 minutes. Milk is sterilised in two ways: batch process; and continuous process. Milk will keep for months as all bacteria are destroyed.

3. **Ultra-heat treated (UHT):** milk is heated to 132°C for one second, cooled rapidly, packed into sterile containers and sealed. UHT milk keeps for months because all bacteria and their spores are destroyed. The flavour changes and vitamins C and B_1 are lost.

4. **Dehydration:** milk is homogenised and evaporated to 60% of its volume, spray or roller dried and packed. Moisture is not present to support the growth of microbes.

5. **Evaporation:** pasteurised milk is evaporated to half its volume, homogenised, sealed and sterilised at 115°C for 20 minutes in sealed cans. It keeps indefinitely.

6. **Condensed:** milk is homogenised, pasteurised, 15% sugar added, and its volume reduced to one-third; it is canned, sealed and sterilised. All bacteria, vitamins C and B group are destroyed. The low moisture content and increased levels of sugar create an unsuitable environment for microbial growth.

Food profile 3. Processing food to add value – Cook-chill foodstuffs

LINK
- Food commodities: milk (p. 86)

Foods are prepared in **two** ways:

1. Cook-chill method.
2. Cook-pasteurise-chill method.

Advantages:
- Extends shelf life, saves time and energy.
- Low temperatures prevent microbial growth.

Disadvantage:
- Some loss of vitamin C.

Cook-chill method

1. Ingredients are prepared and cooked.
2. Food is divided into portion sizes.
3. Food is chilled to 3°C within 30 minutes of cooking.
4. Chilling is completed within 90 minutes.

5. Food is stored between −1°C and 3°C.

6. Food is transported in cold conditions.

7. Food is stored in a refrigerated cabinet in the shop.

8. Shelf life is up to five days.

Cook-pasteurise-chill method

1. Food is prepared, cooked and divided into portions.

2. Hot foods are put into flexible containers.

3. Containers are heat sealed and a partial vacuum forms.

4. Food is pasteurised to 80°C for 10 minutes.

5. Food is chilled to 3°C and stored between −1°C and 3°C.

6. Food is transported in cold conditions.

7. Food is stored in a chilled cabinet in the shop.

8. Shelf life is between two and three weeks.

4. Functional foods

Functional foods contain an ingredient that gives a health benefit above the food's own nutritive value.

New ingredient	Examples	Health-promoting property/benefit
Plant sterols	Benecol, Flora Pro-activ	Reduce build-up of cholesterol and risk of CHD
Probiotics	Bio-yoghurt, yoghurt drinks, e.g. Actimel	Improve the digestive system
Omega-3 fatty acids	Milk, e.g. Supermilk	May reduce risk of cholesterol build-up and CHD
Folic acid	Breakfast cereals (fortified food)	Reduces risk of neural tube defects, e.g. spina bifida

5. Genetically modified (GM) foods

- A GM food is one in which the DNA has been altered.
- A particular characteristic is isolated and transferred to another plant.
- Testing on GM foods is extensive.
- Potential to produce foods to benefit consumers.

GM foods are monitored by the Food Safety Authority of Ireland (FSAI) and European Food Safety Authority (EFSA). Some processed foods sold in Ireland may have GM ingredients, e.g. soya, maize, rapeseed oil.

LINKS
- Consumer responsibilities (p. 221)
- Food Safety Authority of Ireland (p. 120)
- Food legislation: EU (p. 177)

Exam questions and sample answers

Higher Level 2008, Section A, Q8 (6 marks) **HL**

Identify **three** different items of nutritional information that are generally included on pre-packed foods.

 (i) *List of nutrients present and the quantities of nutrients per 100g or per serving.*

 (ii) *List of nutritive additives used.*

 (iii) *Energy value of the food.*

Ordinary Level 2008, Section A, Q7 (6 marks)

(a) Explain the term 'fortified' in relation to food processing.

  Fortified foods have nutrients added to improve the food's nutritive value.

(b) Name **two** fortified foods.

   (i) *Milk – added omega-3 fatty acids (Supermilk).*

   (ii) *Breakfast cereals – added folic acid.*

Higher Level 2007, Section B, Q1 (d) **HL**

Statement at the beginning of the question:

'Mandatory fortification with folic acid of most breads on sale in Ireland is the policy recommended by the National Committee on Folic Acid Food Fortification.' (Press release 2006)

 (i) Define food fortification. (4 marks)

  Food to which minerals or vitamins have been added to improve its nutritive content.

 (ii) Outline the benefits of fortified foods to the consumer **and** to the food manufacturer.

  (3 benefits × 4 marks = 12)

State one **consumer** benefit, one benefit to the **manufacturer** and one **other benefit** (either to the consumer or manufacturer).

Consumer Benefits:

1. *Replacing nutrients lost during food processing.*
2. *Adding extra vitamins and minerals improves nutritive value of food.*

Manufacturer Benefit: *increases sales of products with a 'health benefit' e.g. milk containing omega-3.*

Note the **allocation of marks** in question 2 (b). Most of the marks are awarded for the stages of production.

Higher Level 2005, Section B, Q2 (b)

(b) Profile a food of your choice that has been processed to **extend shelf life.** (24 marks)

   (i) Stages of production
     (4 × 4 marks = 16 marks)

   (ii) Packaging (1 × 4 marks = 4 marks)

   (iii) Labelling (1 × 4 marks = 4 marks)

Choose any **one** of the three food profiles to answer this question. (pp. 128–129)

Food packaging

Packaging is used to:

1. prevent dehydration, oxidation and contamination
2. prevent the transfer of flavours
3. extend shelf life of food
4. prevent damage during storage and transport.

Properties of good packaging

- is safe and hygienic
- looks attractive and is functional
- is environmentally friendly, easy to open and reseal
- is durable, strong, odourless, moisture/vapour proof
- controls the movement of micro-organisms.

Types of packaging

Glass

Advantages	<ul><li>Useful, hygienic</li><li>Rigid/transparent, displays contents</li><li>Protects against contaminants</li><li>Suited to heat treatments</li><li>Easily moulded</li></ul>
Disadvantages	Fragile, breaks easily
Uses	Preserves, pickles, mayonnaise, sauces

Metal

Examples: aerosols, cans, aluminium foil.

Advantages	<ul><li>Good variety of types and uses</li><li>Convenient, easy to store/transport</li><li>Foods can be sterilised in container</li><li>Internal lacquers may be applied</li></ul>
Disadvantages	Unsuitable for use in microwave ovens
Uses	**Tin:** fish, meat, fruit, vegetables **Aluminium cans:** beer, soft drinks **Aluminium foil:** for wrapping food, freezing

Paper

Advantages	<ul><li>Variety of forms, weight and uses</li><li>Economical to produce and print on</li><li>Biodegradable, eco-friendly</li><li>Waxed cartons are strong and durable</li><li>Some are heat-resistant</li></ul>
Disadvantages	<ul><li>Can be fragile</li><li>Absorbs moisture, falls apart</li><li>Most types cannot be resealed</li></ul>
Uses	**Waxed paper:** lining cake tins **Greaseproof paper:** wrapping fish **Paper bags:** flour, sugar **Cardboard:** outer covering for dry foods **Waxed cartons:** fresh soup, cream

Flexible packaging

Examples: cellulose films, polyethylene wrapping, polystyrene and PET bottles.

Advantages	<ul><li>Variety of forms and uses</li><li>Some can be heat sealed</li><li>Moisture proof</li><li>Easy to handle, unbreakable</li></ul>
Disadvantages	<ul><li>Some plastics can contaminate foods</li><li>Not eco-friendly, non-biodegradable</li><li>Produced from non-renewable resource</li></ul>
Uses	To cover food, bottles, food trays, freezer containers, containers for custard, margarine, yoghurt, freezer bags, boil-in-the-bag foods

Environmental impact of packaging

1. **Glass:** recyclable; also goes into landfill.
2. **Metals:** high production/transport costs, non-biodegradable; some are recyclable.
3. **Aerosols** with CFCs damage the environment (the ozone layer).
4. **Paper:** biodegradable, cheap to produce/transport, can be recycled.
5. **Plastics:** cause litter and pollution, limited recycling, plastic goes into landfill.

Problems caused by packaging

1. Use of non-renewable valuable resources.
2. High energy costs, e.g. production and transport.
3. Waste disposal and collection.

4. Litter in urban and rural areas, along roadsides.

5. Materials in landfills can be toxic.

Reducing the environmental impact of packaging

- Reuse, recycle, and refuse excessive packaging.
- Buy unpackaged products, e.g. fruits/vegetables.
- Use cloth shopping bags instead of plastic bags.
- Bring bottles, etc. to recycling banks.
- Send paper for recycling (paper bins).

LINKS
- Consumer choice (p. 218)
- Food safety and hygiene (p. 170)

LINK
- Consumer responsibilities (p. 221)

Exam questions and sample answers

Ordinary Level 2009, Section A, Q10 (part question)   (6 marks)

Explain this **symbol** which may be found on packaging material.   (4 marks)

Recycling symbol

Contains recyclable material or is itself recyclable

Higher Level 2007, Section A, Q9   (6 marks)

(a) State **two** advantages of using flexible films (plastics) as packaging materials.

   (i) Moisture proof.

   (ii) Excellent barrier against micro-organisms.

(b) Identify **one** initiative implemented to address the impact of excess packaging on the environment.

Government levy on plastic shopping bags.

Ordinary Level 2007, Section B, Q1 (d) (20 marks)

Describe **four** ways the consumer can play a role in waste management when selecting and purchasing food commodities. (4 points × 5 marks = 20 marks)

1. *Re-use shopping bags.*
2. *Avoid products with excessive packaging.*
3. *Choose bio-degradable packaging.*
4. *Do not buy pre-packed fruit and vegetables.*

Ordinary Level 2006, Section A, Q7 (6 marks)

Name **three** different types of packaging used in the food industry and give **one different** example of the use of each.

Type of packaging	Example of use
Glass	Jars – preserves
Plastics	Bottles – soft drinks
Cardboard	Egg boxes

Higher Level 2004, Section A, Q6 (6 marks)

Explain the following and give an **example** of the use of each.

(a) **Biodegradable packaging**

Explanation: *breaks down without harming the environment.*

Uses: *paper bags: flour bags*

Cardboard: cereal boxes

(b) **Modified atmospheric packaging**

Explanation: *Air is removed and replaced with a mixture of gases; the item is heat sealed.*

Uses: *rashers.*

Food labelling

Reasons for labelling food

1. to provide information to consumers
2. to give nutritional information
3. to provide information on storage
4. to outline instructions for cooking.

Labelling regulations (packaged and non-packaged foods)

Pre-packed foods	<ul><li>Name of the food</li><li>Net quantity</li><li>List of ingredients in descending order of quantity</li><li>Country of origin</li><li>Manufacturer's name and address</li><li>Instructions for use and storage</li><li>Cooking instructions</li><li>Use by date or best before date</li><li>Name of flavourings</li><li>Indication if 'packaged in a protective atmosphere'</li><li>With sweetener or with sugar(s) and sweeteners</li><li>If alcohol is present (strength)</li><li>If food has been irradiated or contains GM ingredients</li></ul>
Non-packaged or loose foodstuffs	Information must be displayed at the point of sale:<ul><li>Name of food</li><li>Origin, class and variety</li><li>Metric unit price, e.g. price per kg</li></ul>

Nutritional labelling

1. Provides information about nutritive value of foods.
2. Nutrient information is given per 100g or 100ml.
3. Nutrients may be listed per portion or per serving.
4. The minimum/maximum of a particular ingredient must be given in specific cases, e.g. low-fat food.

LINKS

- Dietary guidelines (p. 45)
- Special diets (pp. 52–60)
- Food commodities (p. 70)
- Family resource management (p. 179)

Price and labels

- Selling price must be displayed.
- For pre-packaged foodstuffs, unit price and selling price must be included.
- Unit price per kg/per litre must be displayed beside loose foodstuffs.

Bar codes

A bar code is a series of lines and spaces which contains product information (name, price, brand name) that can be read by a scanner. This information is printed on the customer's receipt and the shop's stock records are adjusted.

Exam questions and sample answers

Ordinary Level 2006, Section B, Q1 (e)   (20 marks)
Name **four** items of consumer information found on food packaging.
                                                (4 × 3 marks = 12 marks)
Explain the importance of **each**.   (4 × 2 marks = 8 marks)

Item of information	Why it is important
List of ingredients	To inform people who have special dietary requirements (e.g. gluten-free)
Country of origin	To support Irish producers
Name of manufacturer	For traceability
Special cooking instructions	To prevent food poisoning

Higher Level 2005, Section B, Q1 (d)
Evaluate the role of food labelling in assisting the consumer when selecting food.   (5 × 4 marks = 20 marks)
Food labelling provides consumers with information about:
1. Ingredients, additives and nutritional value.
2. Preparation, cooking and serving instructions.
3. Storage guidelines and best before date.
4. Dangers to those suffering from allergies.
5. Traceability information.

Food additives and food contaminants

Food additives

Additives are ingredients added to food to improve colour, flavour, texture, shelf life and nutritional value. They must fulfil acceptable and useful functions.

- **Direct additives** are added to foods for specific beneficial reasons.
- **Indirect additives** become part of a product due to handling, packaging or storage.

Main types and sources

Natural	Plants and animals, e.g. chlorophyll
Nature identical	Identical to a natural substance but synthetically made, e.g. ascorbic acid
Artificial	Synthetically made, e.g. esters

Advantages of additives

1. Enhance colour, flavour and texture.
2. Inhibit action of enzymes and micro-organisms.
3. Improve or increase shelf life of food.
4. Maintain or supplement nutritional value.
5. Increase the variety of foods available throughout the year.

Disadvantages of additives

1. May deceive consumers (colours, flavours, textures).
2. Side effects (allergies, hyperactivity, toxin build-up).
3. Cumulative effects on humans not known.

> **LINKS**
> - Food choices (p. 2)
> - Consumer choice (p. 218)

Classification and examples of additives (direct)

Antioxidants (E300–E399)

Functions:

1. To prevent oxidative rancidity (fats and oils).
2. To prevent oxidative discolouring (fruits/vegetables).

Type	Examples and uses
Natural	Vitamin A – fruit products Vitamin C – fruit drinks, jams Vitamin E – vegetable oils
Synthetic	Butylated Hydroxytoluene (chewing gum) – BHT Butylated Hydroxyanisole (stock cubes) – BHA

Colourings (E100–E199)

Functions

1. To improve the natural colour of food.
2. To improve the colour of preserved foods.
3. To replace colours lost during processing.
4. To respond to consumer demand.

Type	Examples and uses
Natural	Caramel – sauces and gravies
	Chlorophyll – canned vegetables
	Carotene – soft drinks
Artificial	Amaranth – blackcurrant products
	Tartrazine – soft drinks

Flavourings (no E numbers)

Functions

1. To enhance/improve the flavour of food.
2. To change the flavour of food.

Type	Examples and uses
Natural	Salt – butter, cheese
	Herbs – stock cubes
	Spices – sauces
Artificial and nature identical	Benzaldehyde – almond flavouring
	Maltol – baked smell
	Esters – pear or rum flavouring
Flavour enhancers	Monosodium glutamate (MSG)

Uses

Breads, crisps, essences, synthetic flavourings, Chinese foods (MSG)

Sweeteners

Function

To sweeten food.

Type	Examples and uses
Natural	Fructose – tinned peas
	Glucose – tinned fruits
	Sugar – cakes, biscuits
Intense sweetener (sweeter than sugar)	Aspartame – soft drinks
	Saccharin – low-calorie products
Bulk sweeteners (same sweetening power as sugar)	Mannitol – confectionery
	Sorbitol – confectionery
	Xylitol – sugar-free chewing gum

Preservatives (E200–E299)

Functions

1. To inhibit growth of enzymes and micro-organisms.
2. To increase/extend shelf life of foods.
3. To increase the variety of foods available.
4. To provide food 'out of season'.
5. To prevent waste.

Type	Examples and uses
Natural	Alcohol – Christmas cake
	Salt – bacon, preserves
	Sugar – sweets, preserves
	Vinegar – preserves
	Smoke – fish and meat
Chemical	Benzoic acid – coffee
	Potassium and sodium nitrate – cured meats
	Sorbic acid – cheese, fruit yoghurt
	Sulphur dioxide – dried fruits

Nutritional supplements

Functions

1. To improve the nutritive value of food.
2. To replace nutrients lost during processing.
3. To satisfy consumer demand for healthier products.

Nutrient	Uses – added to:
Vitamin A and D	Low-fat milk, super milk, margarine
Vitamin B group	Breakfast cereals, flour, TVP
Vitamin C	Fruit drinks
Iron	Breakfast cereals
Calcium	Flour, milk

LINK

- Nutrients (p. 2)

Physical conditioning agents (E400–E499)

Main agents	Functions and uses
Anti-caking	Prevents lumps forming in dried foods *Uses:* cake mixes, powdered milk
Anti-foaming	Prevents foaming and a scum forming *Uses:* packet soups
Antioxidants	Prevent oxidation and rancidity *Uses:* biscuits, cooking oils, crisps
Buffers	Control pH in a food
Bulking agents	Add bulk (but not energy value) to food *Uses:* slimming foods
Emulsifiers	Force water and oil to mix without separating, e.g. lecithin, alginates, pectin *Uses:* desserts, ice cream, mayonnaise
Glazing agents	Give a shiny appearance, seal and prevent food drying out *Uses:* fruits, salads, vegetables
Humectants	Prevent foods drying out, e.g. sorbitol, mannitol *Uses:* confectionery, sweets
Stabilisers	Prevent emulsions separating, e.g. carrageen, guar gum *Uses:* baked goods, ice cream

Legal control of food additives

1. Approved substances undergo testing for safety.
2. Allocation of an E number confirms safety of additive.
3. The EU controls the use and amounts of additives.
4. EU directives do not include flavourings or nutritive additives.
5. Food additives must:
   - perform a useful purpose
   - be safe

LINKS

- Lipids (p. 19)
- Vitamins (p. 26)
- Food processing (p. 126)
- Food packaging (p. 132)
- Food safety and hygiene (p. 170)

- not reduce the nutritive value of the food
- not mislead the consumer
- not disguise faulty processing
- comply with the regulations.

Indirect additives – contaminants

Contaminants are substances which accidentally enter the food chain and can potentially cause damage to humans.

Classification, sources and examples

Class	Sources and examples
Endogenous plant toxins	• *Cyanide:* traces in beans, peas • *Protease inhibitors:* kidney beans, chickpeas
Endogenous animal toxins	• Fish with poisonous tissue (fish poisoning) • Shellfish contaminated with toxic algae (paralytic)
Microbial toxins	**Bacterial toxins** and **mycotoxins** from moulds
Toxic residues	• Metal residues: aluminium, lead • Industrial residues: dioxins • Agricultural residues: antibiotics, pesticides • Radioactive residues: fallout, waste
Chemicals from food processing	• Carcinogens: smoked food products, by-product of cooking methods • Fumigants: used in the sterilisation of food

LINKS

- Food spoilage – microbiology (pp. 144, 152)
- Food safety and hygiene (p. 170)
- Consumer protection (pp. 177, 227)

Exam questions and sample answers

Higher Level 2008, Section A, Q7 (6 marks)

List **three** different classes of food additives and give one example of each class.

Class of food additive	Example (only one required for each class)
Colourings	*Chlorophyll (green)*
Flavourings	*Herbs*
Physical Conditioning Agents	*Emulsifiers*

Higher Level 2005, Section A, Q8 (6 marks)

State **one** function and give an example of **each** of the food additives listed below.

Food additive	Function
Flavour enhancer	To add and improve existing flavours **Example:** *maltol adds a freshly baked smell to bread and cakes*
Emulsifier	To improve consistency of a product **Example:** *lecithin in mayonnaise*
Antioxidant	To prevent oxidative rancidity **Example:** *vitamin C in fruit drinks*

Higher Level 2004, Section A, Q7 (6 marks)

Identify **two** contaminants that may enter the food chain and in each case state a likely source and the possible effect on the body.

Contaminant	Source	Effects on the body
Mercury	Shellfish – industrial pollution of coastal waters	Damages the central nervous system
Chemicals	Used in agriculture, industry and in the home	Damages the central nervous system, nausea, vomiting

Food spoilage – microbiology

There are **three groups** of micro-organism: fungi, bacteria and viruses.

Factors influencing the growth of micro-organisms

Temperature	Mesophiles: optimum 25–45°C Psychrophiles: optimum −5 – +20°C Thermophiles: ideal above 45°C Danger zone = 5–65°C
Food/nutrients	• Saprophytes get food from dead matter • Parasites get food from living matter • Need food for energy and growth • Yeasts need carbohydrate-rich foods • Nutrients are absorbed via cell walls
Oxygen	Aerobic: need oxygen for growth Anaerobic: do not need oxygen Facultative: grow with or without oxygen Microaerophilic: grow in a reduced oxygen environment

Correct pH level	● Bacteria prefer a neutral pH
	● Yeasts prefer a slightly acidic pH
Moisture	● Prefer high-water food sources
	● Cannot use ice, frozen or dried foods
	● Grow best in foods with a water activity above 0.61aw
Time	In favourable conditions bacteria will multiply every 20 minutes
Light	● Grow best without light
	● Destroyed by sunlight

Moulds – multicellular fungi

Characteristics

- Simple plants.
- Cannot manufacture own food; do not contain chlorophyll.
- Saprophytic fungi survive on dead matter, e.g. bread.
- Parasitic fungi feed on living matter, e.g. ringworm.

> **Competitive effects:** when bacteria compete with each other for food, oxygen and moisture.
>
> **Mutualism:** when two organisms benefit from growing near each other.

Classification

Class	Examples
Ascomycetes	Aspergillus, Penicillium
Phycomycetes	Mucor, rhizopus
Basidiomycetes	Mushrooms – large fungi
Saccharomycetes	Yeast

Environmental conditions for growth

Food	Most are saprophytes; grow on a variety of foods. *Examples:* bread, fruit, cheese
Moisture	Prefer moist, humid conditions and moist foods
Oxygen	Aerobic; grow on surface of food, e.g. bread
Warmth	Most are mesophiles; freezing inactivates growth; moulds destroyed by cooking above 75°C
pH level	pH 4–6 (slightly acidic), growth inhibited by very alkaline or acidic environment
Time	Need time to grow and multiply

Basic structure

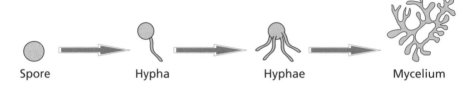

Spore — Hypha — Hyphae — Mycelium

Asexual reproduction

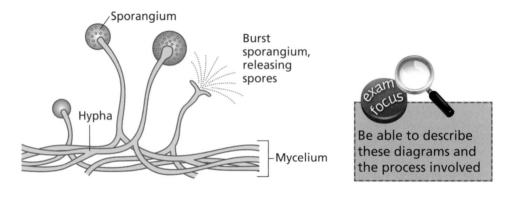

Sporangium

Burst sporangium, releasing spores

Hypha

Mycelium

exam focus

Be able to describe these diagrams and the process involved

Sexual reproduction

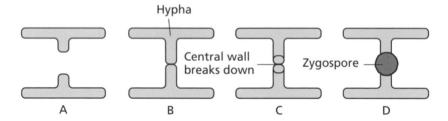

Hypha

Central wall breaks down

Zygospore

A   B   C   D

Common food spoilage moulds

Classification	Example	Details	Food sources
Ascomycetes 20°C to 25°C Septate (cross walls)	Aspergillus	• Saprophytic • Asexual • Conidia • Green-grey or black	• Cereals • Fruit • Black rot on fruit and vegetables
	Penicillium (several species)	• Saprophytic • Asexual • Conidia • Green-blue • *Uses:* blue cheese, antibiotics	• Cheese • Fruit • Bread

Phycomycetes 30°C most favourable Non-septate	Mucor	• Saprophytic • Asexual/sexual • White hyphae • Grey sporangium	• Bread • Meat • Soil
	Rhizopus	• Saprophytic • Asexual • White hyphae • Black sporangium	• Bread • Rot on fruits and vegetables

Large fungi – basidiomycetes

Fungi are visible to the naked eye. Some are edible; others are poisonous. *Examples:* edible mushrooms, truffles.

Development of a mushroom

- A single spore develops hyphae, which form a mycelium.
- Organic material underneath the soil provides food.
- A stalk develops and pushes out of the ground.
- A closed cap forms with gills underneath.
- Cap swells and bursts open, and pink gills become visible.
- Gills darken, basidia form and spores are released from between gills onto the ground and into the air.

Yeast – saccharomycetes

- Unicellular facultative, saprhophytic fungi, destroyed by high temperatures.
- Found in air, on fruit skins, in slightly sweet and acidic foods.
- Important source of B group vitamins, used in health products, food supplements.
- Used to produce bread, vinegar, wine and beer.

Environmental conditions for growth

Food	Feed on carbohydrate foods, e.g. sugars
Moisture	Need moisture/moist conditions to grow
Oxygen	Facultative, survives with or without oxygen
Warmth	Ideal temperature range is 25–30°C, killed above 60°C, inactivated at low temperatures
pH level	Prefers acid environment
Time	Needs time to multiply

Basic structure

Thin, single outer cell walls, filled with cytoplasm containing a nucleus, one vacuole and food storage granules

Reproduction

Yeast reproduces asexually by the process called **budding.**

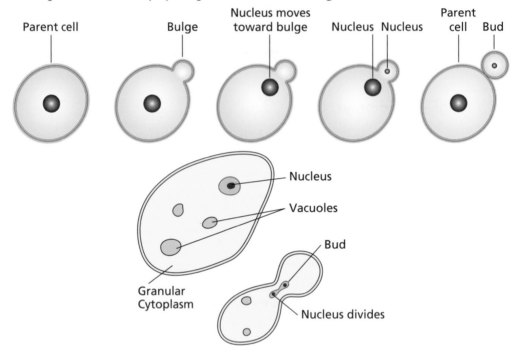

Uses of fungi

Food production, brewing and bread-making, antibiotics, supplements, novel protein foods, cooking.

LINK

● Fermentation (pp. 111, 166)

Disadvantages of fungi

1. Cause food spoilage.
2. Some are poisonous, e.g. amanita.
3. Cause plant diseases, e.g. potato blight.
4. Cause human diseases, e.g. ringworm, athlete's foot.

Bacteria

Bacteria:

- are small, single-celled micro-organisms
- may be parasites or saprophytes, pathogenic or non-pathogenic.

Sources: air, animals, foods, plants, soil and water.

Environmental conditions for growth of bacteria

Food	*Parasitic bacteria* feed on living matter *Saprophytic bacteria* feed on dead or decaying matter
Moisture	Need a good supply of moisture in liquid form for growth, e.g. milk, stew, cream
Oxygen	Needs vary; most are aerobic
Warmth	Extensive range of temperature. Each has a maximum, minimum and ideal range (psychrophile, mesophile, thermophile)
pH level	Most prefer a near neutral pH range
Time	Bacteria double every 20 minutes but rapid growth is limited by the extent of the food sources available
Light	Need darkness; destroyed by ultra-violet rays of the sun

Structure of bacterial cells

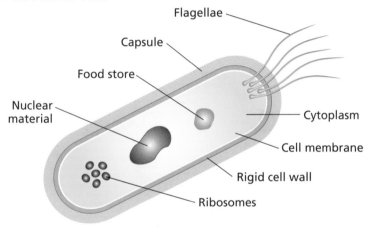

Reproduction

- Bacteria reproduce asexually by binary fission.
- Cells grow and divide into two separate parts.
- A cell wall is formed and the two cells separate.
- Rapid growth ends when bacteria run out of food, oxygen, moisture and space.
- Waste toxins build up and prevent further growth.

Growth curve

The time between each division is referred to as **generation time** (about 20 minutes). Overcrowding results in bacteria competing for food, oxygen and moisture, and death eventually results.

The **growth curve of bacteria** is divided into four phases:

- Lag phase
- Log phase
- Stationary phase
- Decline phase.

Growth curve of micro-organisms

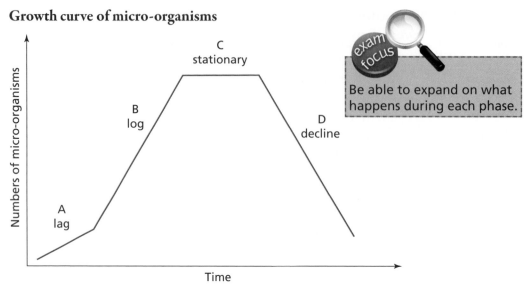

exam focus

Be able to expand on what happens during each phase.

Classification

Bacteria can be classified according to shape or gram staining.

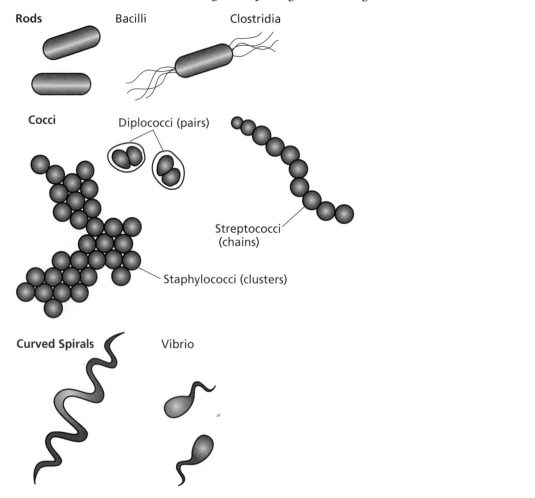

Bacillus (rod-shaped)	1. *Bacilli* – arranged singly. Examples: *Salmonella, E. coli, Listeria*
	2. *Clostridia* – arranged in chains. Examples: *Clostridium botulinum, Clostridium perfringens*
Coccus (round)	1. *Coccus* (single)
	2. *Diplococci* (pairs), e.g. pneumonia
	3. *Streptococci* (chains), e.g. tonsillitis
	4. *Staphylocci* (clusters), e.g. food poisoning
Curved	1. *Vibrios* – short, comma-shaped, e.g. cholera
	2. *Spirilla* – long, spiral, e.g. syphilis

Gram-staining results

Bacteria can be classified into two groups:

1. Gram-positive (*Clostridia, Streptococci*)
2. Gram-negative (*E. coli, Salmonella*).

Gram-positive bacteria	Gram-negative bacteria
Blue-black colour	Reddish, the colour of iodine
Thick single-cell wall	Cell wall has two thin layers
2% lipid in cell wall	20% lipid in cell wall
Generally aerobic	Aerobic and anaerobic
Non-mobile (no flagellae)	Mobile – have flagellae
Spore forming	Do not produce spores
Little resistance to antibiotics	High resistance to antibiotics

Advantages of bacteria

1. Provide starter cultures for cheese, yoghurt, vinegar.
2. Produce vitamins B and K in human gut.
3. Involved in breaking down waste matter.

LINK
- Food spoilage and food poisoning (p. 152)

Disadvantages of bacteria

1. Responsible for food poisoning.
2. Cause diseases in plants, animals and humans.
3. Involved in food spoilage (e.g. sour milk).
4. Cause of dental caries/tooth decay.

LINKS
- Cheese (p. 91)
- Yoghurt (p. 89)
- Alternative protein foods – novel proteins (p. 84)

Endospores

- Tough dormant cells produced by bacilli and clostridia.
- Form when conditions are unfavourable for growth.
- Formed within bacterial cells.
- Resistant to cold, heat and some chemicals.
- Destroyed by dry heat (150°C for one hour) or steam (121°C for 15 minutes).

Toxins (cause food poisoning)

- endotoxins
- enterotoxins
- exotoxins
- mycotoxins

LINK
- Indirect additives – contaminants (p. 143)

Viruses

Viruses are small non-cellular micro-organisms that are responsible for a range of diseases.

Examples:

- SRV – small round structured viruses: shellfish.
- BSE (bovine spongiform encephalopathy) – affects cattle.
- NvCJD (new variant Creutzfeldt-Jakob disease) – human form of BSE.

exam focus
Revise uses of micro-organisms

exam Q

Exam questions and sample answers

exam focus

Higher Level 2006, Section A, Q7 (6 marks)

List **five** conditions required for the growth of moulds.

1. Food, 2. Warmth, 3. Moisture, 4. Oxygen, 5. pH level.

Two marks for the first correct answer and **one** mark for each of the others.

Higher Level 2005, Section A, Q6 (6 marks)

(a) State **two** uses of micro-organisms in food production. (4 marks)
   1. Cheese making: starter cultures, moulds in blue cheese.
   2. Fermentation: yoghurt, wine, beer, yeast bread.

(b) Suggest **one** method of controlling enzymic spoilage in foods. (2 marks)

   Blanching vegetables before freezing inactivates enzymes and prevent enzymic spoilage.

Ordinary Level 2004, Section A, Q7 (6 marks)

(a) Name **two** main types of micro-organisms that are responsible for food spoilage. (2 × 2 marks = 4 marks)
   (i) Moulds
   (ii) Bacteria

(b) Name **two** natural preservatives. (2 marks)
   (i) Sugar
   (ii) Salt

Food spoilage and food poisoning

The main **causes of food spoilage** are:

1. loss of moisture
2. micro-organisms (moulds, yeasts, bacteria)
3. action of enzymes.

Loss of moisture:

- mainly affects fruits and vegetables after harvesting
- results in shrinkage, wrinkling and a limp appearance.

Chemical food poisoning: *caused by* pesticides, antibiotics, chemical contamination of the water supply, accumulation of metals, insecticides and residues from farming and horticulture.

Biological food poisoning: *caused by* poisonous substances found in some foods (e.g. oxalic acid in rhubarb leaves).

Bacterial food poisoning: *caused by* pathogenic bacteria in food.

Types of bacterial food poisoning

Go to Higher Level 2004, Section B, Q2(c) (p. 157).

High-risk foods

Milk, eggs, cooked meats, poultry, reheated food, gravy.

Common pathogenic or food poisoning bacteria

Toxic food poisoning bacteria

1. Clostridium botulinum

Characteristics	<ul><li>Rod-shaped</li><li>Gram-positive</li><li>Forms spores</li></ul>
Habitat/sources	<ul><li>Soil, vegetables</li></ul>
Environmental factors	<ul><li>Anaerobic bacteria</li><li>Optimum temperature 30–37°C</li><li>Destroyed at 121°C for 15 minutes</li></ul>
High-risk foods	<ul><li>Low-acid canned foods</li><li>Vacuum-packed foods</li><li>Smoked fish</li></ul>
Incubation and duration	*Incubation:* 12–36 hours *Duration:* 1–8 days (toxic illness) <ul><li>Mortality rate 5–15%</li><li>Recovery takes months</li></ul>
Symptoms	Blurred vision, diarrhoea, dizziness, headache, slurred speech, paralysis, death

2. Staphyloccus aureus

Characteristics	• Spherical in shape
	• Arranged in clusters
	• Gram positive
	• Non-spore forming
Habitat/Sources	• Nose and throat
	• Unwashed hands
	• Infected skin
Environmental factors	• Facultative
	• Optimum temperature 30–40°C
	• Salt tolerant
High-risk foods	• Unpasteurised milk
	• Cream, milk, custard
	• Cold meats
Incubation and duration	*Incubation:* 2–6 hours
	Duration: 24 hours
Symptoms	Cramps, vomiting, diarrhoea

Infectious food poisoning bacteria

1. Listeria monocytogenes

Characteristics	• Rod-shaped
	• Gram-positive
	• Spore forming
	• Multiplies at low temperatures, can survive heat treatments
Habitat/Sources	Soil, human and animal waste
Environmental factors	• Facultative
	• Optimum temperature is 30°C (mesophile), can grow at 4–43°C
	• Slightly acidic pH range
	• High moisture content
	• Salt tolerant
High-risk foods	Raw meat and poultry, unpasteurised milk, soft cheese, prepared salads, pâté, cook-chill products, raw vegetables
Incubation and duration	*Incubation:* 1–70 days
	Duration: several days
Symptoms	Fever, diarrhoea, septicaemia, meningitis in newborn babies, may cause miscarriage or premature birth

2. Escherichia Coli (E. coli)

Characteristics	• Rod-shaped
	• Gram-negative
	• Non-spore forming
	• Causes infectious food poisoning
Habitat/Sources	• Unwashed hands
	• Animal and human intestines
	• Excreta
	• Contaminated water
Environmental factors	• Aerobic
	• Optimum temperature 30–40°C
High-risk foods	• Unpasteurised milk
	• Raw meats
	• Undercooked mince, burgers, salami
Incubation and duration	*Incubation:* 12–24 hours
	Duration: 1–5 days
Symptoms	Abdominal cramps, bloody diarrhoea, fever, nausea, vomiting
	Serious cases: kidney failure, death

3. Salmonella

Go to Higher Level 2004, Section B, Q2(c) (p. 157) for information.

> **LINKS**
> • Food commodities (milk, dairy products) (pp. 86, 89)
> • Protein (p. 3)

Controlling the microbial spoilage of food

To control microbial spoilage of food, focus on personal, kitchen and food hygiene, and the cooking and chilling of food.

Core principles

1. Remove the factors that contribute to food poisoning.
2. Use good hygiene practices to avoid cross-contamination.
3. Store foods at low temperatures.
4. Cover foods when not in use.

> **LINK**
> • Food safety and hygiene (p. 170)

Personal hygiene

See page 171.

Kitchen hygiene

1. Keep kitchen well ventilated.
2. Check fridge daily; keep fridge clean and dispose of stale foods.
3. Disinfect food preparation and serving areas.

4. Use separate knives to prepare raw meat and raw fish.

5. Use separate chopping boards for raw and cooked foods.

6. Wipe up spills as they occur, wash up as you go along.

7. Wash kitchen cloths, tea towels and hand towels daily.

8. Empty, disinfect and wash kitchen bin daily.

9. Sweep, wash and disinfect kitchen floor daily.

Food hygiene, cooking and chilling

1. Store foods at the correct temperature.

2. Store chilled and frozen food correctly.

3. Label home-prepared frozen foods before freezing.

4. Store raw and cooked meats separately.

5. Use tongs or forks when handling food.

6. Cook foods to a core temperature of 70°C for two minutes.

7. Reheat leftovers only once – heat until piping hot.

8. Follow instructions on package of pre-prepared foods.

9. Cook meat until juices run clear, use a meat thermometer.

Role of micro-organisms in food spoilage

- Souring of foods (cream, milk, yoghurt).
- Spoilage of food (breads, cheese, fruits and jams).
- Produce slime and 'rotten' smells.

Role of enzymes in food spoilage

Enzymes cause spoilage of food through:

1. ripening in fruit and vegetables

2. browning (enzymic browning).

 Controlling enzymatic spoilage of food

Go to Higher Level 2009, Section B, Q3 (below).

Exam questions and sample answers

 Higher Level 2009, Section B, Q3   (50 marks)

'Whether it is pesticides in vegetables, microbes in cooked food products or a breakdown in the food safety management system, hazards can exist anywhere in the supply chain.'

4 points × 3 marks each = 12 marks

(a) Outline the main causes of food spoilage.   (12 marks)

The main causes of food spoilage are:

1. *Micro-organism contamination:*
   - *bacterial contamination*
   - *mould growth on fruit, vegetables and bread*
   - *yeast fermentation in fruit and jam.*
2. *Enzyme action in the ripening process, oxidation, rancidity and decomposition of food.*
3. *Chemical contamination: pesticides, insecticides.*
4. *Moisture loss, e.g. shrinking of fruit and vegetables.*

(b) Explain how the action of enzymes can be controlled in order to prevent food spoilage.   (20 marks)

The action of enzymes can be controlled by:

4 points × 5 marks each = 20 marks

1. *Acids, e.g. lemon juice on apples.*
2. *Blanching vegetables before freezing.*
3. *Using preservatives, e.g. sulphur dioxide in dried fruit.*
4. *Using cold temperatures, e.g. placing salads in fridge.*

(c) In relation to food poisoning explain each of the following:
                                    (3 × 6 marks = 18 marks)

- **Incubation Period**   (6 marks)

  This is the time between the ingestion of the contaminated food and the symptoms of the food poisoning developing. It varies depending on the type of food poisoning.

- **Toxic Food Poisoning**   (6 marks)

  This is caused by eating food contaminated with bacteria which produce and release waste products called exotoxins.

  Examples: Staphylococci, Clostridium Botulinum.

- **Infectious Food Poisoning**   (6 marks)

  This is caused by eating food contaminated with pathogenic bacteria which produce endotoxins within their cells.

  Examples: Salmonella, Listeria.

Higher Level 2004, Section B, Q2(c)

(c) Differentiate between (i) infectious food poisoning **and** (ii) toxic food poisoning.   (2 × 4 marks = 8 marks)

(i) *Infectious food poisoning*
   - *Caused by eating food that contains pathogenic bacteria.*
   - *Bacteria produce and release toxins inside their cells.*
   - *These bacteria have a long incubation period.*
   - *They produce endotoxins which are easily destroyed.*
   - *Heating food destroys endotoxins.*
   - *Examples:* Salmonella, Listeria, E. coli.

(ii) *Toxic food poisoning*
- *Caused by eating food contaminated by toxins produced by bacteria.*
- *Symptoms appear quickly.*
- *Produce exotoxins which are not easily destroyed.*
- *Boiling for 30 minutes is needed to kill them.*
- *Examples:* Staphylococcus aureus, Clostridium botulinum.

(d) Name and give a detailed account of any one type of food poisoning bacteria. Refer to:

Name of Bacteria: Salmonella (4 marks)

(i) **Description:** *rod-shaped, bacilli, gram-negative, non-spore forming, facultative, survives at temperatures of 37°C, 12–36 hours incubation period, lasts 1–7 days.*

Source of infection (2 × 2 marks = 4 marks)
- *Contaminated foods and water.*
- *Unwashed hands, human and animal waste, rodents.*

(ii) **High-risk foods** (2 × 3 marks = 6 marks)
- *Poultry*
- *Eggs*
    (Others: fish, sausages, incorrectly cooked meat.)

(iii) **Symptoms** (2 × 3 marks = 6 marks)
- *Fever, nausea and vomiting.*
- *Abdominal cramps and diarrhoea.*

Food preservation

Principles of food preservation

1. To destroy micro-organisms.
2. To prevent their re-entry into food.
3. To inhibit the activity of enzymes.
4. To maintain colour, flavour, texture and nutritive value of food.

LINKS
- Nutrients (p. 2)
- Food processing (p. 126)
- Food spoilage – microbiology (p. 144)

Reasons for preserving foods (advantages)

1. To extend the shelf life of food.
2. To destroy micro-organisms.
3. To avoid waste by preserving garden produce.
4. To save money by using foods in season.
5. To provide food for emergencies.

Methods of preservation

Home methods	Commercial methods
● Freezing	● Freezing
● Heat treatments:	● Heat treatments
– jams and jellies	● Dehydration
– chutneys, pickling	● Chemical preservation
– bottling	● Fermentation
● Dehydration/drying	● Irradiation
● Chemical preservation:	
– jams and jellies	
– chutneys, pickling	

Preservation involves controlling microbial growth conditions:

Heat treatments: high temperatures destroy enzymes and micro-organisms.

Freezing: low temperatures inactivate enzymes and micro-organisms.

Chemicals: chemicals inhibit enzymes and micro-organisms.

Dehydration: bacteria cannot multiply without moisture.

Vacuum packing: some bacteria cannot survive without oxygen; sealing food prevents their re-entry.

> ## LINKS
> - Nutrients: properties (pp. 3–42)
> - Food processing (p. 126)
> - Food spoilage – microbiology (pp. 144, 152)

Home freezing

Principles of freezing

1. Warmth and moisture are removed.
2. The source of liquid used by bacteria is removed.
3. Blanching vegetables inactivates enzymes.
4. Wrapping foods prevents re-entry of micro-organisms.

Quick freezing (fast-freeze section of the freezer): converts water into small ice crystals at −25°C, causes little damage to cell walls, little loss of liquid on thawing, maintains good colour and texture.

Slow freezing (ice box in fridge): converts water into large ice crystals at 0°C to −25°C, extensive damage to cell walls, loss of nutrients and increased loss of liquid on thawing.

Advantages of freezing

1. Good method of preserving a variety of foods.
2. Bulk freezing saves fuel, time and money.
3. Foods are available out of season; prevents waste.
4. Food can be frozen in useable quantities.
5. Little loss of flavour, colour and nutritive value.

Disadvantages of freezing

1. Freezers are expensive – initial outlay, running costs.
2. Bulk cooking/freezing requires time and work.
3. Danger of buying too many convenience foods/meals.
4. 'Freezer burn'.
5. Keeping the freezer full needs careful planning.

General guidelines for freezing

Preparation	● Choose fresh, high-quality foods
	● Turn on fast-freeze switch 2–3 hours in advance
	● Divide food into useable quantities
	● Blanch vegetables before freezing
	● Cool food before freezing
	● Freeze only one-tenth of the capacity of the freezer in 24 hours
Packaging	● Use suitable packaging material (moisture-proof, vapour-proof)
	● Pack food in small quantities
	● Remove as much air as possible
	● Allow headspace for expansion of liquids
	● Seal food correctly
	● Label food with name, quantity and date
Freezing	● Freeze in fast-freeze section
	● Open freeze foods that stick together, then pack into containers
	● Freeze food according to type
	● Remove frozen food from the fast-freeze section and put in storage area
	● Turn off fast-freeze switch
Storing	● Keep a diary of what is in the freezer
	● Use foods in rotation
	● Store for the recommended time
	● Keep freezer full to reduce running costs

Rules for thawing food

1. Thaw foods slowly and completely in the fridge.
2. Some foods do not require thawing but do require thorough cooking, e.g. commercial ready-prepared meals.
3. Cook all thawed foods fully to prevent food poisoning.
4. Never re-freeze frozen foods: cook and use quickly.
5. Avoid 'thaw drip' from meat contaminating other foods.

Foods suitable for freezing	Foods unsuitable for freezing
Cooked and fresh meats, poultry, fish, sauces, soups, fruits, vegetables, cakes, bread and pastries, sweet and savoury dishes	Foods with high water content and whole eggs
Commercial products, e.g. pizza, ready meals	Bananas, dairy produce and foods containing gelatine

Packaging materials for freezing
See food packaging (p. 132).

Heat treatments

1. Jam-making
Underlying principles of jam-making:

> **key point**
>
> Sugar acts as a preservative by surrounding the bacterial cells and drawing out the water (by a process called osmosis) from the cells.

- Enzymes and micro-organisms are destroyed at 100°C.
- Fruits are softened in the process.
- Sugar (65%) inhibits the growth of micro-organisms.
- Pectin and acids help jams to set.
- Sealing jars prevents the re-entry of micro-organisms.

Fruit, pectin, acid and sugar

Fruit	Choose:
	• good-quality ripe acidic fruits
	• fruits with a high pectin content
	• acidic fruit (apples, blackcurrants)
Pectin	• A polysaccharide found in fruit
	• Present in cell walls of fruit
	• Essential for setting jam
	• Some fruits are richer in pectin than others
	• To get a good set, combine fruits low in pectin with fruits rich in pectin
	• Liquid pectin is available
Acid	• Helps draw out the pectin from cell walls
	• Many fruits are acidic
	• Some recipes add lemon juice (acid)
	• Use of acids improves colour and flavour
	• Helps prevent crystallisation
Sugar	• Acts as the preservative
	• Sugar must be measured accurately (65%)
	• Warm sugar before use
	• Sure-set is a preserving sugar with added pectin and acid; has a shorter boiling time

The stage of maturity of the fruit influences the amount of pectin present:

Fruit	Contains	Setting quality
Under-ripe fruits	Pectose	Poor
Ripe fruits	Pectin	Good
Over-ripe fruits	Pectic acid	Poor

Pectin content of fruit (some examples):

Rich in pectin	Apples, blackcurrants, gooseberries
Medium pectin	Apricots, plums, raspberries
Low in pectin	Late blackberries, rhubarb, strawberries

Results of test for pectin (methylated spirits)
- High in pectin → large single clot.
- Medium pectin → two or three soft clots.
- Low pectin → several small soft clots.

Fruits with medium or low pectin levels must have pectin added by using fruits rich in pectin, liquid pectin or preserving sugar.

Setting tests for jam
1. Temperature test.
2. Cold plate test.
3. Flake test.

Revise: method of making jam.

Jam-making problems

Crystallisation	Too much sugar (over 65%), sugar not dissolved before boiling, insufficient boiling, insufficient acid, overcooking
Fermentation	Too little sugar (less than 65%), poor quality fruit, insufficient boiling
Mould growth	Too little sugar, over-ripe fruit, damp storage conditions
Poor set	Incorrect ratio of pectin, sugar and acid, insufficient boiling
Shrinkage	Cellophane cover loose on jar, warm storage conditions

2. Chutney making

Chutneys are made from a mixture of fruits, vegetables, salt, sugar (brown), spices (whole, in a muslin bag) and vinegars (5% acetic acid).

Chutney has a consistency similar to jam. The flavour of chutneys improves with storage. Leave for about three months before use.

Underlying principles of chutney making

1. High temperatures destroy micro-organisms.
2. Vinegar acts as a preservative by lowering the pH level; prevents microbial growth.
3. Sugar acts as a preservative by dehydrating the bacterial cells (osmosis); prevents their growth.
4. Sealing jars prevents the re-entry of micro-organisms.

Commercial preservation

Examples: bottling, canning, chemical preservation, dehydration, freezing, irradiation, pasteurisation and sterilisation.

Types of commercial preservation:

1. canning and bottling
2. pasteurisation, sterilisation and UHT.

> **LINKS**
> - Food commodities (p. 70)
> - Food profiles (pp. 128–30)

1. Canning/bottling

Underlying principles of canning/bottling

1. High temperatures destroy enzymes, micro-organisms and spores.
2. Food is sterilised in cans or glass.
3. Airtight containers prevent re-entry of micro-organisms.

The canning process – a summary

1. Food is prepared.
2. Vegetables are blanched.
3. Meat/fish is cooked.
4. Cans are filled with food, sauce/brine/oil/syrup.
5. Air is removed from cans.
6. Cans are hermetically sealed (airtight).
7. Cans and contents are sterilised.
8. Cans are cooled and labelled.

Aseptic canning process – a summary

1. Cans and foods are sterilised separately.
2. Food is sterilised for a short time at 120–150°C.
3. Food is placed into sterile cans and sealed hermetically.
4. Cans are cooled and labelled.

Canning high- and low-acid foods

Canning temperatures and times differ depending on the acid content of foods.

High-acid foods	Heated to 100°C for less than 30 minutes to destroy pathogenic bacteria
Low-acid foods	Heated to 115°C for more than 30 minutes to destroy bacterial spores

Effects of canning

1. Micro-organisms and enzymes are destroyed.
2. Loss of heat-sensitive vitamins – B group and C.
3. Changes in colour, flavour and texture.
4. Food may have salt, fat and sugar added.

2. Commercial dehydration

Underlying principles of dehydration:

1. removing moisture to prevent microbial growth
2. enzymes are inhibited.

Methods of dehydration – a summary

Sun drying	• Drying fruits and vegetables in hot countries
	• Food prone to contamination and attacks from animals, birds and insects
Accelerated freeze drying (AFD)	• Food is frozen quickly at –30°C
	• Water is converted to ice crystals
	• Food is passed through a heated vacuum cabinet
	• Ice crystals change to a vapour by the process of sublimation
	Uses: coffee, dried fruits and vegetables, meat
	Effects of AFD:
	• loss of vitamins B and C
	• change in shape and weight of food
	• oxidative rancidity (foods containing fat)
	Advantages:
	• longer shelf life
	• good flavour
Fluidised bed-drying	• Warm air is circulated around food to prevent it sticking
	• Food is agitated to prevent sticking
	• Temperature, humidity and air flow are monitored until the moisture level is reduced
	Uses: vegetables

Roller drying	• Prepared food is poured over revolving heated rollers, dried and scraped off in powder or flakes, cooled and packed • Moisture reduced to 10–14%. **Uses:** breakfast cereals, dried milk
Spray drying	• Liquid is sprayed through fine nozzles into a heated chamber (165°C) • Dried powder falls to the bottom of the chamber • Powder is cooled, packed and labelled **Uses:** powdered eggs and milk

> **LINK**
> • Properties of protein (denaturation) (p. 8)

3. Commercial freezing

Underlying principles of commercial freezing

1. Low temperatures are used to prevent growth of micro-organisms.
2. Moisture in food is converted to ice.

> **LINK**
> • Home freezing (p. 159)

Methods of commercial freezing

Blast freezing	Cold air (−30°C to −40°C) is blown over food as it moves through a tunnel on a conveyor belt *Uses:* meat, vegetables
Contact or plate freezing	Food is arranged between two cold metal surfaces. Food freezes in a short time *Uses:* burgers, fish, fish fingers, meat
Cryogenic freezing	Food is sprayed with liquid nitrogen to freeze foods in a short time *Uses:* prawns, strawberries
Flow freezing or fluidised freezing	Cold air (−30°C) is blown under foods, keeping them moving and preventing them sticking together, and freezing them in the process *Uses:* berries, peas, sweetcorn

4. Commercial chemical preservation

Underlying principles of chemical preservation

1. Chemicals dehydrate and destroy microbial cells by osmosis.
2. Acids lower pH levels, inhibit enzymatic activity and micro-organisms.
3. Alcohol denatures bacterial cell protein.
4. Antioxidants inhibit enzymatic action and prevent rancidity.

Common chemical preservatives

Preservative	Uses
Anti-oxidants	Fruits, fats, oils
Acids	Chutneys, pickles, relishes
Nitrates/nitrites	Cured meats
Salt	Cheese, bacon, sausages, foods in brine
Smoking	Produces aldehydes and phenols
Sugar	Jams, jellies, canned or bottled fruit
Sulphur dioxide	Forms sulphuric acid, which acts as a preservative

 ## 5. Fermentation

Underlying principles of fermentation

1. Carbohydrates and sugars are broken down by the action of yeast or bacteria to produce alcohol and carbon dioxide.
2. By-products of fermentation are in themselves preservatives, e.g. alcohol, vinegar.

> **LINKS**
> - Yeast (pp. 111, 147)
> - Yoghurt (p. 89)

Examples of fermentation in action

Food	Raw ingredient	Organism
Bread (baking)	Flour	Yeast
Wine (brewing)	Grapes	Yeast
Yoghurt	Milk	Lactic acid bacteria
Pickles	Vegetables	Yeasts and bacteria
Vinegar	Wine, cider	Yeasts and acetobacter bacteria
Blue cheese	Milk	Lactic acid bacteria and mould

6. Irradiation

Underlying principles of irradiation – ionising gamma radiation is passed through food to:
- sterilise it
- delay ripening
- destroy pathogenic and food spoilage bacteria
- kill insects
- prevent sprouting.

Irradiated foods carry an internationally recognised label/symbol Radura.

Advantages of irradiation

Revise the principles of irradiation and add the following:
- Reduces use of chemicals
- Increases shelf-life

Disadvantages of irradiation

1. Unsuitable for foods with a high fat content.
2. Loss of nutritional value, e.g. vitamins.
3. Consumer concerns over levels of radiation.
4. Concerns over using irradiation on inferior products.

Effects of preservation on food

> **LINKS**
> - Freezing (pp. 159, 165)
> - Commercial dehydration (p. 164)
> - Canning/bottling (p. 163)

Comparative evaluation of methods of preservation

Use the approach suggested for **comparative evaluation questions**. Include 'Areas to Investigate' and use a table format to present your answer.

Evaluation of frozen and canned peas – a summary

Areas to investigate	Freezing	Canning
Ingredients	Fresh peas	Fresh peas Water, additives Colouring
Type of packaging	Plastic bags	Metal cans
Labelling information	• Name of product • Weight of product • Number of servings • Ingredients • Nutrition information • Storage instructions (star rating) • Cooking instructions • Best before data • Commitment to quality • Customer care data • Address of producer	• Name of product • Ingredients • Nutrition information • Cooking instructions • Storage instructions • Customer care data • Weight • Symbols (low GI, recycling, guaranteed Irish)
Shelf life	Up to one year	• Unopened product has a long shelf life • Once opened eat within two days

Effects of processing	• Micro-organisms are inactivated • Enzymes are inactivated • Nutritional value is close to that of fresh peas	• Micro-organisms are inactivated • Enzymes are inactivated • Loss of water-soluble vitamins B and C • Loss of colour, flavour and texture • Increase in salt content
Risks of spoilage	Repeated defrosting and refreezing can lead to microbial growth	Dented, pierced or damaged cans/food may result in food poisoning
Cost	€1.69 (450 g)	€1.24 (410 g); drained weight 250 g
Culinary use	• Easy to use • Quick to cook	• Easy to use • Quick to cook

LINKS

• Food commodities (vegetables) (p. 97)
• Food safety (p. 170)

Exam questions and sample answers

Higher Level 2006, Section A, Q8 (6 marks)

Name **two** commercial methods of freezing and suggest a food suitable for each method.

Method of freezing (2 × 2 marks = 4 marks)	Food suitable for method (2 × 1 mark = 2 marks)
Flow freezing	Peas
Cryogenic freezing	Strawberries

Ordinary Level 2004, Section A, Q6 (6 marks)

Name **three** different methods of preserving food and give an example of a food preserved by **each** method.

Method of preservation	Example of food
Heat	Fruit ⟶ jams
Chemicals (salt, sugar)	Vegetables ⟶ pickles
Freezing	Meat, fish

Higher Level 2005, Section B, Q2(a)

'Preservation aims to ensure that the colour, flavour, texture and nutritive value of the food preserved is as near as possible to the fresh food.'

Nutritional Value of Fresh, Frozen and Canned Peas:

Nutritional information per 100g	Energy (kcals)	Protein (g)	Carbohydrate (g)	Vitamin C (mg)	Vitamin A (μg)	Sodium (mg)	Iron (mg)	Thiamine (mg)
Fresh peas (raw)	67	5.8	10.6	25	300	1	1.9	32
Frozen peas (raw)	53	5.7	7.2	17	300	3	1.5	32
Canned peas	47	4.6	7	8	300	230	1.6	13

(a) Using the information in the table, comment on:

(i) Effects of **freezing** on the Vitamin C content of peas.

Give **one** possible reason. (1 × 6 = 6 marks)

Effect: *vitamin C content has been reduced from 25 mg in fresh peas to 17 mg in frozen peas.*

exam focus

Read the table.

Reasons for effect: *vitamin C is water soluble and is unstable at high temperatures. Peas are blanched at high temperatures before they are frozen. Vitamin C is destroyed by blanching and processing.*

(ii) Effects of **canning** on the Vitamin C, Sodium and Thiamine content of peas.

Give **one** possible reason. (3 × 6 marks = 18 marks)

Effect on vitamin C: *vitamin C content has been reduced from 25 mg in fresh peas to 8 mg in canned peas.*

Reason: *high temperatures and processing times in canning destroys some of the vitamin C.*

Effect on sodium: *sodium content has increased from 1 mg in fresh peas to 230 mg in canned peas.*

Reason: *large amounts of salt are used in canning peas.*

Effect on thiamine: *thiamine content has been reduced from 32 mg to 13 mg.*

Reason: *B group vitamins, including thiamine, are unstable at the high temperatures used in canning.*

Ordinary Level 2006, Section B, Q2(c) (16 marks)

Freezing is one method of storing fish for a period of time. Outline the general rules to be followed when freezing **fresh food**. (4 points × 4 marks = 16 marks)

1. *Turn on the fast-freeze switch 3 to 4 hours before freezing.*
2. *Freeze one tenth of the freezer's capacity in any 24 hours.*
3. *Freeze quality foods in useable quantities or portions.*
4. *Always blanch vegetables before freezing.*

Food safety and hygiene

Safe food preparation

To avoid contamination and prevent food poisoning:

1. Follow strict hygiene practices.
2. Prepare foods in hygienic conditions.
3. Separate raw and cooked foods.
4. Maintain correct temperatures when storing, preparing and cooking foods.

> **LINKS**
> - Food spoilage and poisoning (p. 152)
> - Food spoilage – microbiology (p. 144)

The aims of good food hygiene practices/systems are to:

- destroy any micro-organisms
- prevent their re-entry into the food
- prevent contamination and cross-contamination
- prevent carriers of food poisoning bacteria (humans) causing an outbreak of food poisoning.

Reducing the risk of food contamination

During food preparation	During cooking
1. Handle food as little as possible	1. Keep equipment and cooker spotlessly clean
2. Wash fruit and vegetables	2. Thaw frozen meat, fish and poultry fully before cooking
3. Prepare raw and cooked foods separately	3. Ensure that meat, fish and poultry are cooked fully (82°C in centre of meat)
4. Prepare meat, fish and poultry separately	4. Do not handle cooked foods
	5. Avoid reheating foods

Guidelines for food storage

(a) Non-perishable and dry foods (cupboards)

1. Store foods in clean, dry, well-ventilated cupboards.
2. Store dry goods in a clean, dry, well-ventilated place.
3. Use in rotation, check stocks, replace as required.
4. Store opened dry foods in airtight containers.

Examples: flour, rice, cans, jars.

Hazards: insects, microbial contamination.

> **key point**
>
> The danger zone for contamination is between 5°C and 65°C.

(b) Frozen foods (freezer)

Examples: meat, fish, convenience meals, vegetables.

Hazards: microbial growth (incorrect temperature).

> **LINK**
> - Guidelines for home freezing (p. 160)

(c) Chilled foods (fridge)

1. Store chilled foods in the fridge at below 4°C.
2. Allow for circulation of air in fridge.
3. Cover all food in the fridge.
4. Store foods in the recommended areas in the fridge.
5. Check use-by date; use food in date order.
6. Place raw foods below cooked foods.

Examples: convenience meals, fresh soup, yoghurt.

Hazards: mould growth, microbial growth.

(d) Fresh fruit and vegetables

Examples: apples, pears, carrots, onions, salads.

Hazards: enzyme activity, mould growth, microbial contamination, pests.

> **LINK**
> - Fruit and vegetables (pp. 94–9).

(e) Perishable foods

Store perishables in fridge for 1–3 days.

Examples: dairy products, eggs, meat, fish.

> **LINKS**
> - Food spoilage – microbiology (p. 144)
> - Food spoilage and food poisoning (p. 152)

Reheating procedures – guidelines

1. Cool quickly, cover and store leftovers in the fridge.
2. Use leftover foods within two days.
3. Reheat foods only once.
4. Reheat to 100°C to destroy micro-organisms.

Personal hygiene

1. Wash hands using disinfectant soap, hot water and a nail brush.
2. Wash hands before handling all foods, after using the bathroom, after sneezing and coughing, after handling pets and waste.
3. Remove jewellery, tie back/cover hair, wear an apron.
4. Keep nails cut short and clean (no nail varnish).
5. Do not touch hair or face when preparing food.
6. Cover all cuts with a waterproof dressing.
7. Do not smoke near food, do not cough over food.
8. Do not handle food if ill, e.g. diarrhoea, vomiting.

Kitchen hygiene

High standards of kitchen hygiene require:

- durable, smooth, non-absorbent, easy to clean surfaces
- effective lighting, ventilation, waste and recycling systems
- colour-coded chopping board system
- clean water supply and effective drainage system.

Work surfaces	Wash and disinfect daily
Floors	Sweep, wash and disinfect daily
Wall surfaces	Wash regularly
Equipment	Wash, dry and store in clean cupboards
Food storage	• Clean cupboards regularly • Check and wash out fridge weekly
Chopping boards	• Use separate boards for raw and cooked foods • Wash boards each time they are used
Kitchen cloths	• Use different cloths for different purposes • Wash, disinfect and change daily
Kitchen bins	• Empty daily • Wash, disinfect and dry daily • Keep covered when not in use
Spills	Wipe up immediately
Pets	Never let pets into the kitchen

LINKS

- Food spoilage – microbiology (pp. 144, 152)
- Food preparation and cooking processes (p. 107)

 ## Hazard analysis and critical control points (HACCP)

The **HACCP system:**

1. HACCP is a **system of analysis** that identifies potential food hygiene and safety hazards that might occur at specific points in food production.
2. These **'danger points'** can be identified, monitored and controlled in order to prevent contamination.
3. **HACCP can be applied** to all areas of food production from seed to the kitchen table.

Setting up a HACCP system – a summary

1 Set up a HACCP team
Members representing all areas involved

▼

2 Develop a flow chart for all aspects of food production

▼

3 Identify and analyse potential hazards
Identify anything that might cause harm to consumers. This can occur at any stage of production, from purchase of raw materials to point of sale.

Main hazards/contaminants	Examples
Biological	Moulds, yeasts, bacteria
Chemical	Pesticides, cleaning agents
Physical	Glass, human hair, metal

Analyse hazards and examine implications for consumer safety.

▼

4 Carry out a risk assessment
A **risk** is the probability of a hazard occurring during food production. The risks present can be high, medium or low.

▼

5 Identify critical control points (CCPs)
A **critical control point** is a step in the food production process where hazards must be controlled.
Controls can be applied in order to eliminate, prevent or minimise hazards.
The CCP is the final opportunity to correct a hazard.

LINK
- Go to the food production areas table on the next page to see who might be involved.

▼

6 Decide on control measures to eliminate or reduce risk
What has to be done, when, by whom.

▼

7 Implement control measures

▼

8 Monitor and record control strategies

▼

9 Implement further action if necessary

▼

10 Evaluate the HACCP system regularly

Food production areas and who/what is involved

Purchase of raw materials	Supplier, deliveries, premises, records, sampling
Delivery of raw materials	Delivery vehicles, temperatures, unloading
Storage of raw materials	Chilled, frozen, dry
Preparation of food product	Cleaning, monitoring, equipment, environment
Application of baking, cooking or heating methods	Times, temperatures
Cooling food product	Times, temperatures, storage
Assembly of food product	Equipment, monitoring, staff
Storage	Temperatures, containers, time
Display	Temperatures, dates
Reheating	Core temperatures
Delivery/sale	Vehicles, temperatures, unloading, records, date stamps

Advantages of HACCP

1. Identifies potential hazards.
2. Eliminates or reduces potential hazards.
3. Focuses employees on food safety and food hygiene.
4. Records implementation of food safety legislation.
5. Provides an accurate summary of food production.

ISO 9001

- ISO (the International Organisation for Standardisation) is a federation of national standards bodies that sets standards of quality to ensure that consumer needs are met.
- The ISO quality scheme for food companies is operated by the National Standards Authority of Ireland (NSAI).
- ISO 9001 guarantees quality of design, development, production and servicing.
- ISO 9001:2000 supports the implementation of a process approach to a quality management system.
- Food companies who have been accredited ISO 343 have achieved a high standard of food hygiene.

Check out these websites:
- Department of Agriculture, Fisheries and Food (www.agriculture.gov.ie)
- Department of Health and Children (www.dohc.ie)
- Department of the Environment, Community and Local Government (www.environ.ie)
- local authorities
- Public Analyst's Laboratories (PAL)
- Health Services Executive local offices
- Food Safety Authority of Ireland (FSAI) (www.fsai.ie)
- National Consumer Agency (www.consumerconnect.ie).

LINK

- Food legislation (p. 177)

HL

Exam questions and sample answers

Higher Level 2008, Section B, Q3

'In the hustle and bustle of today's world, more and more people are eating convenience food and "food to go" . . . however, poor handling practices can cause food poisoning.' (FSAI)

(a) Discuss the importance of temperature control during the storage and cooking/reheating of food in order to minimise the risk of food poisoning.

(4 × 4 = 16 marks)

To minimise the risk of food poisoning:

- *Storage*
  1. *Cool food before refrigerating or freezing.*
  2. *Refrigerate fresh food at 0°C to 5°C or freeze quickly at −25°C and store at −18°C.*
  3. *Never refreeze frozen food, e.g. poultry: cook and use straight away.*
- *Cooking/reheating*
  1. *Defrost frozen foods thoroughly in the fridge before cooking.*
  2. *Cook poultry and joints of meat thoroughly, at the correct temperatures and for the correct time.*
  3. *Serve cooked foods immediately: keep hot at temperatures above 65°C.*
  4. *Reheat food quickly at temperatures above 100°C.*

(b) Describe the stages in a basic HACCP system for making a hot meat dish. Refer to (i) possible hazards and (ii) the corresponding control measures to be implemented. (24 marks)

Stages	Potential hazards	Control measures
Purchase	● Damaged ingredients, e.g. bruised vegetables ● Contamination by bacteria, chemicals, pests ● Ingredients not stored at correct temperature	● Buy from reputable supplier ● Check vegetables are not mouldy ● Check there are no signs of contamination ● Check raw and cooked foods are stored separately at correct temperature ● Check packaging
Storage before use	● Growth of moulds, yeast and bacteria ● Cross-contamination ● Damaged packaging	● Store chilled foods below 4°C ● Store frozen foods below −18°C ● Store raw and cooked ingredients separately ● Check packaging
Preparation	● Growth of bacteria ● Cross-contamination	● Implement hygiene standards ● Use separate equipment for raw and cooked ingredients (colour-coded boards) ● Wash hands frequently
Cooking	Growth of bacteria	● Cook at correct temperature for correct time ● Core temperature of 74°C for 2 minutes
Serving	● Surviving bacteria ● Contamination by food handlers ● Dirty utensils	● Use clean utensils ● Hold food above 63°C ● Food handlers must follow hygiene rules

(c) Outline the role of the Environmental Health Officer in relation to food safety. (2 × 5 marks = 10 marks)

The EHO:

- is involved in the registration of new food premises
- inspects food premises, restaurants, hospital kitchens, shops and food manufacturers
- deals with complaints regarding standards of hygiene in food premises.

Food legislation

The purposes of food legislation are to:

1. protect human health
2. inform consumers
3. prevent fraud
4. facilitate trade.

Food Hygiene Regulations (1950–89)

The regulations:

1. Prohibit the sale of food that is diseased, contaminated or unfit for human consumption.
2. Require that adequate precautions are taken to prevent food contamination at all stages of production.
3. Allow the seizure and destruction of unfit food.
4. Require specific food businesses to be registered.
5. Require that food stalls are licensed annually.

European Communities (Hygiene of Foodstuffs) Regulations 2000

These EU regulations require that food businesses:

1. Operate and maintain hygienic practices at all stages of production.
2. Ensure that staff are trained in hygiene practices.
3. Ensure that HACCP is implemented.

Hygiene regulations apply to all stages of production and sale: premises, delivery areas, storage, preparation, transportation, water supply, staff training and personal hygiene.

Labelling Regulations (1982, 1991)

Regulations cover labelling, presentation and advertising of foodstuffs. The regulations state that labels:

1. should be clear, legible and indelible
2. should be written in a language understood by consumers
3. must not mislead the consumer
4. should not be covered or hidden by pictures or written information.

Liability for Defective Products Act 1991

This Act covers the liability for damage caused wholly or partly by a defect in a product.

LINKS
- Food processing (p. 126)
- Food packaging (p. 132)

Sale of Food and Drugs Acts (1875, 1879, 1899, 1936)

These Acts protect consumers against fraud and adulteration of foodstuffs, which may be damaging to human health.

It is illegal to:

- mix, colour, stain or powder any article of food with an ingredient which would damage health
- sell food items that are not of the nature, substance and quality demanded by the consumer.

Health (Official Control of Foodstuffs) Regulations 1991

In order to prevent danger to public health, these regulations set out guidelines for:

- general food hygiene from production to retail sale
- HACCP as part of quality assurance
- the setting of food composition standards
- penalties for breaking the regulations.

The Act allows for inspection of food premises by enforcement officers, who may prescribe penalties.

Exam question and sample answer

Higher Level 2006, Section B, Q3(c)

Explain how European Union law regulates the use of food additives.

(2 × 4 marks = 8 marks)

1. *All approved additives are assigned E numbers.*
2. *Additives must present no hazard to the health of consumers.*

Family Resource Management and Consumer Studies

aims To learn and revise:
- Family resource management
- Management of household financial resources
- Housing finance
- Household technology
- Textiles
- Consumer studies.

Family resource management

Resource management terms

Management – the effective use of resources to handle or run something, e.g. managing a home, people, money, etc.

Resources – anything that people use to achieve goals, e.g. time, people, skills, equipment and money.

Resource management – using resources wisely to achieve goals.

Family resource management – planning, controlling and evaluating the use of resources in order to achieve goals and improve the quality of family life.

The topics in this chapter are examined in **Sections A** and **B** and are **integrated** across questions.

Purposes of family resource management

1. To use resources wisely.
2. To improve the quality of family life.
3. To help individuals achieve goals.

Management systems – three basic types

Open system	Depends on, and interacts with, systems outside the family to achieve goals
Closed system	All activities occur within the family or community
Contingency system	A change in one area of a system affects another, e.g. unemployment

The family as a managerial unit

The family uses an **open managerial system**, which interacts with other, external, systems.

Management skills are needed in different aspects of family life:

- financial management – budgeting, saving, paying bills
- meal planning – decision-making, shopping
- childcare – education, safety, health, hygiene
- cleaning, laundry, maintenance and gardening
- problem-solving
- decision-making
- conflict management.

(HL) Components of management

There are **three** components of management: **inputs**, **throughputs** and **outputs**.
Inputs are made up of demands and resources.

Inputs	Examples
(a) Demands	● *Needs:* food, clothing, shelter ● *Values:* what we believe to be right and wrong ● *Goals:* what we aim to achieve ● *Events/family commitments:* vary between families
(b) Resources	● *Human resources:* people, skills, time ● *Material resources:* money, equipment ● *Environmental resources:* water, land/space ● *Social resources*

Throughputs involve processing the inputs. Throughputs link inputs and outputs.
Throughputs consist of:

> **Planning**
> Clarifying goals, gathering information, considering options and consequences, setting standards and sequencing activities
> *Examples:* contingency, directional or strategic plans
>
> ↓
>
> **Organising**
> Allocating tasks and resources: may be task-centred or person-centred
>
> ↓
>
> **Implementing**
> Putting a plan into action, being in control, adjusting plan as necessary

Outputs are the **end results** of the inputs and throughputs. They are obvious in:

- goals achieved or demands met/not met
- resources used
- plan followed and completed
- satisfaction that the plan has worked
- changes in family values and/or goals.

Evaluation and feedback: evaluation of inputs, throughputs and outputs provides feedback, which is useful for future input stages.

The decision-making process

Decision-making involves examining two or more alternatives and making a choice between them based on personal values and goals.

Decision-making is influenced by **primary** (family and friends) or **secondary reference groups** (other people).

Basic steps in the decision-making process

1. Define the decision to be made or identify the goal.
2. Examine the alternatives or possible solutions.
3. Consider the consequences of each solution.
4. Make a decision: choose a solution.
5. Draw up a list of resources.
6. Develop an action plan.
7. Implement the plan.
8. Evaluate the outcome.

Types of family decisions

- Accommodation
- Consensual
- 'De facto'

Communication

Communication

- is the process of exchanging information
- may be verbal or non-verbal
- is a two-way process.

Characteristics of effective communication

1. Message sent is clear.
2. Receiver hears and understands the full message.
3. Receiver understands the verbal/non-verbal aspects of the message.
4. Receiver relates to the message and responds to the sender of the message.

Key factors affecting family management – a summary

1. Family members' stages in the life cycle.
2. Size and composition of family.
3. Employment pattern.
4. Management of dual roles.
5. Gender roles.
6. Culture.
7. Values/standards.
8. Socio-economic status.

Be able to elaborate on each of these points in exam questions.

Exam questions and sample answers

Higher Level 2009, Section A, Q9 (6 marks)

(a) Explain the purpose of resource management.

1. To use resources wisely to achieve goals.

2. To improve the quality of family life.

(b) Give **one** example of efficient family resource management.

Using money management systems and budgeting to plan effective use of the family income.

Higher Level 2006, Section B, Q4

Case Study – A Summary

> Colm and Jane Brown live with their teenagers – David aged 15 and Yvonne aged 17. Monday is a hectic day in the household. Colm leaves for work at 7.30 a.m. and returns at 5.30 p.m. Jane works from 9.00 a.m. to 4.00 p.m. David and Yvonne have training for the local swimming team from 4.30 p.m. to 5.30 p.m. Yvonne also goes to guitar lessons at 6.30 p.m. As they live in a rural area transport is necessary for all activities. The family try to apply a management system to ensure that everything runs smoothly.

(a) Explain why a good management system can contribute to a well-run home and the well-being of all family members. (4 points × 4 marks = 16 marks)

A good management system benefits this family because it:

1. Involves a system of collective decision-making.

2. Uses all available resources in an effective manner.

3. Meets the demands of each family member.

4. Uses the management skills of organising, analysing, scheduling, negotiating, communicating, etc.

(b) Using the components of management explain how the Brown family could apply a management system to ensure that Mondays run smoothly in the household. (18 marks)

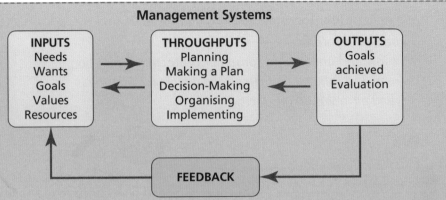

Components	Application of a management system – a summary
Inputs (demands and resources)	**1. Demands (Mondays):** ● Colm leaves for work at 7.30 a.m., returns at 5.30 p.m. ● Jane works 9.00 a.m. to 4.00 p.m. ● David and Yvonne are at swimming from 4.30 p.m. to 5.30 p.m. ● Yvonne goes to her guitar lesson at 6.30 p.m. ● Transport is required for all evening activities **2. Resources available and needed:** Human: parents' time and driving skills Material: two cars needed (if children are to be driven to each activity)
Throughputs (planning, organising and implementing)	**1. Planning** Goals: Colm and Jane must leave for work on time and be home in time to take David and Yvonne to evening activities. Children need to be ready for evening activities (homework done, etc.) **Resources:** parents' time and car/s **2. Organising and allocating tasks and resources** Time: Jane drives children to swimming at 4.30 p.m. Colm drives Yvonne to guitar lessons at 6.30 p.m. **Unforeseen situation:** Colm not home on time, **therefore** Jane drives Yvonne to her guitar lesson. **3. Implementing the plan** Parents and children put the plan into action as arranged
Outputs (goals met, resources used, plan followed)	**1. Were the goals achieved?** Yes. Colm and Jane arrived home from work on time. The children attended the evening activities on time according to the plan. The procedures were followed, resources used as planned and the end result was satisfactory. **2. Any changes for next Monday?** None, but there is a back-up plan if Colm does not arrive home on time from work; Jane drives the children to activities.

(c) Give details of **four** consumer responsibilities. (16 marks)

1. *To be well informed.*
2. *To know and understand consumer protection legislation.*
3. *To read and follow instructions given by manufacturers.*
4. *To read all labels on products.*

LINK
- Consumer responsibilities
  (p. 221)

exam focus

Elaborate on each of these points and give concrete examples.

Ordinary Level 2005, Section A, Q9 (6 marks)
(a) State the purpose of family resource management. (2 marks)
   To use resources wisely in order to achieve family goals and to improve the quality of family life.
(b) List **two** factors that affect the management of family resources. (4 marks)
   (i) Size and composition of family.
   (ii) Stages in life cycle of family members.

Management of household financial resources

The household as a financial unit

1. Families contribute to the national economy.
2. Family spending generates revenue for the government.
3. Taxes paid are used for state services.
4. Income provides the family's financial resources.
5. Income provides for needs, wants and luxuries.
6. Families may be self-sufficient or dependent on the state.

LINK
- Functions of the family
  (p. 238)

Factors affecting household income

1. Age	Income may increase with age due to promotion
	Income reduces in retirement
	Teenagers may do paid part-time work
2. Culture	Cultures may value income differently with regard to how family income is spent:
	Disposable income spent on luxuries
	Most income spent on basic needs

3. Gender	• Pay equality legislation (Anti-Discrimination Pay Act 1974, Employment Equality Act) guarantees equal pay and conditions for men and women • More men than women are in paid work • Few women are in senior positions
4. Socio-economic status	• Parents' socio-economic group, education and salary influence a person's opportunities and income • Lower socio-economic groups spend less income on luxuries • Higher socio-economic groups have better opportunities and higher incomes

Sources of household income – some examples

1. Wages and salaries.
2. Social welfare allowance and benefits.
3. Pensions.
4. Investments and savings (interest/dividends).

Financial terms

Gross income – income *before* any deductions are made.

Net income – income *after* deductions are made.

exam focus

For your exam it is **very important** to check the information relating to the **latest government budget** as arrangements change with each budget.

Deductions from wages/salary

Compulsory (statutory)	Voluntary (non-statutory)
1. PAYE (income tax)	1. Health insurance
2. Universal social charge	2. Saving schemes
3. PRSI (social insurance)	3. Superannuation (pension)
4. Pension (public service)	4. Union subscription
	5. Loan repayments

Statutory/compulsory deductions

PAYE (income tax)

- Tax is deducted from each employee's salary/wages.
- The tax deducted is sent directly to the government by the employer.
- Each citizen has a Personal Public Service Number (PPSN).
- Self-employed people are responsible for their own tax returns.

Tax credits

Tax is calculated on gross income and tax credits are applied.

The **annual tax certificate**, *'Notification of determination of tax credits and standard cut-off-point',* provides taxpayers with information on tax credits and tax liability.

Check the **current** tax rates, tax credits, allowances, levies and any other pay-related deductions.

Use a table like the one below to record the tax rates and credits for the current year.

Tax rates and tax bands – sample table

Personal Circumstances	2011	Leaving Certificate year
Single/Widowed without dependent children	€ 32,800 @ 20% Balance @ 41%	
Single/Widowed qualifying for one parent family tax credit	€ 36,800 @ 20% Balance @41%	
Married couple with one income	€ 41,800 @ 20% Balance @ 41%	
Married couple with two incomes	€ 45,400 @ 20% (with an increase of € 23,800 max.) Balance @ 41%	

PRSI (Pay Related Social Insurance) 2010

1. PRSI is a compulsory deduction.
2. Employees and employers share the costs of PRSI.
3. PRSI is based on a percentage of the employee's income.
4. Benefits include unemployment, maternity or disability benefit, contributory old age pension, etc.
5. To claim benefits, employees must have made a minimum number of 39 contributions in the previous tax year.
6. Some groups are exempt from paying PRSI.

Universal Social Charge (USC)

The USC is a tax payable on gross income from all sources, but before pension contributions.

2011 rates of Universal Social Charge

- 2% on the first €10,036
- 4% on the next €5,980
- 7% on the balance

Persons over 70 years are not liable at the rate of 7% but instead pay at 4%.

Exempt Categories include those with incomes less than exceed €4,004, all Department of Social Protection payments and income already subjected to DIRT.

Pension levy

This levy is applied to people working in the public service.

Pensions

Types of pension

Types	Conditions
1. Contributory old age pension (state pension)	People over 65 Minimum number of contributions Not means tested
2. Non-contributory old age pension (state pension)	People over 66 who do not qualify for contributory pension Means tested
3. Occupational pension	Workers pay percentage of salary into a pension fund set up by employers
4. Personal/private pension	Individuals pay into private pension fund

Additional allowances for some pensioners

- Living Alone Allowance
- Over-80s' Allowance

Additional benefits for pensioners

- Medical card.
- Free travel.
- Household packages (electricity, gas, TV licence, telephone rental).

Social Welfare and Pensions Act 2005

This Act is based on the EU Pensions Directive. It protects the consumer and may investigate pension schemes.

Social welfare payments

There are **three categories** of social welfare payment:

1. Social insurance payments.
2. Social assistance payments.
3. Universal payments.

Household expenditure

Essential expenditure	Discretionary expenditure
Money used for essentials: 1. **Fixed:** mortgage/rent, insurance, electricity 2. **Irregular:** food, clothes, education, health, household maintenance	**Disposable income:** money spent by individuals according to personal choice, e.g. holidays, savings

Budget planning

A budget is a plan for spending money over a specific period of time.

Reasons for budgeting

1. To develop good money management habits.
2. To control spending and reduce financial stress.
3. To plan for irregular and regular bills.
4. To identify areas where economies can be made.
5. To set short-term and long-term saving goals.

Budgets need to be

- Re-organised as family needs/priorities change.
- Examined as income changes, e.g. employment/unemployment.
- Checked annually or more often if necessary.

LINK
- Functions of the family (p. 238)

key point

Personal budgets **and** family budgets can be calculated using the same method.

Sample budget and allocations

Expenditure on:	Allocation	Example: € 400 per week (net)	Fill in your own example here:
Food	25%	100	
Housing	25%	100	
Household	15%	60	
Clothing	10%	40	
Transport	5%	20	
Health	5%	20	
Education	5%	20	
Personal/leisure	5%	20	
Savings	5%	20	
Total	**100%**	**400**	

Areas of expenditure and examples

- **Housing/shelter:** rent/mortgage, insurance, maintenance.
- **Household:** heating, cooking, lighting, furniture.
- **Clothing:** clothes, footwear, dry cleaning.
- **Transport:** petrol/diesel, bus, train.
- **Health:** medical insurance, dentist, doctor, pharmacy.
- **Personal/leisure:** entertainment, sports, holidays, gifts.
- **Savings:** long-term, short-term for emergencies.

LINK
- Meal management and planning (p. 106)

Preparing a household budget

1. List all regular net income (omit irregular income).
2. List planned expenditure (fixed, irregular).
3. Add up the totals, divide by 52 to calculate weekly expenditure.
4. Always allocate money in budgets to savings.
5. Make provision for special events, e.g. birthdays.
6. Keep receipts and evaluate the budget regularly.

Decide to budget on a weekly, monthly or annual basis.

MABS – Money Advice and Budgeting Service

- Set up under the Department of Social and Family Affairs.
- Helps low-income families or individuals at risk of debt.
- Helps people plan budgets and repayment arrangements.
- Assists people to develop money management skills.
- Informs families of special schemes.
- Helps families to source cheaper sources of finance.

Methods of paying for goods and services

Method and use	Advantages	Disadvantages
Cash	Convenient, quick and easy, no extra costs, less risk of overspending	Dangers of carrying cash
Cheque	Safe, convenient, overdraft can be arranged, Chip and Pin system	Charges for cheque and cheque book
Debit card (e.g. Laser): current account with funds	Safe, convenient, easy to use, cash-back facility, widely used and accepted, cannot overspend	Government charge for card; may be a transaction charge
Credit card	Set credit limit, Chip and Pin system for security	Interest charged at various rates
24-hour banking	Pay bills over the phone; convenient (can be done at a time that suits the consumer)	Transaction charges may apply
Online banking	Pay bills over the Internet, accessible 24 hours, can be accessed from virtually anywhere	Transaction charges may apply
Direct debit	Safe, easy to set up, convenient, bills paid on time	May involve setting-up charge, payment charge
ATMs	Easy to use, convenient, can pay bills and withdraw money	Transaction charges may apply
Credit transfer/giro	Easy to use, convenient, all details on giro form	Transaction charge, must go to bank

Credit: 'buy now, pay later'

Credit allows consumers to buy goods or services and to repay the money along with interest and other charges on a regular basis.

Forms of credit include term loans, overdrafts, credit cards, credit unions, hire purchase.

> LINK
>
> • Consumer choice (p. 218)

> *exam focus*
>
> Check the latest information relating to conditions of use for **each** of the methods of paying for goods and services before your exam.

Advantages and disadvantages of credit

Advantages	Disadvantages
1. Consumer has use of goods while paying for them	1. High interest rates
2. Useful for large items or luxury items, e.g. home, car	2. Easy to get into debt, impulse buy and overspend
3. Do not need to save	3. Borrowers might not maintain repayments
4. Little need to carry cash	4. Repossession of goods if repayments are not made
5. Interest-free period on credit cards	5. Goods not owned by consumer until final instalment is paid

Points to check before entering into a credit agreement

1. Is it a need, a want or a luxury?
2. Repayment arrangements (cost, when and for how long).
3. Rates of interest charged; other hidden charges.
4. Consequences if unable to pay.
5. When do you own the product?

Consumer legislation

1. Hire Purchase Acts (1946, 1960)

All agreements must state the following:

- Identify the agreement as 'hire purchase'.
- Names and addresses of all parties involved.
- Description of the goods.
- Cash price of goods and hire purchase price.
- Number of repayments and dates on which they are due.

- APR – annual percentage rate.
- Details of ten days' 'cooling off period'.
- Information on termination of agreement, recovery of goods (repossession) and penalty clauses.

Note: conditions for hire purchase are now part of the Consumer Credit Act 1995.

2. Consumer Credit Act 1995

- Consolidates all consumer credit legislation (from advertising to contracts or written agreements).
- Provides protection for consumers (the borrowers) in relation to consumer loans and credit agreements, hire purchase, overdrafts, leasing, mortgages, etc.
- Monitors credit advertisements: must show APR, cost of credit, security or deposit required, details of penalties, etc.
- Is implemented by the National Consumer Agency.

Savings

Advantages of saving

1. Provides security for emergencies.
2. Encourages planned spending.
3. Reduces the need to borrow.
4. Reduces stress associated with debts.
5. Savings earn interest.
6. Establishes a good record of ability to save/pay.

Methods of saving

When considering saving schemes, check:

- rate of interest (shop around)
- ease of access to funds/withdrawal
- risk/return (terms and safety of scheme)
- tax payable (tax-free or DIRT applied).

exam focus

Keep focused!
Savings options available are liable to change. **Check** the latest information and draw up a summary table of five saving schemes.

Summary table of saving schemes – an example

Type of account	Risk/terms	Interest rates	Ease of access	Tax
1				
2				

Bank/building societies – examples

Demand deposit accounts	• Short-term savings • Savings are guaranteed • Variable low interest rates • Easy to access • Withdraw money any time (ATM)
Notice accounts	• Short-term deposits • Higher interest rate • Subject to DIRT • 15 to 30 days' notice needed
Special term accounts	• Funds invested for fixed term • Interest rate variable/fixed

An Post (2010 information)

Deposit account	• Easy to access, safe • No fees, minimum deposit • Interest payable • Subject to DIRT
Instalment savings	• Fixed monthly instalments • Minimum/maximum investment limit • No transaction fees • Tax-free over 5 years
Savings certificates	• State guaranteed • No fees charged • Minimum/maximum investment limit • Interest over 5 years + 6 months • Interest calculated every 6 months • 7 working days' withdrawal notice
Savings bonds	• State guaranteed • No fees charged • Minimum/maximum investment limit • Interest over 3 years • Interest calculated each year • 7 working days' withdrawal notice

Insurance

- Insurance provides financial protection against a risk.
- The risk is shared with an insurance company.
- Premiums are paid (terms and conditions apply).

Insurance terms

Insurance – protects against something that **might** happen.

Assurance – protects against something that **will** happen.

Broker – an agent who sells insurance policies and receives commission on a sale.

Policy – written details of the terms and conditions.

Premium – the money paid to the company in monthly instalments or annually.

Claim – request/demand for compensation.

Categories of insurance

- **Obligatory insurance:** PRSI, car insurance
- **Voluntary insurance:** salary protection, health, home and contents, life.

Guidelines for choosing insurance

1. Check family needs and circumstances.
2. Seek independent advice.
3. Shop around.
4. Compare policies on offer.

Life assurance

- Life assurance is taken out on an individual's life.
- Provides financial security for the family.
- May include an element of saving (check policy).

Types of life assurance

1. **Term life assurance**
   - Cheap form of assurance, provides security.
   - Insured person's life is covered for set period.
   - No payment if insured person survives term.
   - Terms vary greatly across schemes.

2. **Whole of life assurance**
   - More expensive.
   - No time limit: covers person for entire life.
   - Payment made to family if insured person dies.

3. **Endowment assurance**
   - Most expensive form of assurance.
   - Savings element and whole-life cover.
   - Agreed monthly premium payments.

Mortgage protection policy

- Type of term assurance taken out alongside a mortgage.
- Conditions set down by institution when granting mortgage.
- Loan is repaid if the borrower/either spouse dies (if it is a joint mortgage).

Property insurance

A fixed sum is paid monthly with mortgage repayments or annually to the insurance company.

Types include:

- house and building insurance
- contents insurance
- all-risk insurance.

Others:

- car insurance
- travel insurance.

Private health insurance

Types of health-related insurance:

1. Income protection/health insurance.
2. Serious/critical illness cover.
3. Private medical insurance.

Benefits of private health insurance

1. Variety of schemes.
2. Options of semi-private or private rooms.
3. Covers medical treatment abroad.
4. Tax relief available.

Salary protection insurance

If a person has to retire from work due to illness or injury, an income based on a percentage of the original salary is paid until the person retires.

Exam questions and sample answers

Higher Level 2009, Section A, Q11   (6 marks)

Explain **each** of the following state benefits and give **one** example of each.

1. Social Insurance Payments

   Made to a person who has contributed the minimum amount of PRSI payments (39 weeks); payments are not means tested.

   Example: contributory old age pension.

2. Social Assistance Payments

   Payments made to a person who does not qualify for social insurance payment; payments are means tested.

   Example: non-contributory old age pension.

Higher Level 2005, Section A, Q10 (6 marks)

In relation to the **management process**, explain and give an example of **each** of the following:

	Explanation and example – a summary
Input	Demands (needs, wants, goals, values) and resources (human and material) brought into a management system
	Example: skills, time, energy, equipment
Output	Goals reached, satisfaction, evaluation and feedback
	Example: goal has been met, no changes need to be made

Ordinary Level 2009, Section A, Q11 (6 marks)

Net income is 'take-home' pay after deductions have been made. Name **two** compulsory deductions and **two** voluntary deductions that may be made from an employee's salary/wage.

Compulsory deductions	Voluntary deductions
1. PRSI	1. Health insurance
2. Income tax/PAYE	2. Savings, e.g. NIS

Ordinary Level 2008, Section A, Q10 (6 marks)

(a) Name **two** forms of credit.

(i) Overdraft from bank.

(ii) Credit cards.

(b) State **one** advantage and **one** disadvantage of using credit.

Advantage: useful in emergencies.

Disadvantage: encourages impulse buying and overspending

Ordinary Level 2006, Section B, Q3(a), (b)

Case Study

'Jack and Jane O'Brien have two children aged five and three. Jack works five days a week and Jane stays at home to look after the children. They currently live in a three-bedroomed rented house and are saving to buy a home of their own.'

(a) Explain why it is important for the O'Brien family to set up a budget.

(3 points × 4 marks = 12 marks)

Planning a budget:

1. Allows for savings to be made towards buying a home.

2. Provides financial security to cover essential expenses.

3. Prevents overspending and impulse buying.

(b) List the main sources of expenditure for this family.

(5 points × 3 marks = 15 marks)

1. *Rent for accommodation.*
2. *Food.*
3. *Savings towards buying a house.*
4. *Fuel and light.*
5. *Clothing.*

Ordinary Level 2005, Section B, Q4

(50 marks)

John is 25 years old. His net weekly income is €370. He shares a house with three others and commutes to work each day by bus. He is a member of the local health and fitness club that has an annual membership charge of €350. He is planning to buy a car next year.

(a) Using the information given above, plan and set out a weekly budget for John to ensure that he uses his money wisely. (24 marks)

Area of spending	Percentage of income	Approximate allocation
Rent	25%	92.50
Food	25%	92.50
Household	15%	55.50
Travel	5%	18.50
Savings	15%	55.50
Health	5%	18.50
Clothes	5%	18.50
Leisure	3%	11.00
Club membership	2%	7.50
Total	**100%**	**€370**

(b) (i) Name and give details of **one** saving scheme that John could use in order to save for a car. (ii) Give **two** reasons for your choice. (16 marks)

(i) (8 marks: name = 4 marks; details = 4 marks)

Saving scheme: *An Post Saving Bonds.*

Risk/return balance: *no risk, state-guaranteed, no fees.*

Investment required: *minimum/maximum limit.*

Rate of interest: *interest over three years.*

Ease of access: *easy; seven working days withdrawal notice.*

Tax: *interest is tax-free.*

exam focus

Check current saving opportunities.

(ii) (2 points × 4 marks = 8 marks)

Reasons for Choice

1. *State guaranteed, no tax on interest*
2. *A reasonable amount can be saved in three years*
3. *Establishes a regular savings pattern*

(c) Name <u>two</u> items of information as required by the Consumer Credit Act (1995) that must be included in an advertisement for buying goods on credit. (10 marks)

1. *APR and how it is calculated.*
2. *Extra charges or types of restrictions.*

Housing finance

Mortgages

A mortgage is a loan from a lending institution to buy a home, which must be repaid over a set time, e.g. 20–30+ years.

Sources of mortgages: banks, building societies, local authorities.

> **LINK**
> - Summary answer to Higher Level 2008, Section B, Q4 (p. 200)

General conditions

1. Amount of money borrowed	80–92% of purchase price or valuation, whichever is lower
2. Borrower's deposit	10% of the purchase price
3. Credit history/rating (creditworthiness)	Savings record – shows ability to repay loan, little debt
4. Proof of income	P60; self-employed people must show audited accounts and a tax clearance certificate
5. Length of mortgage	Age of applicant influences length of loan
6. Type of property	Must be surveyed, in reasonable condition, value for money
7. Building insurance	Statutory obligation
8. Mortgage protection policy	Compulsory requirement: if the person dies before mortgage is paid off the debt is cleared

The **mortgage agreement** states the amount of each payment, interest payable, date due each month, term of mortgage.

Types of interest rate

1. Variable – rise and fall in line with ECB rates.
2. Fixed – for a set time.
3. Tracker – tracks the ECB rate.

Types of mortgage

1. Annuity.
2. Endowment.
3. Pension linked.

> **exam focus**
>
> Check out the types of mortgages available during your exam year.

Mortgage relief – tax relief at source (TRS)

Tax relief may be applied to mortgage loans under certain conditions. Note: '*Mortgage interest relief will be abolished by the end of 2017*' *(Budget 2010)*.

Local authority housing

Local authorities provide housing for individuals who are unable to provide a home from their own resources.

Local authorities:

- provide assistance or loans
- enable people to buy, rent or improve homes
- provide help to those who fail to meet the conditions of lending institutions.

Applicants must:

1. be in need of a home
2. be unable to finance a home themselves
3. be unable to get a mortgage (refused by lender)
4. meet an income eligibility test.

Local authority schemes and general conditions

Tenant purchase	• Must be tenants of local authority for one year • Buy house outright or through shared ownership scheme • House is priced at market value • Discount on the value of the house applied for each year of tenancy of a local authority house (max. 10 years)
Shared ownership	• Aimed at those who cannot buy their entire home in one go • Ownership is shared between the individual and the local authority • Applicants must buy 40% of the value of house (minimum) and pay rent to the local authority on the remaining 60% • Regular payments of mortgage and rent: outgoings are lower than regular mortgages
Mortgage allowance scheme	• Allowance of €11,450 is paid over five years to tenants or tenant purchasers of local authority houses • Allowance is paid directly to lender • Mortgage repayments are reduced for the first five years
Affordable housing	• Helps low-income families buy a home • Purchasers must need housing • Loans are repaid over 25 years • Loans must not exceed a set percentage of the household income

Factors affecting housing choices

LINK
- Family Home Protection Act 1976 (p. 255)

(a) Socio-economic factors

1. Life cycle and ages of family members.
2. Special needs, e.g. child or elderly person in family.
3. Budget available, family income.
4. Proximity to amenities, transport, school, shops.
5. Proximity to work, family, friends.

(b) National housing policy

1. Formulated by Department of the Environment, Heritage and Local Government, implemented by local authorities.
2. Aims to provide affordable quality housing.
3. Supports a sustainable national housing programme.

(c) Trends in housing development

1. Increase in city apartment living.
2. Development of a variety of home ownership schemes.
3. Development of housing estates in rural areas.
4. Smaller exclusive gated communities/estates.
5. Inner-city renewal developments.

exam focus

Be able to describe the latest National Housing policy.

(d) Availability of housing during economic recession

1. Demand for buying a home is low.
2. Individuals are unable to get mortgages due to low salaries, recent unemployment and banking restrictions.
3. More people are renting than buying, rents have fallen.
4. Demand for local authority housing exceeds supply.
5. Large number of empty houses and unfinished housing schemes across Ireland.

LINKS
- Key factors affecting family management (p. 182)
- Family structures (p. 234)
- Functions of the family (p. 238)
- Making a will (p. 256)

Exam questions and sample answers

Higher Level 2008, Section A, Q11 (6 marks)

Identify **two** features of the national housing policy in Ireland.

(i) *Provides quality social and affordable housing suited to the needs of individuals.*

(ii) *Supports home improvements/renovations via grants.*

Ordinary Level 2005, Section A, Q12 (6 marks)

Outline **three** factors that determine a person's choice of housing.

(i) Economic: budget, location, cost of house.

(ii) Social: life cycle stages of family, sense of belonging, special needs.

(iii) Environmental: energy rating of house, proximity to motorway and phone masts.

Ordinary Level 2004, Section B, Q3(c)

(c) Give an account of the factors that affect an individual's choice of accommodation.

(6 points × 4 marks = 24 marks).

Refer to:

Give two factors for (i), (ii) and (iii), and elaborate on each point.

(i) **Social factors**

1. People like to feel a sense of belonging to the place where they live.

2. Proximity to amenities, shops, hospitals, library, entertainment and schools is important.

(ii) **Economic factors**

1. Cost determines whether one rents or buys. Cost is determined by the location, size and condition of the house and cost of service charges, insurance, interior and exterior maintenance.

2. There may be a danger of negative equity.

(iii) **Trends in developments**

1. Smaller exclusive, expensive, gated communities.

2. Higher-density mixed housing in cities and towns.

Higher Level 2008, Section B, Q4 – summary answer (50 marks)

'Developments in housing are influenced by lifestyle patterns and demographic trends.'

(a) Discuss how (i) socio-economic factors and (ii) trends in housing development influence housing choices.

(5 points × 4 marks = 20 marks)

You **must** refer to both (i) and (ii).

(i) **Socio-economic factors:**

1. Life circumstances, income, age, stage in life cycle.

2. Money available, cost of homes on market.

3. Location, environment, amenities.

(Elaborate on/explain each point.)

(ii) **Trends in housing development:**

1. Energy-efficient home designs.

2. Availability of a variety of home ownership schemes.

(Elaborate on/explain each point.)

(b) **Identify** and **elaborate** on the general terms and conditions that have to be fulfilled before a mortgage is granted. (5 points × 4 marks = 20 marks)

1. *Amount to be borrowed: 80–92% of purchase price or valuation, whichever is lower. This varies between lending institutions, e.g. banks, building societies.*

2. *Deposit: borrowers are expected to have 10% of cost price.*

3. *Credit record: applicant must have a good record, no bad debts, show an ability to save and to pay bills.*

4. *Income: must supply proof of income, e.g. salary slip or P60.*

5. *Term of loan: can range from 15 to 40 years.*

exam focus

Give current examples for each of these points.

(c) Explain the term **mortgage protection** and state why mortgage protection is necessary. (2 × 5 marks = 10 marks)

Mortgage protection is a life assurance policy taken out on the value of the mortgage by the mortgage borrower on their principal residence. (5 marks)

If the borrower dies the insurance company repays the loan to the lending institution. The policy covers both home owners. (5 marks)

Household technology

Examples of technological developments

- **Food preparation:** blenders, liquidisers, processors.
- **Cooking:** fan ovens, double ovens, dual grills, microwave ovens, halogen rings, contact grills.
- **Cleaning:** vacuum cleaners, dishwashers, steam cleaners.
- **Laundry:** washing machines, dryers.
- **Household surfaces:** stainless steel, ceramic, plastic.
- **Entertainment:** DVDs, PlayStation, Wii, home cinema.
- **Security:** alarms, lights, automatic gates.
- **Communication:** Internet, mobile phones, Skype.
- **Automation:** lighting, water, heating and appliances.
- **Maintenance:** electric drills, garden equipment.
- **Computer packages:** budgeting, accounts, spreadsheets.

Contribution of technology to home management

1. Reduces workload; tasks completed quickly.
2. Improves quality of home life; more leisure time.
3. Energy-efficient appliances save money.
4. Appliances are fitted with safety devices.
5. Higher standards of food and kitchen hygiene.

LINK
- Food preparation and cooking equipment (pp. 112, 202–212)

Guidelines for choosing household appliances

Cost	● Consider budget available ● Shop around, compare costs, get value for money ● Buy the best you can afford ● Check purchase, installation and running costs, length of warranty
Brand	● Choose a reliable, well-known brand ● Buy from a reputable dealer ● Check for quality symbols
Energy	Check energy-efficiency rating (A to G)
Design and construction	● Durable, must be easy to use ● Easy to care for/clean and maintain ● Colour and shape should suit the home ● Check whether extra services are needed, e.g. power points, plumbing, ventilation
Safety	Check safety symbols and features
Size	● Family needs, size of household ● Space available, check measurements
Guarantee	● Check terms of guarantee (parts, time, labour) and warranty ● Check after-sales service if a fault develops

Household appliances

LINKS
- Consumer choice (p. 218)
- Consumer responsibilities (p. 221)
- Consumer protection (p. 227)

Types of appliance

With a motor	With a heating element	With a motor and a heating element
Food processor, vacuum cleaner, carving knife, washing machine	Coffee maker, electric cooker, deep-fat fryer, electric kettle, frying pan, iron, sandwich maker	Fan heater, washing machine, tumble dryer, dishwasher

Small appliance with a motor – food processor

A food processor is a versatile motor appliance that saves time and energy, speeds up food preparation and is easy to use and maintain.

Construction

Food processors are made up of:

1. A **base unit**, containing:
   - a motor enclosed in a strong metal or plastic casing
   - a flex and three-pin plug with appropriate fuse
   - a variable speed button/switch with on/off switch.
2. A **bowl unit**, containing:
   - a plastic or metal bowl with a lockable funnelled lid
   - a central spindle to hold blades and discs
   - a feed tube and pusher.
3. **Attachments**: a selection of metal and plastic blades and discs.

Attachments and uses

Steel chopping blade	Puréeing fruits, soups, sauces; chopping parsley, vegetables, meats; making breadcrumbs, mayonnaise
Grating discs (fine, medium, coarse)	Slicing, dicing, grating cabbage, carrot and potatoes
Whisk attachment	Meringues, sponge cakes, sauces
Juice extractor	Fresh orange juice, lemon juice
Liquidiser	Soups, sauces, purées
Dough hook	Breads, pastry, cake mixtures

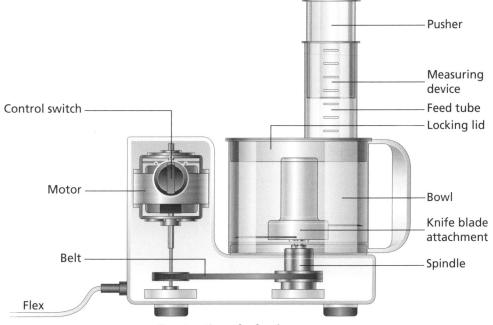

Construction of a food processor

Working principles of a food processor

> **LINK**
> - Go to Higher Level 2009, Section B, Q4(b) (p. 211)

Size/capacity
Standard size is two litres; smaller and larger capacities are available.

Guidelines for use

> **LINK**
> - Go to Higher Level 2009, Section B, Q4(b) (p. 211).

Guidelines for care and cleaning
1. Stop at intervals to allow the motor to cool down.
2. Never force switch or locking mechanism.
3. Unplug before cleaning.
4. Do not use abrasives.
5. Allow motor to cool before cleaning.
6. Never immerse motor in water. Wipe base with a damp cloth, dry with a clean cloth.

Small appliance with a heating element – electric kettle

Construction
- Available in a variety of colours, shapes and sizes.
- Made in chrome, stainless steel or coloured plastic.
- Most have fitted lids (easily opened or removed).
- Pouring spout with filter to remove limescale.
- Heat-resistant handles.
- Water level indicator.
- Vents for steam to escape.
- On/off switch.
- Indicator light.
- Concealed heating element.
- Thermostat which turns off kettle at 100°C.

Lid

Heat-resistant handle

Water level indicator

Indicator light
On/off switch
Concealed heating element
Lead

Construction of an electric kettle

Standard capacity: 1.7 litres

Working principles

1. Kettle is plugged in and turned on.
2. Electricity causes element to heat up.
3. Element heats water by conduction and through convection currents.
4. Thermostat automatically switches the kettle off when water reaches boiling point.
5. 'Boil-dry' safety switch is a feature of most kettles.

Guidelines for use

1. Follow the manufacturer's instructions.
2. Switch on using dry hands.
3. Unplug and switch off before filling.
4. Ensure that the element is covered with water.
5. Never overfill.
6. Allow the kettle to cool before refilling.
7. Use only for heating water.

Guidelines for care and cleaning

1. Switch off and unplug before cleaning.
2. Never immerse the kettle in water.
3. Clean filters in spout daily.
4. Descale if necessary.
5. Wipe outside with a warm, damp cloth.
6. Dry with a clean cloth.
7. Never use abrasives to clean kettles.

Large refrigeration appliance – a refrigerator

The function of a refrigerator is to keep perishable food fresh for a specific length of time under cold conditions by preventing the action of micro-organisms.

Types of refrigerator

1. Standard refrigerator (fits under the counter).
2. Larder refrigerator (no ice box).
3. Fridge-freezer (different capacities).

Design and construction

- A variety of types, designs, colours and finishes.
- Outer layer of insulated enamelled steel.
- Inner lining of moulded polystyrene.
- Layer of insulating material between the steel and polystyrene.
- Door with magnetic catch and rubber door seals.
- Thermostat to control temperatures.
- Selection of adjustable plastic-coated shelves.
- Storage drawers.
- Adjustable door bottle rack and moulded compartments.
- Icebox at the top of refrigerator.
- Automatic light inside the cabinet.

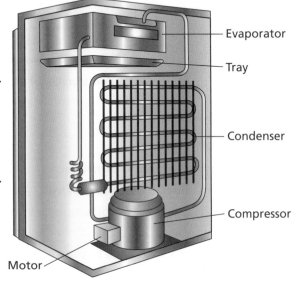

Construction of a fridge

Size/capacity: average is 150 litres; ranges from 50 litres to 280 litres

Special features of modern refrigerators

1. Compartments, adjustable shelves and storage areas.
2. Chilled drinks dispenser for water and/or fruit juices.
3. Internal ice maker and/or external ice dispenser.
4. Automatic defrosting.
5. Zoned refrigeration.
6. Frost-free refrigerators.
7. Digital temperature displays.
8. Integrated fridge doors for kitchen cabinets.

LINK
- Working Principle: go to HL 2007, Section B Q4 (p. 207).

Exam question and sample answer

Higher Level 2007, Section B, Q4 – Refrigeration   (50 marks)

'Refrigeration appliances are an integral part of modern-day kitchens.'

(a) Set out a detailed study that you have undertaken on a refrigeration appliance. Refer to:

   (i) **Type of refrigeration appliance**   (2 marks)

   Refrigerator

   (ii) **Working principle**   (4 points × 3 marks = 12 marks)

   1. A **compressor**, at the base of the refrigerator, is activated by an electric motor and forces a **gaseous refrigerant** into a condenser.
   2. Condenser cools the refrigerant, which changes to liquid.
   3. The **liquid refrigerant** passes into the **evaporator**, where it is cooled and evaporated into a gas by removing heat from inside the refrigerator.
   4. The **evaporated refrigerant** returns to the compressor, where the cycle begins again.

   (iii) **Guidelines for use**   (4 points × 3 marks = 12 marks)

   1. Follow the manufacturer's instructions.
   2. Avoid opening the door unnecessarily, which raises the temperature.
   3. Cool all foods before placing them in a fridge and cover to prevent dehydration.
   4. Prevent cross-contamination by storing raw and cooked foods separately.

   (iv) **Modern features**   (2 points × 3 marks = 6 marks)

   1. Chilled drinks dispenser
   2. Zoned refrigeration

   (v) **Energy efficient rating**   (2 points × 2 marks = 4 marks)

   1. Choose a fridge with an A+, A or B energy rating. A+ is the most efficient and cheapest to run and G is the least efficient.
   2. Energy rated appliances are environmentally friendly.

(b) Give a detailed account of the star rating system found on refrigeration appliances.   (3 × 4 marks = 12 marks)

Star Ratings – *Refrigeration Appliances*

Star rating	Temperature	Storage time
*	−6°C	1 week
**	−12°C	1 month
***	−18°C	3 months
****	−18°C to −25°C	Up to 1 year

Methods of defrosting

1. Automatic.
2. Manual.
3. Push-button.

Guidelines for use

1. Open refrigerator only when necessary.
2. Cool warm/hot food before storing in the fridge.
3. Cover foods to stop drying out and transfer of flavours.
4. Store foods in the recommended area.
5. Store raw and cooked meats separately.
6. Store foods for the recommended time; use in rotation.
7. Allow for circulation of air around food.

Guidelines for care and cleaning

1. Position fridge away from any heat source.
2. Clean regularly, i.e. weekly.
3. Wash with a solution of warm water and bread soda.
4. Wipe the outside of the fridge daily.
5. Avoid build-up of ice.
6. Wipe up spills immediately.
7. Keep the back of the appliance free of dust.
8. When not in use, unplug and leave door open.

LINK
- Star Ratings (p. 207)

LINK
- Food safety and hygiene (p. 170)

Microwave ovens

Types of microwave oven

1. Standard microwave.
2. Microwave with grill.
3. Combination microwave.

Foods suitable for microwave cooking

- Evenly shaped food without sharp corners.
- Foods for re-heating, e.g. meals, sauces, soups.
- Ready-made meals and individual dishes.
- Fish, meat, poultry, fruit, vegetables.

Construction of a microwave oven

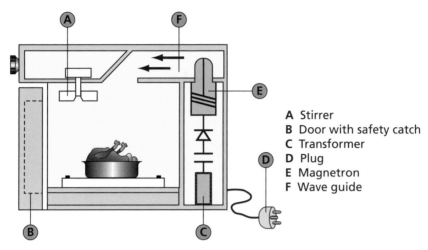

A Stirrer
B Door with safety catch
C Transformer
D Plug
E Magnetron
F Wave guide

Working principles

1. Microwave oven is turned on.
2. Transformer steps up the standard voltage.
3. Magnetron converts electrical energy to electromagnetic energy or waves.
4. Energy enters the oven via the wave guide.
5. Wave stirrer directs microwaves around the oven.
6. Waves are (a) reflected off the walls of the oven, (b) transmitted through the containers and (c) absorbed by the food to a depth of 2–4 cm.
7. Water molecules vibrate rapidly, creating heat, which cooks, re-heats or defrosts the food. Heat travels to the centre of the food by conduction.
8. Water comes to the surface and prevents the food crisping or browning.

> **LINK**
> ● Methods of cooking (p. 109 and Chapter 3: Extension 1, www.moresuccess.ie)

Guidelines for use

1. Follow the manufacturer's instructions.
2. Never turn on the microwave when empty.
3. Use recommended cooking containers, **never** metal.
4. Arrange food in a circle, cover food.
5. Pierce foods with skins to prevent from bursting.
6. Allow recommended 'standing time' before serving.
7. Use recommended heat-resistant cling film.
8. Never leave unattended – overcooking can cause a fire.
9. Use oven gloves to remove dishes.
10. Stir liquids to prevent 'hot spots'.

Care and cleaning of a microwave oven

1. Follow manufacturer's instructions.
2. Unplug microwave oven before cleaning.
3. Avoid abrasives, use hot soapy water.
4. Wipe door seal and interior of oven, rinse and dry.
5. Remove turntable, wash, rinse and dry.
6. Wipe up spills immediately.
7. Get oven serviced by a qualified engineer.

Advantages

- Economical method of cooking.
- Cooks foods quickly, defrosts foods quickly.
- Food retains natural colour, flavour and nutrients.
- Saves on washing up, saves time and energy.
- Foods can be served in dishes in which they were cooked.

Disadvantages

- Foods do not brown satisfactorily in basic models.
- Tough cuts of meat cannot be used (will not tenderise).
- Unsuitable for fried and roast foods, cakes and batters.
- Foods/dishes need standing time before serving.
- Extra time needed when cooking larger amounts of food.

Containers and microwave ovens

	Examples
Suitable	Glass, Pyrex, plain china, earthenware, heat-resistant plastic, oven-proof dishes
Unsuitable	Foil containers, metal dishes, metal-trimmed dishes, thick dishes, glazed pottery

Exam questions and sample answers

Higher Level 2008, Section A, Q9 (6 marks)

State the function of **each** of the following parts of the microwave oven.

(i) Transformer: *increases domestic voltage from 220V to a higher frequency.*

(ii) Magnetron: *converts electrical energy into microwave energy.*

Ordinary Level 2008, Section A, Q9 (b)

(b) State how the consumer should dispose of electrical appliances. (2 marks)

Consumers should:

- Return old appliances to shop when purchasing replacements.
- Take to designated recycling centres.

Higher Level 2009, Section B, Q4 (50 marks)

'Today's kitchen appliances must offer convenience, technology and style that keep up with the way we live.'

(a) Discuss how technology has contributed to the efficient management of the home. (4 × 4 marks = 16 marks)

Technology has contributed to:

1. Saving time through equipment that enables tasks such as food preparation, cooking, cleaning and washing to be done quickly, e.g. food processors, blenders. More time is available for other activities.

2. Reduction in workload through labour-saving equipment, e.g. dishwashers, washing machines. Tasks are completed quickly and easily.

3. Improvement in the quality of home life. Automated security systems, communication and entertainment systems, e.g. the Internet for shopping, online banking; mobile phones and Skype for easy access to family and friends.

4. Energy efficiency, e.g. A-rated appliances, energy rating certificates for the home, automated heating, lighting and water systems. These save money and energy.

(b) Set out details of a study you have undertaken on one type of electric appliance suitable for a kitchen. (26 marks)

Type of appliance: *food processor (appliance with motor).*

Diagram of Food Processor

(See page 203.)

Working principle:
(3 points × 3 marks = 9 marks)

> Any appliance suitable for use in a kitchen is acceptable when answering this question.

1. The food processor is plugged in and switched on. A motor causes the shaft and blades to rotate.

2. Rotating blades beat, chop, liquidise, slice or whisk ingredients in an enclosed metal or plastic container.

3. A safety lock system prevents the lid being removed when the motor is working.

Guidelines for use: (3 points × 3 marks = 9 marks)

1. Follow the manufacturer's instructions. Never operate appliance with wet or damp hands.

2. Choose correct attachments and fix in correct position.

3. When feeding small pieces of food through feed tube use food pusher, **never** spoons or fingers.

Energy efficiency: (2 points × 3 marks = 6 marks)
1. *The attachments work at a fast speed to complete tasks quickly, using less energy than doing them by hand.*
2. *Food processors use less time when chopping vegetables, whisking egg whites, cream and mayonnaise, grating cheese, carrots and cabbage, extracting juice from fruits, making breads and cakes (with the dough hook).*

(c) Explain how the rights of the consumers are protected by the **Sale of Goods and Supply of Services Act (1980).** (4 points × 4 marks = 16 marks)
1. *Confers a legally binding contract between the buyer and the seller when one buys a product or service.*
2. *Goods and services must be fit for their purpose.*
3. *Goods must be of merchantable quality.*
4. *Goods must be as described, and must correspond to any sample on display.*

Textiles

Uses of textiles

- household linen (bed, table and kitchen)
- interior textiles (cushions, rugs, upholstery)
- clothing (shirts, coats, etc.).

Functions of clothing

1. To enhance one's appearance and give confidence.
2. To protect against the weather, e.g. hats, coats.
3. To keep us safe from chemicals, disease, fire, injury.
4. To identify workers, e.g. gardaí, nurses, soldiers.
5. To express one's personality.

LINKS

- Management of household financial resources (p. 184)
- Consumer choice (p. 218)

Functions of household textiles

1. To decorate our homes.
2. To create a comfortable atmosphere.
3. To provide warmth and insulation.
4. To absorb sounds, making the home more relaxing.
5. To provide privacy.

Choosing household textiles (selection criteria)

When choosing textiles, consider the following factors:
1. Function of item: end use of textile.
2. Fitness for purpose: suitability, drape and weight.
3. Cost: buy the best you can afford.
4. Properties: check desirable/undesirable properties.

5. Care and maintenance: washable, etc.
6. Personal taste: likes and dislikes.
7. Aesthetic appeal: colour, pattern, etc.
8. Safety: e.g. flame-retardant.

Care of fabrics

Scientific principles

1. Use detergents to suit the fabric.
2. Choose the correct water temperature.
3. Agitate fabrics to loosen dirt and remove stains.
4. Add fabric conditioners to reduce static electricity.
5. Remove water using a method which will not damage the fabrics or their finishes.

Detergent	Ingredients in detergents include bleach, enzymes, fluorescents, conditioner and surfactants
Water	Efficiency of wash is determined by type of water – hard or soft
Temperature	Incorrect temperatures damage fabrics
Agitation	Amount of agitation is determined by type of fabric, e.g. silk = gentle agitation
Conditioners	Soften fabrics, reduce static and aid ironing

Textile care labelling codes

Symbol	Application
95°	White cotton and linen articles without special finishes.
60°	Cotton, linen or viscose articles without special finishes where colours are fast at 60°C.
50°	Nylon, polyester/cotton mixtures, polyester, cotton and viscose articles with special finishes, cotton/acrylic mixtures.
40°	Cotton, linen or viscose articles where colours are fast at 40°C but not at 60°C.
40°	Acrylics, acetate, triacetate (including mixtures with wool), polyester/wool blends.
40°	Wool (including blankets) and wool mixtures with cotton or viscose and silk.
✕	Do not wash
30°	Delicate fabrics

95° – cotton, linen, hot boil wash
60° – hot wash, cotton, linen or viscose
50° – nylon, polyester/cotton blends
40° – cotton, linen, viscose
40° – (one bar) acrylics, acetate, triacetate
40° – (two bars), wool, wool blends
30° – non-colour fast fabrics, silk

Ironing Symbols

 Cool (120°C) acrylic, nylon, acetate, triacetate, polyester.

 Warm (160°C) polyester mixtures, wool.

 Hot (210°C) cotton, linen, viscose or modified viscose.

 Do not iron.

Handwash

 Articles which must not be machine washed.

Drying Symbols

Dry flat

 Fibres may stretch if line dried.

Drip dry

 Fibres may stretch or crease if wrung.

 Line dry

 Tumble drying beneficial

 Do not tumble dry

Cleaning Symbols

Dry cleaning

 Normal goods dry cleanable in all solvents.

 Normal goods dry cleanable in perchloroethylene, white spirit, Solvent 113 and Solvent 11.

 Normal goods dry cleanable in white spirits and Solvent 113.

Some fabrics may be affected by different solvents, e.g. silk.

Chlorine bleach

May be treated with chlorine bleach.

Do not use chlorine bleach.

Do not dry clean

Properties and care of fibres

1. Wool

Properties	Care required
• Absorbent and soft	• Hand wash or dry clean (read label)
• Damaged by bleach	• Medium machine wash at 40°C
• Shrinks	• Dry flat, avoid stretching
• Scorches easily	• Use a warm iron setting
• Weak when wet	• Do not use bleach
• Pills easily	• Do not tumble dry

2. Cotton

Properties	Care required
• Absorbent, dyes readily	• Hand wash with hot water *or* machine wash at 95°C (100% cotton) or at 40°C or 50°C (cotton blends)
• Strong	
• Burns/scorches easily	• Bleach can be used
• Creases easily	• Iron when damp with a hot iron
• Cheap cotton becomes limp	
• Shrinks	

3. Polyester (synthetic fibre)

Properties	Care required
• Resists creasing, mildew	• Machine wash in warm water
• Washes well, dries quickly	• Wash cotton/polyester blends at 50°C
• Non-absorbent, attracts dirt	• Cool iron
• Develops static build-up	

4. Viscose (regenerated fibre)

Properties	Care required
• Creases easily	• Medium machine wash at 50°C
• Weak when wet	• Must not be wrung out
• Shrinks at high temperatures	• Press/iron at low temperature
• Absorbent, drapes well	

Fabric finishes include: anti-static, anti-pilling, crease-resistance, mercerising, shrink-resistant and stain-resistant finishes.

> **LINK**
> • Consumer choice (p. 218)

Household textiles – safety considerations

Only choose:

- low-risk fabrics
- fabrics treated with flame-retardant finishes
- CMHR foam filling in furniture.

Low-risk fabrics: wool, polyester.
High-risk fabrics: cotton, acrylic.

> **key point**
> CMHR = combustion-modified high resilience foam

Flame-retardant finishes

Fabrics with flame-retardant finishes will self-extinguish when the flames are removed.

Types of flame-retardant finish

1. Coated fabrics: not permanent, cheap.
2. Inherent flame-retardant finishes (fibres treated prior to weaving): durable, expensive.

Example: Proban – an expensive durable flame-retardant finish.

- A phosphorus/nitrogen layer is applied to fabric.
- Insoluble polymers form in the fabric.
- On lighting, fabrics do not melt or smoulder and flames will self-extinguish.

Effects of flame-retardant finishes

- Makes fabric more expensive.
- Care needed when cleaning.
- Reduces risk of igniting.
- Self-extinguishing when removed from flames.
- Allergic reaction in some people.

Fire Safety (Domestic Furniture) Order (1988, 1995)

Purpose is to reduce the risk of household fires from textiles.

The **Fire Safety Order** covers:

1. *Types of fillings and covers* used for upholstered domestic products, e.g. armchairs, beds, cushions, loose covers, pillows, sofas, children's cots and pushchairs.
2. *Labelling arrangements* for textile products.

Note: it *does not* cover bed linen, carpets, curtains, pillowcases and sleeping bags.

The regulations require that:

1. Manufacturers use CMHR.
2. Fabrics must pass a series of fire safety tests.
3. Permanent safety labels must be attached securely, be clearly legible and durable.
4. Products must have a swing or display safety label.

Types of safety label

1. **Red triangle:** filling meets the safety requirements, states that a fire-resistant interliner is present, states that outer fabric is not match-resistant.

2. **Green square:** filling and covering fabric meet safety requirements for resistance to cigarettes and match ignition.

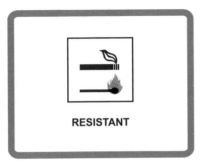

RESISTANT

Filling material(s) and covering fabric(s) meet the requirements for resistance to cigarette and match ignition in the 1988 safety regulations

CARELESSNESS
CAUSES FIRE

3. **Permanent label:** stitched permanently to fabric, provides a warning ('Carelessness causes fire') details about the manufacturer (name, address, identification number), description of filling and cover materials.

Exam question and sample answer

Ordinary Level 2009, Section B, Q4 (a,b) (50 marks)

(a) Comment on the importance of each of the following when selecting textiles for clothing: (24 marks)

(i) **Suitability for purpose** (6 marks = 6 marks)

Properties should make the fabric suit its purpose, e.g. raincoats should be waterproof, upholstery should be flame-retardant, easy-care fibres for sportswear.

(ii) **Personal choice** (6 marks)

Likes and dislikes will influence the type of fibre in the fabric, e.g. some people prefer natural fibres to man-made fibres, others may be allergic to wool.

(iii) **Aesthetic appeal** (6 marks)

The attractiveness of a fabric is determined by colour, texture, drape and feel of fabrics.

(iv) **Cost** (6 marks)

Natural fabrics, e.g. wool, silk, linen, are more expensive than man-made fabrics. Budget will determine the quality and type of fabric chosen.

(b) Describe **four** functions of household textiles. (16 marks)

1. To provide warmth, e.g. duvets.
2. To provide privacy, e.g. curtains.
3. To provide protection, e.g. oven gloves.
4. To provide insulation, e.g. curtains.

(c) Name **and** explain the effect of **one** fire-retardant finish. (10 marks)

Name: *Proban* (4 marks)

Effect: *On lighting, this finish chars, does not melt or smoulder and self-extinguishes. This lowers the risk of the fabric catching fire.* (6 marks)

Consumer studies

What is a consumer?

A consumer is any person who buys or uses goods or services.

Consumer choice

Factors affecting consumer choice – key points:

1. *Household income:* single, dual, multiple sources.
2. *Personal values:* wants, needs and goals, likes/dislikes.
3. *Cost:* budget available, value for money.
4. *Family and friends:* their view of a product/service.
5. *Merchandising/advertising:* encourages spending.
6. *Salespeople:* persuade consumers of the value of a product/service.
7. *Packaging:* quality, eco-friendly, attractiveness.
8. *Labelling:* information on care, nutrition and safety.
9. Design, colour and functionality.

exam focus

Consumer Studies is examined in both Sections A and B in Higher and Ordinary Level papers and is integrated across questions.

LINKS

- Food commodities (p. 70)
- Food processing (p. 126)
- Food packaging (p. 132)
- Management of household financial resources (p. 184)
- Household technology (p. 201)

The purchasing process

Classification of retail outlets

Outlet	Examples	Features
Department stores	Arnotts, Clerys	• Wide range of goods • Arranged in departments, e.g. shoes, electrical, cosmetics, furniture
Multiple chain stores	Dunnes Stores, Penneys	• Same company, many branches • Same design and layout • Self-service • Shared advertising • Good value for money
Supermarkets	Superquinn, Tesco	• Self-service, open plan • Wide range of goods • Own brands are cheaper • Internet shopping offered
Discount stores	Argos	• High turnover • Lower prices • Order goods from catalogue • Limited pre-packed stock

Independent shops	Local butcher, jeweller, greengrocer	<ul><li>Local, often family-owned shops</li><li>Higher prices (higher overheads), limited stock</li></ul>
Voluntary supermarkets	Combined supermarket and independent shop e.g. Spar	<ul><li>Good range of products</li><li>Local owner</li><li>Own brands as well as other popular brands</li></ul>

Other retail outlets/shopping systems:

- mail order shopping
- online or Internet shopping
- television buying
- street markets
- house parties.

Retail psychology

Retail psychology involves the study of human behaviour and decision-making when buying products and services.

Techniques to encourage consumer spending

In-store stimuli	Background music, colours, aromas
Layout of store	<ul><li>**Structured:** grid layout with aisles</li><li>**Unstructured:** free-flow layout</li></ul>
Product placement	<ul><li>Luxury items placed at eye level</li><li>Essentials lower down or at back</li><li>Products grouped by association</li><li>Special offers at the end of aisles</li></ul>
Product blocking	'Blocking' makes consumers notice products
Shelf position	Products with highest profit margins at eye level
Impulse goods	Magazines and sweets at checkout
Late-night opening	Accommodates workers and families
Loyalty schemes	Club card, tokens for other products
Merchandising	'Two for one' offers encourage spending
Size of decompression zones	Consumers adjust to shopping area
Home delivery service	Useful for people without transport
Car delivery service	Helping consumers take groceries to their car

Shopping patterns

Factors that influence shopping patterns include:

Consumers expect quality goods and services.

1. Shopping traditions in the family.
2. Income, e.g. restrictive or non-restrictive.
3. Marketing and advertising strategies.
4. Environmental awareness.
5. Opening times of shopping outlets, e.g. 24-hour shopping.
6. Time available, e.g. if limited, use online shopping.
7. Dependence on others for transport.
8. Proximity to retail parks/shopping centres.

Consumer research

Consumer research involves collecting, analysing and processing information from consumers.

Research methods: surveys, interviews, customer panels and questionnaires.

Types of research

1. Desk research
- data collected via Internet, state agencies, etc.
- quick method of collecting data
- inexpensive method of collecting data
- information is too general, little detail.

2. Field research
- involves going out into the marketplace
- data collected via surveys, interviews and observations
- data more accurate and detailed than desk research
- time-consuming and expensive.

Advantages of consumer research

1. Creates a consumer profile, e.g. age, gender, income.
2. Identifies consumers' likes and dislikes.
3. Highlights weaknesses in marketing strategies.
4. Identifies current and potential market sizes.
5. Identifies the competitors in the market.

Advertising

Functions of advertising

1. To sell goods and services.
2. To inform consumers of new products.
3. To improve the popularity/sales of old products.

4. To create an environmentally friendly image.

5. To promote a company as a consumer-friendly organisation.

Advantages of advertising

1. Provides consumers with information about a product.

2. Creates interest in new/old products, increases or maintains sales.

3. Encourages competition, may reduce prices.

4. Provides a range of employment opportunities.

Disadvantages of advertising

1. Increases cost of product/service.

2. Creates a desire in people to buy lifestyle products.

3. Encourages consumerism, buying of non-essentials.

4. Puts pressure on low-income groups.

5. Can reinforce stereotyping.

> **LINK**
> - Food packaging (p. 132)

Consumer rights and responsibilities

Consumer rights

Consumers are entitled to the **right to**:

1. honest information (labelling laws, instructions)

2. redress (repair, replacement or refund)

3. high standards of safety (safety symbols, warning symbols)

4. choice (competition is encouraged)

5. value for money (never confuse cost and value)

6. high-quality services and goods (merchantable, fit for purpose).

Consumer responsibilities

Consumers are expected to:

- be informed when making decisions
- be familiar with consumer protection laws
- read the labels provided about goods and services
- examine products, investigate services before buying
- understand symbols and warnings on labels
- use the product as intended and follow the instructions
- keep receipts and guarantees.

Sources of consumer information

1. Points of sale, e.g. showrooms, salespeople.

2. Magazines, newspapers, brochures, leaflets.

3. TV, radio, Internet, billboards.

4. Friends and family.

5. Labelling information.

6. Official centres.

Consumer signs and symbols

Hazardous substances	
Harmful/Irritant	
Toxic	
Highly Flammable	
Corrosive	
Quality and safety	
Irish Standard mark/Caighdean Éireannach	
Guaranteed Irish	
Communauté Européenne	CE
BSI Kitemark	
BSI Safety Mark	
National Standards Authority of Ireland	NSAI

Double insulated	
Irish mark of electrical conformity	

The consumer and the environment

Consumers have a responsibility to protect the environment by developing a waste management system in the home, and by re-using and/or recycling products.

Failure to protect the environment results in:

- reduction in non-renewable resources (coal, oil)
- global warming, climate change, pollution
- disappearance of tropical rain forests
- drought, flooding, famine, migration.

LINKS

- Food commodities (p. 70)
- Food processing (p. 126)
- Food packaging (p. 132)
- Household technology (p. 201)
- Textiles (p. 212)

Managing resources

Renewable resources come from naturally recurring resources, e.g. biomass, geothermal heat, hydropower, solar power, wind power, tidal power. Renewable resources:

- can be used to generate electricity
- have little effect on the environment
- are clean and efficient – but set-up costs are high.

Non-renewable resources come from fossil fuels, e.g. coal, gas, oil, peat, uranium.

- They will run out.
- They are sources of air pollution.
- Nuclear power produces waste.

Waste management

Waste management involves prevention, minimisation, re-use, recycling, energy recovery and disposal. Consumers should refuse, re-use and recycle. **Sustainable development** promotes the use of renewable resources and ensures that the least possible amount of damage is done to the environment.

exam focus

Check out the Waste Management Pyramid (search the Internet) and central/local government Waste Management Plans.

Refuse, re-use and recycle

Responsible waste management involves:

1. recycling organic and inorganic waste products
2. re-using products in the home, e.g. glass jars
3. bringing products to recycling centres/points
4. buying products with the EU Eco-label or the green dot
5. selecting biodegradable and phosphate-free products
6. disposing of freezers and fridges correctly.

WEEE Directive (Waste Electrical and Electronic Equipment)

Producers must organise the collection and treatment of waste electrical and electronic equipment. A specific fee is charged at point of sale when buying electrical and electronic goods to cater for this waste management system.

Advantages of recycling

- Reduces costs of waste disposal.
- Reduces litter and pollution.
- Conserves non-renewable resources.
- Creates new businesses and employment.

Recycling symbols

Be able to name each symbol and state what it represents.

1. **Green dot**
   Companies are members of Repak, have made a contribution to cost of recycling products.

2. **Recycling symbol**
   Goods or packaging are made from recyclable materials or can be recycled.

3. **Eco-label**
   Little damage caused to the environment.

4. **PET label**
   Polyethylene terephthalate – certain plastics can be recycled.

Energy

Ireland supports a policy of sustainable energy.

SEAI (Sustainable Energy Authority of Ireland)

- Is a statutory authority.
- Aims to improve energy efficiency.
- Promotes the move to renewable energy resources.
- Aims to reduce the effects of energy production and use.
- Advises government on policies and measures.

Energy labelling – Energy rated A to G

See Household appliances (pp. 202–12).

Sources of energy

Wind	Wind turbines produce energy, in coastal and hilly areas
Solar	Panels built into roofs, also used to power public devices, e.g. parking meters
Hydropower	Harnessing energy from fast-flowing rivers
Biomass	Sustainable energy source, e.g. wood
Geothermal	Harnessing energy from heat in the earth

Energy consumption efficiency

Appliances	Use appliances with good energy ratings; use the 'half load' button on washing machines; unplug televisions and video machines when not in use; use Nightsaver electricity, etc.
Lighting	Use CFL bulbs; switch off lights when not in use
Insulation	Lag hot water cylinders; fix timers to immersion heaters; use draught-proofing; insulate the house, place timers and thermostats on central heating systems; turn down heating thermostats by a couple of degrees; replace old windows with double glazing
Others	Dry clothes in the fresh air; take a shower instead of a bath; use rechargeable batteries and a charger; add solar systems to new homes; replace fossil fuels with solar, wind or biomass energy

Air pollution

Causes

- chlorofluorocarbons (CFCs)
- carbon monoxide from cars, buses, etc.
- burning fossil fuels.

Consequences/effects

- depletion of ozone layer
- acid rain (damage to soil, buildings, plants)

- global warming, climate change
- respiratory problems.

Preventing air pollution (preventative actions)

- buy energy-efficient appliances
- choose renewable fuels
- avoid products containing CFCs
- buy ozone-friendly aerosols.

Water pollution

Causes

- industrial and farm waste
- fertilisers, pesticides and chemicals
- oil spillages
- illegal dumping of toxic waste.

Consequences/effects

- destroys plants, animals and birds
- damages rivers
- damages fishing and tourist industry
- water becomes unsafe to drink.

Preventing water pollution (preventative actions)

- opt for phosphate-free products
- reduce use of pesticides and fertilisers
- install effective sewage and water systems
- enforce legislation – impose penalties.

Noise pollution

Causes

- traffic (cars, buses, trains)
- equipment (household, garden)
- noisy animals
- house and car alarms
- loud music, e.g. discos.

Consequences/effects

- headaches
- lack of sleep
- tension, stress and ill-health
- rows between neighbours.

Preventing noise pollution (preventative actions)

- good insulation (triple glazing)
- live away from busy public roads
- turn down music systems, TVs and radios.

Consumer protection

Consumer rights are protected by legislation and the courts, statutory government agencies and voluntary agencies.

Sale of Goods and Supply of Services Act 1980

- Covers goods, services, guarantees and illegal signs.
- A legal contract exists between the buyer and the seller when a product or service is purchased.
- Implemented by the Office of the Director of Consumer Affairs in Ireland.

The Act states that goods or services should:

- be of merchantable quality
- be fit for purpose, suitable for use
- as described on labels
- correspond to sample on display.

Services:

- must be supplied by qualified and skilled people
- must be provided with due care, following safety procedures
- materials used must be of merchantable quality.

Redress for consumers

Under the Act, if goods are faulty or services are unsatisfactory consumers may be entitled to a replacement, repair, refund or partial refund or repeat of a service.

Guarantees

A guarantee:

- is covered by the Sale of Goods and Supply of Services Act 1980
- is a contract between the consumer and the manufacturer
- has a time limit, e.g. one year
- does not affect a consumer's rights.

Under the Act, guarantees should:

- be legible and refer to specific goods
- name the product
- name the person/company offering the guarantee
- give the company address
- show the duration of guarantee from date of purchase

- outline procedures for making a claim
- state what the manufacturer will do – what the customer should expect to receive in the event of a fault
- identify any extra charges claimant might pay, e.g. postage.

Signs

Signs that are illegal because they limit the rights of consumers:

- 'No cash refunds'
- 'Credit notes only given'
- 'No exchange of goods'.

Electronic Commerce Act 2000

- Established under the EU.
- Protects consumers when shopping online (e-bookings and agreements).

Consumer Information Act 1978

- Protects consumers against false or misleading information or claims about goods or services (advertisements, information in brochures)
- Applies to price, product or service, and credit agreements.

Statutory and voluntary bodies protecting consumers

Statutory bodies	Voluntary bodies
National Consumer Agency (NCA)	Consumer Association of Ireland
Office of the Ombudsman	Advertising Standards Authority of Ireland
National Standards Authority of Ireland (NSAI)	
Citizens Information Board	
European Consumer Centre, Ireland	

National Consumer Agency (NCA)

The NCA is a statutory body which was set up in 2007 by the Irish government. Its main work is divided into five areas: targeted research; information; enforcement of laws; advocacy; education and awareness.

Functions

- Promotes and defends consumer rights.
- Informs consumers of their rights.
- Promotes a consumer culture via education and awareness.
- Enforces consumer law/legislation.
- Represents consumers at all levels of policy development levels through research and advocacy.

Office of the Ombudsman, Ireland

The Ombudsman is appointed by the government. The role of the office is laid down in law by the Ombudsman Act 1980 and the service is independent and free.

Role of the Ombudsman

- To investigate unresolved complaints against public bodies: government departments, local authorities, the Health Service Executive, agencies that deliver health and social services on behalf of the HSE, An Post and all bodies covered by the Disability Act 2005.
- Valid complaints are reported by the Ombudsman to the department in question and recommendations are made to resolve the matter.

National Standards Authority of Ireland (NSAI)

The NSAI:

- is a state body that sets, monitors and develops standards of safety and quality in Ireland
- ensures Irish products meet EU and international standards and is an accreditation body for ISO 9000.

Citizens Information Board

The board is a statutory body that provides the public with accurate information and advice on a range of public and social services areas, for example consumer rights, social welfare, health services, family law, housing, income tax, local services and redundancy. Information is provided through:

- a website (www.citizensinformation.ie)
- a phone service
- Citizens Information centres.

The Citizens Information Board was assigned responsibility for MABS (Money Advice and Budgeting Service) in July 2009.

European Consumer Centre, Ireland

- Located in Dublin (a walk-in centre).
- Provides information on consumer rights in the EU.
- Participates in the European Consumer Centres Network (ECC-Net), research and surveys.
- Co-operates with national consumer organisations and enforcement agencies, e.g. National Consumer Agency.
- Provides feedback to the European Commission.

Consumer Association of Ireland

- A non-profit-making, independent organisation
- Publishes *Consumer Choice* magazine.

- Carries out independent research and surveys.
- Aims to improve consumer legislation.
- Represents consumers in state bodies, agencies and industry.
- Advises government on consumer issues.

Advertising Standards Authority of Ireland (ASAI)

- Independent, voluntary body.
- Ensures advertisements are legal, decent, honest and truthful.
- Investigates consumer complaints.

Making complaints – procedures to follow

- Do not use the product if you notice a fault.
- Stop using the product if it develops a fault.

Complaining in person

1. Return the product and the receipt to the retailer.
2. Ask to speak to the manager if the assistant is unable to help.
3. Explain the nature of the problem, produce the product and receipt.
4. Keep to the facts and calmly ask what the retailer will do to solve the problem.

Solution: might involve replacement, refund or repair.

Complaining in writing

Put the complaint in writing to the manager or director, outlining clearly:

1. item purchased (manufacturer's name, make, model)
2. date of purchase
3. copy of receipt of purchase
4. nature of the problem
5. outline of return visit to the shop, name of the person spoken to
6. action you expect the company to take.

Keep a copy of the letter.

If your complaint fails, consider legal advice or the small claims procedure.

Small claims procedure

The Small Claims Court:

- is a system within the local District Court
- is a cheap, fast and easy way of dealing with small claims
- can be used by consumers and businesses (since 11 January 2010).

A solicitor is not required.

Claims handled by Small Claims Court include:

- faulty goods
- bad workmanship or minor damage to property.

Procedure for claimants

- Claimant completes an application form with three sections: claimant's name, address and telephone number; respondent's information; facts of the claim.
- Claimant signs form and sends with fee to the Small Claims Registrar.
- Small Claims Registrar registers the complaint.
- A copy of the complaint is sent to the respondent.
- Respondent must respond within 15 days.
- Undisputed claims are settled without going to court.
- Registrar tries to settle disputed claims.
- If there is no resolution there will be a court hearing.

Exam questions and sample answers

Higher Level 2009, Section A, Q10 (6 marks)

Give details of **two** merchandising techniques used by retailers to encourage consumer spending.

(i) In-store stimuli, e.g. music, baking aromas.
(ii) Loyalty schemes, e.g. club card points.

Higher Level 2009, Section A, Q12 (6 marks)

State **one** advantage of using renewable energy sources.
Renewable energy sources are sustainable.
Name **two** forms of renewable energy.
(i) Solar energy/power.
(ii) Biomass.

Ordinary Level 2008, Section A, Q9(a) (4 marks)

(a) Name **two** renewable energy resources and **two** non-renewable energy resources.

Renewable energy	Non-renewable energy
Wind energy	*Coal*
Hydropower	*Oil*

Higher Level 2005, Section B, Q4 (50 marks)

'Studies show that impulse buying can account for 65% of purchases in supermarkets.' (*Consumer Choice*, May 2001)

(a) Describe **four** in-store techniques that supermarkets use to encourage consumer spending. (4 points × 5 marks = 20 marks)

Product placement, positioning and association are key techniques used in shops to encourage spending.

1. **Essentials,** *e.g. milk and bread, are located at the back of the store and consumers are forced to pass expensive products just to buy essentials.*

2. **Luxury items** are placed at eye level, while cheaper own-brand products are placed on lower shelves.

3. **Special offers** are placed at the end of aisles.

4. **Biscuits and cakes** are located close to tea and coffee.

(b) Name **three** research methods used to gather information on the consumer.
(3 × 3 marks = 9 marks)

1. Surveys; 2 Telephone interviews; 3 Loyalty cards.

State **one** benefit of consumer research to (i) the retailer and (ii) the consumer.
(2 × 5 marks = 10 marks)

(i) The retailer: identifies the type of consumer (needs, wants, luxuries).

(ii) The consumer: creates competition in the market, may reduce prices.

(c) Outline the **role** of any one voluntary agency concerned with consumer protection.
(11 marks)

Name: Consumers' Association of Ireland (CAI)
(3 marks)

Role:
(2 points × 4 marks = 8 marks)

1. Provides consumers with information through the media and Consumer Choice (monthly magazine).

2. Promotes improvements in consumer legislation.

Ordinary Level 2008, Section B, Q4
(50 marks)

Consumer Case Study

'On a shopping trip Tom bought a new camera and two T-shirts, Kate bought two cotton summer tops, one woollen jumper and denim jeans. When they arrived home Tom discovered that the camera did not work. Kate was disappointed with the colour of the jeans. They both decided to return the following week with the camera and the jeans and demand their money back.'

(a) As consumers, what rights do Tom and Kate have in relation to getting a refund on the camera and jeans?
(2 × 7 marks = 14 marks)

Tom: has a right to a refund, replacement or a repair if he has a receipt.

Kate: has no right to a refund but out of goodwill the shop might give her a refund or offer her jeans in another colour.

(b) List **three** responsibilities Tom and Kate have as consumers.
(3 × 4 marks = 12 marks)

1. To be informed about goods and services.

2. To read and understand labels and instructions.

3. To use the product as intended.

(c) Outline **three** factors that Kate should take into consideration when caring for the woollen jumper.
(3 × 4 marks = 12 marks)

1. Read and follow the care label instructions.

2. Wash at low temperatures at minimum wash.

3. Pull back into shape before drying flat.

5 Social Studies: The Family in Society

aims To learn and revise:

- The family
- Marriage
- Family law.

exam focus

The topics in this section are examined in Section B of the exam. In the exam, be able to elaborate on the points given and back up your answers with **factual, up-to-date information**. Use bullet points when answering questions, keep to the facts or the point, elaborate on the information you give, do not give personal opinions and avoid essay-style answers.

Sociological terms

Sociology – the systematic scientific study of the organisation and functioning of human society.

Society – a group of people who share a similar way of life.

Social groups – groups of people linked by a common purpose. Social groups may be primary or secondary.

- **Primary social groups** – small groups whose relationships are seen as permanent, e.g. family and close friends.
- **Secondary social groups** – larger groups of people whose relationships are more impersonal and less permanent, e.g. school community, voluntary groups and work groups.

Culture – the beliefs, customs, language, norms, mores, values, roles, knowledge and skills passed on from one generation to another.

Norms – accepted established patterns of behaviour: the social rules that people are expected to follow, e.g. going to school.

Mores – accepted customs, norms and values that are considered important by a society, e.g. being respectful.

Values – the principles and beliefs held by a society about what is 'right' and 'wrong'.

Role – the expected pattern of behaviour of an individual according to their status or position.

Status (ascribed or achieved) – the position held by people relative to others within the society and the respect or prestige given to that position by others.

Socio-economic grouping – the classification of people according to income and wealth, e.g. lower-income, middle-income and higher-income groups.

Social mobility – the movement of people between socio-economic groupings due to changes in education, income, occupation and social circumstances.

Kinship – the blood relationship links that exist between people.

Socialisation – the lifelong process of learning how to fit into a society. There are two types:

- primary socialisation: in the family
- secondary socialisation: in school, workplace, community.

Social change – changes that take place in a society due to events (national or global) or scientific and technological developments.

Social controls – the methods (sanctions, rewards or punishments) used to ensure that people follow the acceptable norms, mores and values of society.

Social institutions – the organised social arrangements in a society, e.g. marriage.

The family

The Irish Constitution defines the family as the 'natural, primary and fundamental group of society'.

The family is:

- a group of people related to each other through blood, marriage or adoption
- 'the basic unit of society which acts as a support for its members and transmits values from one generation to the next'.

The family exists in all societies in different forms. The **family of origin** is the family in which we grow up. The **family of procreation** is the family we form as adults when we have our own children.

Family structures

Types of family structure

- nuclear
- extended
- blended/reconstituted
- lone-parent
- foster.

Nuclear family

1. Small in size, consists of parents and children.
2. Mobile, moves for a variety of reasons, e.g. career.
3. Democratic – shared decision-making.
4. Egalitarian – roles are shared.
5. Economically dependent on a small number of people.
6. Often both parents work outside the home.
7. Accepts change more easily than an extended family.
8. Less reliable and more isolated in a crisis.
9. Short-lived: grown-up children move away from home.

Extended family

1. Based on traditional family structures.
2. Large in size, members are interdependent.
3. Authoritarian and generally patriarchal.
4. Segregated roles, gender-specific in nature.
5. Family is immobile because it is large.
6. Long lasting, several generations interdependent.
7. Good network of support in a crisis.
8. Less accepting of change than a nuclear family.

Blended family

1. A new unit formed by two adults and their children from previous relationships/marriages.
2. Occurs due to separation and divorce.
3. Family size changes, number of children may increase.
4. Changes in placement of children according to age.
5. Discipline may be a source of conflict between parents.
6. Links with multiple sets of grandparents/family groups.
7. Relationship with non-resident parent may be difficult.
8. Can be more isolated than nuclear or extended family.
9. Balancing finances across two families is difficult.

Lone-parent family

1. Consists of one parent and her/his children.
2. Results from death, divorce, separation, unplanned pregnancy, spouse in prison, or personal choice.
3. Increased workload, parent may be isolated.
4. Reduced ability/opportunities to work outside home.

5. Financial difficulties due to high cost of childcare.
6. Greater risk of poverty and unemployment.
7. Increased dependence on state benefits.
8. Emotional difficulties, depression and stress.

LINK

● Management of household financial resources (p. 184)

HL Social, economic and technological changes affecting the family

Social changes

1. Decline in the extended family and traditional roles.
2. Increase in new family forms and more egalitarian roles.
3. Decrease in family size due to family planning.
4. Acceptance of divorce, separation and co-habitation.
5. Decrease in religious influence; a more secular society.
6. Education and career achievements are priorities.
7. Focus on individualisation and personal choice.
8. Improved educational and work opportunities for women.
9. Most people complete primary and secondary education.
10. Increase in leisure time, more time for family.
11. Greater cultural and religious diversity.

Economic changes

1. Smaller family sizes as a result of higher cost of living.
2. Increased cost of buying a house, two incomes required.
3. Young couples find it difficult to get a mortgage.
4. Childcare arrangements are expensive.
5. State benefits provided (for lone parents, low-income groups).
6. Unemployment increased between 2008 and 2011.
7. Higher levels of emigration due to unemployment.

Technological changes

1. Modernisation of machinery, appliances and equipment for agriculture, the home, work and communications.
2. Less segregation of roles in workplaces.
3. Less time and labour spent on monotonous tasks.
4. Advances allow working, shopping and banking from home.
5. Technology helps families keep in touch, e.g. email.
6. Television provides a 'window' to societies, cultures and economies across the world.

LINK

● Household technology (p. 201)

Development of the family in Ireland

Before industrialisation (1900–1960)

Family form	Extended family was the usual structure.
Family size	Large: children viewed as an economic asset, worked from an early age, high child mortality rates.
Economic status	Households functioned as residential and work units. The father controlled the finance (breadwinner).
Roles	Household tasks were organised along segregated roles. Authority was gender-related, vested in the father (patriarchal). Sons had higher status than daughters.
Position of women	Women considered inferior to men legally and socially. Marriages were often arranged for females and dowries offered.
Employment	Limited work opportunities: badly paid and determined by level of education. Limited access to education without finance. Emigration was common. The mechanisation of farming resulted in unemployment; emigration increased.
Religion	Strict religious upbringing.
At home	• Introduction of *rural electrification* (1946) and *water schemes* (1960s) improved home life for women and children. • 1950s: improvements in standards of living, women's health and decrease in child mortality rates.

After industrialisation (1960–1990)

Family form	Nuclear families emerged, urban-based, decline in extended family. People married younger. Romantic love the basis for marriage, decrease in arranged marriages.
Family size	Smaller in size, lower child mortality rates. Children not viewed as economic assets. Regulations were put in place to reduce child labour.
Economic status	Husband viewed as the main breadwinner, some married women worked outside the home. Emergence of the dual-income family. Improved standard of living. Increase in life expectancy, with improved nutrition and healthcare.
Education	Increased educational initiatives and opportunities for all. Education viewed as important. Children able to attend both primary and secondary school. Free secondary education introduced in 1967.
Roles	Husband viewed as the breadwinner, wife as the homemaker and carer, focus was on children, their development and family life. Decline in status and role of older family members. More egalitarian roles emerged mid-1970s.

| Position of women | Many women working in the home. Improved life expectancy and family planning. |
| Employment | More married women in the workforce from the mid-1970s. Higher wages and more leisure time. Reduction in working hours. |

Contemporary Irish families (1990s–2008)

Family form	More lone-parent and blended families. Introduction of divorce (1996), increased rates of separation and co-habitation.
Family size	Smaller family size, more reliable methods of family planning.
Economic status	Emergence of full employment and dual-income families. Higher standards of living, more choices available. Influx of migrant workers.
Position of women	More married women in the workforce.
Roles	Demand for greater gender equality in the home and workplace. Demand for childcare facilities. Parents stressed.
Religion	Decline in religious influence.
State support	State supporting family functions, e.g. financial, education and socialisation.
Technology	Benefits in the home, work and education.

Life in Ireland 2008–present

1. Increased unemployment across all sectors of workers.
2. Increased emigration and migration.
3. More financial problems, lower standards of living.
4. Inability by some families to make mortgage repayments.
5. High costs of childcare, stress within families.
6. Extra demands on state supports.

exam focus

Before exams check out the latest employment/ unemployment data

Functions of the family

Protection	• Family protects vulnerable members • Provides a safe environment for all
Reproductive function	• Ensures the survival of the human race • Regulates adult sexual behaviour • Unregulated sexual behaviour results in unwanted pregnancies, STDs and AIDS
Nurturing and rearing function	• Provides basic physical needs • Child develops a well-balanced personality in a safe, secure and loving environment

Emotional function	Meets the emotional and psychological needs of the child by providing reassurance, encouragement, love and security
Economic function	Adults in the family work to earn money to provide for the needs of the family
Education function	<ul><li>Primary centre of early learning</li><li>Family supports the state in the education of children by supervising homework, praising and encouraging the child and by providing a stimulating home environment</li></ul>
Socialisation function	<ul><li>The primary centre of socialisation</li><li>Introduces children to the traditions, norms, and values of society</li><li>Acts as an agent of social control by showing children what is acceptable and unacceptable behaviour</li></ul>

LINKS

- Dietary and food requirements (Chapter 2)
- Family resource management (p. 179)
- Management of household financial resources (p. 184)
- Housing finance (p. 197)

State interventions in family functions

1. **Protective**
   - May place children at risk in foster care.
   - Cares for the elderly and those suffering from long-term illness through home help, public health nurse, sheltered accommodation, sheltered working environments.
   - Provides Child Benefit monthly.

2. **Educational/intellectual**
   - Provides full-time free education from 5 to 18 years.
   - Provides assessments to identify learning difficulties.
   - Provides learning support, resource teachers and special needs assistants (SNAs).

3. **Nurturing**
   Assisted by pre-schools, primary and secondary schools.

4. **Economic**
   Provides unemployment benefit, old age pension, social and affordable housing, medical cards, disability allowance and public health services.

5. **Socialisation**
   - Provision of pre-schools, primary and secondary schools.
   - Provision of parenting courses.

6. **Caring**
   Parenting skills courses provided in community centres.

Exam question and sample answer

Higher Level 2008, Section B, Q5 (50 marks)

'Fewer than one in five households in Dublin City are now made up of the traditional family of husband, wife and children.' (CSO Census of Population 2006)

(a) Analyse the reasons for the decline of the traditional family in society.
(5 × 4 marks = 20 marks)

Reasons include:

1. *Increase in number of people seeking separation or divorce.*
2. *More lone-parent and blended families*
3. *Different attitudes to marriage (co-habiting instead of marrying).*
4. *Changing family roles, both parents working outside the home, childcare provided by others.*
5. *Smaller families due to effective family planning.*

(b) Describe how the changing roles within the family have had an impact on individuals.
(3 × 6 marks = 18 marks)

(i) **Changing Role of Parents**
   - *More women working outside the home and are not financially dependent on their husbands as in the past.*
   - *Men are more involved in childcare and household activities due to the nuclear family structure.*
   - *Education is considered as important for males and females, and many women work in highly paid jobs. Women may be the breadwinners and husbands may be at home caring for children.*
   - *Due to the pressures of work parents experience role conflict and role overload.*

(ii) **Changing Role of Grandparents**
   - *Have more time to spend with grandchildren.*
   - *Provide emotional support for their adult children and their grandchildren.*
   - *Enjoy a more relaxed relationship with grandchildren.*
   - *Play an important role in childcare.*
   - *Often assist adult children financially.*

(iii) **Changing Role of Children**
   - *Share in household tasks according to age.*
   - *Are expected to become independent and do their best.*
   - *Are expected to be role models for younger children.*
   - *Have become more involved in family decision-making.*

(c) Describe **one** strategy for resolving conflict within the family.

(3 × 4 marks = 12 marks)

When resolving family conflict:

1. Have open and honest communication/discussions.

2. Listen carefully with interest to the other person.

3. See both sides and reach a compromise.

Marriage

Marriage may be defined as 'a voluntary, legally binding union between a man and a woman to the exclusion of all others'. Some countries have provisions for same-sex marriages or partnerships.

Cultural variations

1. **Choice of a partner:** mutual consent of couple, marrying someone of the same background, arranged marriages, e.g. Hindus, Sikhs, Muslims, endogamy (particular race, religion, social class).

2. **Number of partners:**

Monogamy	• One partner
	• Serial monogamy: marries and divorces many times
	• Legally binding until death or divorce
	• Most common type of marriage for Christians and western societies
Polygamy	• More than one partner
	• More acceptable outside western societies
	Polyandry:
	• One woman and two or more husbands
	• Prevents the division of land
	• Can be found in some Tibetan families
	Forms of polyandry:
	• fraternal (husbands are brothers)
	• non-fraternal (husbands are not related)
	Polygyny:
	• One man and two or more wives
	• Practised in Islamic countries and some African countries

3. **Locality:** patrilocal, matrilocal and neolocal.

4. **Transfer of inheritance:** eldest son, between spouse and all offspring, inheritance to children born outside marriage – varies across the world.

5. **Minimum age for marriage:** 18 years in Ireland. Some countries do not have a minimum age.

key point

Bigamy occurs when a person who is legally married to one person enters another marriage.

Marriage and the law in Ireland

1. Both partners must be aged over 18 years.
2. The marriage must be voluntary.
3. Both partners must be free to marry.
4. Partners must not be too closely related by blood or marriage.
5. Three months' written notice must be given to the district registrar.
6. The marriage must take place in a registered location.

LINKS
- Family structures (p. 234)
- Functions of the family (p. 238)

key point

1st January 2011 – The Civil Partnership and Cohabitation Act 2010 became effective.

Rights and responsibilities in marriage

- The partners are entitled to the company of each other (live together).
- Expected to be loyal and faithful to each other.
- Conjugal rights.
- To provide for a dependent spouse and children.
- Joint guardianship and custody of children.

LINK
- Family law (p. 255)

Preparation for marriage

In the home

- Ideas on marriage are based on experiences in the home.
- Parents are the first role models for married life.
- A supportive and contented relationship between parents provides the basis for a happy marriage.
- A caring and loving home environment, where good communication, honesty and trustworthiness are evident, helps the development of happy relationships.

At school

- Marriage is studied in a variety of subjects: SPHE, RSE, Health Education, Religion and Home Economics.
- Students discuss topics related to relationships and marriage.

Pre-marriage courses

- Provide opportunities for couples to discuss the realities and expectations of marriage.
- Pre-marriage courses are offered by: ACCORD, Marriage and Relationship Counselling Service.
- Areas discussed include: relationships, roles and responsibilities, children, family planning, finance, marriage and family law, setting up home, problems.
- Financial experts, lawyers, doctors, marriage counsellors and home economists act as facilitators.

Marriage breakdown

Reasons for marriage breakdown include:

1. Marrying for the wrong reason, e.g. pregnancy.
2. Getting married at too young an age.
3. Background differences (social, cultural or religious).
4. Unrealistic expectations associated with romantic love.
5. Social problems (alcoholism, violence).
6. Infidelity, loss of trust.
7. Changing attitudes towards marriage.

Choices available when a marriage breaks down

Marriage counselling

- Couples look for help to avoid marriage break-up.
- Counselling is provided by ACCORD, Marriage and Relationship Counselling Service.
- Both spouses must attend.
- Trained professionals help couples to communicate difficulties in a non-threatening environment and to reach resolutions through discussion.

Family Mediation Service

- Run by the Family Support Agency.
- Helps couples who have decided to separate to reach agreement on all issues related to their separation.
- A mediator supports couples in a co-operative, non-threatening, confidential atmosphere.
- Couples reach agreement about:
  - arrangements for children (parenting and custody)
  - the family home and property
  - financial matters.
- A written document records the details of the agreement between the couple and this can be taken to a solicitor to formalise the agreement.

Legal nullity

- The marriage never existed in the eyes of the law.
- A marriage is **void** if one of the following was the case prior to or on the day of marriage.
  1. Either party was already married (bigamy).
  2. A legal requirement was not met.
  3. Lack of consent of one of the parties.
  4. A partner was on drugs or drunk during the ceremony.
  5. Non-consummation due to homosexuality or impotence.
  6. Psychiatric problems.

Catholic Church annulments
- The marriage never existed in the eyes of the Church.
- Church annulments have no legal standing.

Separation

Reminder – check for any amendments to family law before your exam.

Types of separation:
1. Deed of Separation or legal separation
2. judicial separation.

Deed of Separation or legal separation
- Arranged through mediation.
- A written legal agreement between a couple.
- Outlines the terms of the separation relating to their future rights, and their obligations to each other and their children.
- Both partners must agree to all terms.
- A solicitor draws up the Deed of Separation.
- The written contract is signed in front of witnesses.

Judicial Separation Act 1989
- This was amended by the Family Law Act 1995.
- It is implemented when a couple fail to agree on the terms of a separation.
- It involves a court judgment under the Act.
- Grounds for a judicial separation include:
  1. One spouse committed adultery.
  2. Couple have been living apart for one year by agreement **or** for three years without consent.
  3. One spouse deserted for more than one year.
  4. Absence of normal marital relationship for one year prior to application.

Divorce
- Introduced into Ireland in 1996.
- Governed by the Family Law (Divorce) Act 1996.
- A divorce may be granted when:
  1. The parties have lived apart for four of the five previous years.
  2. There is no prospect of reconciliation.
  3. Provisions have been made for spouse, children and other dependents.
- The divorce hearing is held in the Family Court.
- Direction is provided on maintenance, child custody and access, property and pension adjustment.

Exam questions and sample answers

Higher Level 2009, Section B, Q5 (50 marks) HL

(a) Identify and elaborate on the rights and responsibilities of a couple within a marriage relationship. (5 points × 4 marks = 20 marks)

1. *Each spouse is entitled to the other's company (conjugal and cohabiting rights).*
2. *Couples expect each other to be faithful and loyal.*
3. *Couples are joint guardians of their children and must provide together for the children's basic, moral and social needs.*
4. *Spouses must provide financial support for dependent spouse and children.*

(b) Discuss the benefits of pre-marriage courses for couples preparing for marriage. (3 × 6 marks = 18 marks)

Pre-marriage courses provide couples with:

1. *Information about the expectations and reality of marriage e.g. the legalities of marriage, commitment, relationships, family planning, conflict resolution, rearing of children and problems that might occur.*
2. *An opportunity to discuss their own vision of marriage and all the above topics. Couples examine personal qualities and discuss issues that may have a negative effect on their marriage.*
3. *Information on buying a home, financial responsibility and budgeting.*

(c) Explain how Irish family law protects the rights of family members in the event of marriage breakdown. (3 × 4 marks = 12 marks)

1. *The Family Law Divorce Act 1996 makes provision for dependent family members. Spouses have the right to remarry.*
2. *The Judicial Separation Act 1989 permits the legal separation of spouses and makes provision for dependents.*

> **LINK**
> • Marriage (separation) (p. 244)

3. *The Family Home Protection Act 1976 states that neither spouse can sell or re-mortgage the family home or have essential services cut off.*

Ordinary Level 2008, Section B, Q5 (50 marks)

'Marriage is one of the oldest institutions but – contrary to popular belief – so too is divorce of one kind or another.' (Dr Linda Connolly, Senior Lecturer in Sociology, UCD)

(a) Discuss (i) the rights and (ii) the responsibilities of a couple within the marriage relationship. (*Answered above*) (24 marks)

(b) Outline the benefits to a young couple of attending a pre-marriage course. (2 × 4 marks = 16 marks)

> **LINK**
> • Marriage (p. 241)

1. *Couples discuss their feelings, visions and role expectations with openness in a safe environment.*
2. *Course offers practical advice on housing, finance, child-rearing, family planning and family life.*

(c) Explain how the Family Mediation Service helps couples who are experiencing difficulties in their marriage.   (2 × 5 marks = 10 marks)

The Family Mediation Service:

- *encourages open communication and helps reduce conflict*

  Elaborate a little more on these two points.

- *helps separating couples negotiate their own separation agreement with regard to custody arrangements, parenting of children, finances, the family home and other property.*

Family as a caring unit

Family roles

- Each family member plays a role.
- Each individual fulfils many roles.

key point

A role is the expected pattern of behaviour of an individual, determined by society's expectations.

Roles and responsibilities of children

1. To learn how to behave in an acceptable manner.
2. To be role models for younger siblings.
3. To follow the rules set down by parents, to show respect.
4. To help out with basic tasks, e.g. making their beds.
5. To learn about responsibility, to follow rules.
6. To become socially competent, be happy and secure.

LINK
- Family resource management (p. 179)

Roles and responsibilities of adolescents

Adolescence is a period of transition from childhood to adulthood. Role expectations are difficult as adolescents try to:

- become more responsible for themselves
- help out in the home in preparation for life
- learn from role conflicts that may arise
- use independence and freedom wisely
- study hard and achieve their potential.

Roles and responsibilities of parents

1. To provide for children's physical, psychological and social needs.
2. To act in a respectful, loving and caring manner.
3. To show what is right and wrong, to set clear limits.
4. To act as good role models for their children.
5. To balance discipline with encouragement and love.
6. To provide a stimulating and safe environment.
7. To spend time together as a family.
8. To modify the role as children get older.

Answer exam questions in point/bullet form and expand on each point. Keep to the facts.

Older person's roles and responsibilities

1. To live active and healthy lives.
2. To plan for retirement and to maintain independence.
3. To develop new, active roles on retirement.
4. To provide active support to younger family members.
5. To share knowledge and wisdom with younger generations.
6. To continue to be involved in family and community life.

Gender roles

- **Gender** refers to being male or female.
- **Gender role** refers to the pattern of behaviour expected from a man or woman.
- **Gender equity** means treating men and women equally at home, at school and in the workplace.

Gender issues in family roles

Traditional stereotyped gender roles are reinforced by:

- assigning different household tasks to girls and boys
- encouraging separate types of games for boys and girls
- suggesting boys are independent, ambitious and strong
- suggesting girls should be content and dependent
- encouraging girls to take up 'caring' professions
- encouraging boys to consider scientific professions.

Factors affecting changing roles in families

Social factors

Type of family	• Fewer extended families • More nuclear, blended, lone-parent families
Family size	• Smaller families • More resources spent on children
Roles	• More egalitarian roles; both parents involved in family life • Shared decision-making • Changing role of women in the home • Both parents involved in child rearing
Employment	• Shorter working week, more time spent with children • Increase in women working outside the home, fathers may be at home • Increase in unemployment 2008–2011

Grandparents	Frequently provide child care and financial help
Education	• Education and achievement are valued • Skilled workforce has emerged • More adults seeking places on training courses due to unemployment
Adolescence	Recognition of adolescence as a period of transition, more involved in decision-making at home and school

Economic factors

1. Increase in standard of living, dual-income families.
2. Couples are unable to get mortgages due to reduced income, unemployment and inability to repay loans.
3. High cost of childcare, grandparents are more involved.
4. Young adults have become more financially dependent on parents.
5. Adolescents may choose to work part time, but opportunities are limited.
6. Families experiencing financial difficulties are supported by state welfare system.

LINK

• Family resource management (p. 179)

Role conflict

- Occurs when roles are not clearly defined and when one role interferes with another.
- Arises when there is a clash between role expectations.
- Arises when expectations of individuals are to be met.
- Role conflict creates stress for teenagers and adults.

Examples:

1. Individuals may experience role conflict when a family role interferes with the demands of a work role.
2. For men a role conflict might arise when they are no longer the breadwinner in the family, e.g. because the mother has a better-paid job or because they have become unemployed.

Relationships in the family

Examples:

- child/parent relationship
- adolescent/parent relationship
- sibling relationships
- grandparent/grandchild relationship
- relationships across the extended family.

Child/parent relationship

A good child/parent relationship:

1. Provides for the child's physical, psychological and social needs.
2. Is the most important first relationship for children.

3. Influences children for life as parents show their ability to care for and love their children.

4. Emphasises and develops honesty, justice, a sense of responsibility and maturity in a secure and safe environment.

5. Provides opportunities for children to experience praise, security, approval and acceptance.

6. Develops self-esteem and confidence in children so that they are capable of forming healthy relationships.

> **LINK**
> - Importance of good communication in a family (p. 250)

Rights of children within the family

Under the **UN Convention on the Rights of the Child**, children are entitled to:

- protection from physical, emotional and sexual abuse
- be allowed to develop physically, spiritually, emotionally and socially
- love, understanding, freedom and dignity
- education within the family
- free primary and secondary education
- freedom from discrimination, exploitation and cruelty
- provision for special physical or emotional needs.

> **LINK**
> - Child Care Act 1991, 1997 (p. 255)

Adolescent/parent relationship

1. Adolescence is a time of transition from childhood to adulthood.
2. Relationships between adolescents and parents change (sometimes conflict occurs).
3. Peer expectations may clash with parental expectations.
4. Understanding and listening are needed on both sides.
5. Educational achievements, friends and social life may become a source of conflict.

Conflict between adolescents and adults

1. Conflict arises in the transition period from childhood to adulthood.
2. Learning responsibility, independence and decision-making can be difficult for teenagers.
3. Adolescents often object to the imposition of rules.
4. Parents worry about the influence of the peer group, changes in attitudes and mood swings, alcohol, drugs, boy/girl relationships.
5. Parents may find their 'child' has developed a new personal value system.
6. Adolescents become more independent, outspoken and challenging.
7. Adolescents and parents seem to have little in common.
8. Parents may not be sufficiently informed about recent changes in the world of adolescents, e.g. music, fashion, electronic gadgets, online social networks, etc.
9. Parents may feel isolated as their child moves from childhood dependence to adult independence.

Generational conflict

Causes of generational conflict

1. Different generations may have different norms, mores and values.
2. Young people may have more liberal views than their parents.
3. Young people may feel misunderstood.
4. Older people may feel undervalued and unwanted.
5. Grandparents may question the parenting skills of their adult children.
6. Children and parents may have different expectations about educational achievement and future goals.

Dealing with generational conflict

1. Maintain an open system of communication.
2. Develop a fair, consistent system of discipline.
3. Set limits – boundaries should be clear.
4. Avoid confrontation; wait until people are calm.
5. Never use physical punishment.
6. Provide an atmosphere where young people feel secure.
7. Consider the issue from both points of view.
8. Check what each person wants.
9. Examine the possible solutions.
10. Negotiate and compromise if possible.

Key words in resolving conflict are listening, showing interest, openness, honesty and compromise.

Importance of good communication in a family

1. Determines the quality of the relationships between family members, develops respect for others.
2. Ensures that all family members can express their ideas, feelings and thoughts in a safe environment where their views are valued.
3. Requires the development of good listening skills.
4. Supports a positive approach to solving disagreements.
5. Enables all involved to reach agreed solutions together.
6. Prevents misunderstandings.

Communication is a two-way process.

Role of older people in the family

Older people in families play an important role by:

- passing on norms, mores and values to the next generation
- enriching society through sharing knowledge and life experiences
- spending free time with grandchildren, helping their social development
- providing a childcare option for their adult children
- offering financial assistance to younger family members.

Grandparent/grandchild relationships

- Tend to be less formal, more relaxed with fewer rules.
- Are very special relationships.
- Grandparents teach grandchildren how to respect others.
- Grandchildren learn how to communicate/negotiate.

Independence of older people in the family

To maintain quality of life and independence, **older people need:**

- an acceptable level of privacy
- an independent lifestyle to maintain self-esteem
- respect and freedom to make their own choices
- recognition of their role within family and society
- clarification in relation to role expectations
- protection and care if unable to look after themselves
- involvement in family life, not excluded or ignored.

Economic situation

- Pensions give financial independence.
- Free travel allows freedom to visit new places.
- Medical cards remove stress for poorer pensioners.
- Reduced income may be a problem for some older people.

Problems associated with ageing

Problems associated with getting older include deterioration of eyesight, hearing, memory and mobility; loneliness; change in status; change in roles; and reduced income.

Accommodation options for older people

- Living at home alone (with family close by).
- Living with family (own section within the house).
- Home care in their own home.
- Sheltered housing scheme in the local community.
- Residential care (private or public nursing home).

Exam question and sample answer

Ordinary Level 2007, Section B, Q5   (50 marks)

'Adolescence is the time between the ages of 10 and 18 when your thinking, your feelings and your body are changing.' (Angela MacNamara)

(a) Identify **two** factors, outside the family, which may influence a teenager's behaviour.   (2 × 4 marks = 8 marks)

   1. *Part-time work can interfere with school and study.*
   2. *Teenagers are influenced by the media, e.g. magazines.*

(b) Discuss: (15 marks)

   (i) **Three** aspects of adolescent behaviour that
       may lead to conflict between parents, other
       adults and teenagers.

   1. *Relationships may take priority over
      school and study. Students may fall
      behind in homework and do badly in
      school tests.*

   *Elaborate and explain each
   of these points to give a
   complete answer.*

   2. *Teenagers may feel that parents are
      out of touch with music, fashion and technology.*
   3. *Peer group attitudes may conflict with those of parents.*

   (ii) **Three** ways of dealing with conflict.   (3 × 5 marks = 15 marks)

   1. *Creating an open, comfortable atmosphere for everyone.*
   2. *Listening to each other and hearing other viewpoints.*
   3. *Setting boundaries and limits, reaching a compromise.*

(c) Each family member has a role and a number of responsibilities within the family
    unit. Describe **one** role and **two** responsibilities of teenagers/adolescents.

   Role: *to be good role models for younger children in the family.*

   Responsibilities:

   1. *To attend school, do homework and do one's best.*
   2. *To do their share of household tasks.*

Family members with special needs

(a) Special physical needs

Examples	Deafness, blindness, wheelchair bound
Difficulties	● Lack of mobility ● Dependence on others; lack of independence ● Lack of access to education and employment
Family response	● Modifying the family home and car ● Encouraging self-esteem and confidence ● Encouraging independent living
Statutory aid	● National Disability Authority ● Rehab Group ● Grants to adjust homes ● Equality Authority
Voluntary support	● Irish Wheelchair Association ● National Association for the Deaf ● National Council for the Blind of Ireland ● Special Olympics Ireland

(b) Special mental needs

1. Mental disability, e.g. Down Syndrome	
Difficulties	● Lack of independence, poor access to education and employment
Family response	● Love, encouragement, emotional support, care and attention ● Membership of organisations
Statutory aid	HSE
Voluntary support	● Down Syndrome Ireland ● Special Olympics

2. Addictions, e.g. drugs, alcohol, gambling	
Difficulties	● Family problems, e.g. debt, lies ● Unemployment ● Breakdown of relationships
Family response	● Assistance from outside agencies ● Provide emotional support ● Protect children ● Membership of organisations
Statutory aid	● Psychiatric services and hospitals ● HSE
Voluntary support	● Alcoholics Anonymous (AA) ● Alateen ● Narcotics Anonymous

3. Psychiatric problems, e.g. depression, schizophrenia	
Difficulties	● Unemployment ● Low self-esteem ● Relationship/family problems ● Misunderstandings
Family response	● Emotional support and understanding ● Encouragement ● Help from outside agencies
Statutory aid	● Psychiatric services and hospitals ● HSE
Voluntary support	● Schizophrenia Ireland ● Aware

(c) Special emotional needs

Autism	
Difficulties	• Unable to express emotion • Inability to form relationships • Disruptive behaviour (some cases)
Family response	• Provide love and emotional support • Endeavour to understand problems • Join support groups • Provide a caring and safe home
Statutory aid	• Health Service Executive (HSE) • Department of Education and Skills
Voluntary support	• Autism Ireland • Hope Project
Abuse	
Difficulties	• Guilt, anxiety, depression • Lack of trust • Family breakdown • Inability to express emotion
Family response	• Provide love and emotional support • Join a support group • Arrange counselling
Statutory aid	HSE
Voluntary support	• Rape Crisis Centre • Women's Aid

Rehab – voluntary support

- Independent, non-profit-making organisation, non-governmental status at UN.
- Supports social and economic inclusion of people with disabilities.
- Helps individuals to maximise skills and talents at work and in the community.
- Campaigns for reforms and equal opportunities.
- Participated in development projects in Africa.
- 200 centres across Ireland and UK.

National Disability Authority – statutory aid

- Defends and protects the rights and entitlements of people with disabilities.
- Membership includes parents (including parents with disabilities), carers and people working in the area of disability.
- Four main departments involved: Policy and Public Affairs, Research and Standards Development, Corporate Services and Centre of Excellence in Universal Design.

Family law

Family Law (Maintenance of Spouse and Children) Act 1976

- Entitles a dependent spouse and children to financial support from his/her partner.
- A child is dependent if aged under 18 years or under 23 years and in full-time education or has a disability.
- Maintenance is requested following a separation or divorce, even if both spouses live in the same home.
- If the parties cannot reach an agreement the District Court can decide on the amount of maintenance to be paid based on income and needs.
- A parent may apply for maintenance of a child even if the parents are not married.

Domestic Violence Act 1996

- Covers the protection of individuals who are threatened by physical, mental or sexual abuse.
- The Act states that a spouse/partner may apply to the courts for a:
  1. **Protection Order:** temporary order while waiting for a Safety or Barring Order
  2. **Safety Order:** Prevents abuser using violent behaviour towards spouse/partner/children; may extend to five years.
  3. **Barring Order:** Abuser must leave the home, order can last for up to three years.

Higher Level: revise Judicial Separation Act 1989 (p. 244).

Family Home Protection Act 1976

- Act states that neither spouse can mortgage, sell, lease or transfer the family home without the written consent of the other.

LINK
- Housing finance (p. 197)

- Applies regardless of whose name is on the title deeds – family homes are generally in joint ownership today.

Child Care Act 1991, 1997

- Outlines a range of regulations providing for the protection of children who are at risk (neglected, assaulted, ill-treated or sexually abused).
- A child is defined as being under 18 years of age.
- The Gardaí have the authority to remove a child from the home and place them in care if they are at risk.
- **An Emergency Care Order** permits the HSE to remove a child from their home for up to eight days.
- **A Supervision Order** is granted where it is necessary to monitor a child.

Making a will

Reasons for making a will

1. Your wishes are carried out by an executor.
2. Money and property go to those you wish to have them.
3. Eliminates family stress and disagreements.
4. Parents ensure that children are cared for by naming a specific person.
5. If no will is made the estate is distributed according to the Succession Act 1965.

The **Succession Act 1965** outlines what should happen in the case of an individual dying without leaving a will in the following cases:

- a spouse and no children
- a spouse and children
- no spouse but children
- without a spouse or children
- no parents
- no siblings.

Procedures for making a will

1. Employ a solicitor.
2. Make a list of assets, current value and location.
3. Compile a list of beneficiaries to include names, dates of birth and current contact addresses.
4. Appoint two executors.
5. Divide the estate (cash and specific property) between the beneficiaries (keep in mind restrictions imposed by the Succession Act 1965).
6. Outline your wishes regarding funeral arrangements and burial place.
7. Draw up the will in a written form.
8. Sign the will in the presence of two witnesses (witnesses do not need to know contents).
9. Keep in a safe place (bank or solicitor's office).

Exam question and sample answer

Higher Level 2007, Section B, Q5 (part question)

'"Special needs" refers to a diverse range of needs often caused by medical, physical, mental or developmental condition or disability.' (Scoil.net)

(a) Identify and elaborate on the difficulties that a family unit may experience when a member of the family has special needs.   (3 × 6 marks = 18 marks)

  1. *Individual may **lack mobility** and have difficulty accessing public transport systems and facilities. They may be dependent on family members or the state to provide transport.*

2. **Lack of educational and employment** opportunities results in social isolation, prejudice and depression.

3. **Lack of adequate financial support** may put extra pressures on family as the family income may be inadequate to provide for the needs of the individual.

(b) Discuss how a family might respond to the needs of a member who has a physical or mental disability. (4 × 5 marks = 20 marks)

The family might respond by:

1. **Modifying** the family home and family car to make life easier for those with physical disabilities.

2. Providing **financial assistance** if the family income allows.

3. Providing **emotional encouragement and support** to ensure that the individual leads a happy and fulfilling life.

(c) Outline the role of the Rehab Group. (3 × 4 marks = 12 marks)

1. Independent non-profit-making organisation providing education, training and employment for people with physical and intellectual difficulties.

2. Provides health, social and home care services.

3. Campaigns for equality of opportunity for people with disabilities.